Acclaim for

BOOKBINDER'S DAUGHTER

"A daring memoir that escorts the reader from love to terror and back again. Judith Fisher's story is a stunning journey into the delicate dynamics of a family in crisis. Yet Judith is tenacious, smart, and reflective—the very qualities that enable humans to conquer their shadows and emerge into the light beyond. Readers who have struggled with their own demons (and haven't we all?) will find this book instructive and inspiring.

— Linda Lambert, author of seven award-winning
   leadership books

"Real lives are so much more interesting and inspirational than textbook clinical cases or even fictionalized characters, because you know the miracles really did happen. In *Bookbinder's Daughter* we see transformation happening as the memoir unfolds. Out of the darkest of times as an adolescent arises a radiant woman."

—David Skibbins, PhD, author of the Tarot Mystery Series,
   Working Sober and *Becoming a Life Coach*

"*Bookbinder's Daughter* is a brave, inspiring memoir, a tale of unrelenting resilience and redemption. Judith Fisher tells all —her horrific experiences, seemingly impossible challenges, and sweet triumphs — with stunning honesty. I love knowing her through this book, and feel so gifted by the beauty of her transformative life."

— Katie Atherton, LCSW

"What does it take to find serenity after a childhood fraught with the rage of an emotionally fragile mother and an adolescence darkened by mental hospitals, rape, and suicidal despair? In vivid and moving vignettes, Judith Fisher takes the reader on an emotional journey from Cobleskill, New York, to her life as principal of a healing arts center on the Mendocino Coast. Along the way she has achieved another dream: to become a writer whose words 'bring light into the dark places where people hide their secrets from themselves and others' and show them they are not alone — they too can survive and heal."

—Maureen Eppstein, Executive Director,
   Mendocino Coast Writers Conference

"As the prologue suggests (read it and you'll be compelled to read the book), *Bookbinder's Daughter* is akin to sitting in a living room with Judith over a cup of coffee as she shares her life story. And what a life story it is! With the fascinating feel of a can't-put-down novel, her detailed descriptions take you right into the middle of a life that makes you wonder how she survived. A memoir of falling to the depths only to rise, again and again."

—Joel Crockett, president, Four-Eyed Frog Books

BOOKBINDER'S DAUGHTER

A Life Lost and Found

JUDITH A. FISHER

Judith A. Fisher

LOST〰
COAST
PRESS

BOOKBINDER'S DAUGHTER:
A Life Lost and Found
Copyright © 2014 by Judith A. Fisher

Lost Coast Press
155 Cypress Street
Fort Bragg, CA 95437
(800) 773-7782
www.cypresshouse.com

Cover and book design by Michael Brechner / Lost Coast Press
Cover and interior illustrations courtesy of the author
Back cover author photo © Seve Cardosi

Publisher's Cataloging-in Publication Data

Fisher, Judith A., 1944-
Bookbinder's daughter : a life lost and found : a memoir / Judith A. Fisher. --
1st ed. -- Fort Bragg, CA : Lost Coast Press, c2014.
p. ; cm.

ISBN: 978-1-935448-29-7

Summary: The poignant memoir of Judith A. Fisher, who, at age seventeen, experienced appalling mistreatment including electroshock treatments and an attempted rape in a mental hospital, but survived and went on to become a healthy adult and a successful businesswoman, wife, and mother.--Publisher.

1. Fisher, Judith A., 1944- 2. Ex-mental patients--United States--Biography. 3. Mentally ill children--Treatment--New York (State) 4. Shock therapy--Patients--Biography. 5. Electroconvulsive therapy for teenagers--Patients--Biography. 6. Psychiatric hospitals--Corrupt practices--New York (State) 7. Self-realization. 8. Self-actualization (Psychology) I. Title.

RC464.F57 A3 2014   2014938121
362.2/092--dc23   201407

Printed in the USA on partially recycled text stock

2 4 6 8 9 7 5 3 1

First edition

DEDICATION

To my daughter, Heidi,
And my husband Peter

To Love—what it's all about—
And for those who have not yet told their stories

Contents

Prologue

SHATTERING THE SILENCE, 1972

"You mean your parents locked you up?" Sally's eyes, usually a soft pale blue beneath her shaggy blonde pixie, become bright and sparkle with interest.

"How could they? I mean, you were only, what, seventeen? I can't believe it!" She edges closer to the coffee table, nearly sitting on it.

What am I doing here? My guard is down. I slump back into the enveloping wing chair, hug my knees, wonder how the subject came up. Sadness creeps in, like wet sand dragging me out to sea in its undertow. Defeat. Yet too, something hopeful, a spark, that allows me to sit up and answer her questions. She has so many. I'm in new territory, and nervous, never having told the story before.

The day sizzles, unbearably hot. I wear shorts and a tee shirt, barefoot in the house. Afternoon light dances through the tall redwoods to the west. A fan whirrs overhead, but there's no cooling the stale air. My silence speaks first, before I can bring myself to begin. And in that steamy room, my legs begin to shake.

Start at the beginning. Where is that anyway? It all feels so painful. Northfield School for Girls? The dorm? My parents? I cringe. Each detail sends shivers through my body, and waves of shame. Dull memories, stored away for years, begin to make their way to the surface, gasping for air. And still, the shaking.

"The first hospital, Albany, wasn't that bad. My parents took me there for tests, psychiatric evaluation, they said, with no indication I'd be there for long. A week or two, a rest, just to get my head together after all that had happened at school. I almost welcomed it, needed to be away from Northfield and my mom and dad. It would have been okay, except for that damn orderly and the attack. That's when it all got screwed up." As my story unfolds into the evening, it takes three hours to get it all out, moved along by Sally's urgent questions. *Be still!* I command my quivering legs, and for a moment feel a particle of control seep in. I sigh and take a few deep breaths, like clean mountain air.

"When they left me at the second hospital, outside New York, it felt like the bottom. Mom was crying, and I knew things were bad. I didn't realize exactly where I was — a private psychiatric hospital — that things would become even worse, never be the same; that they were leaving me there."

Can I get through the whole story? The tension in my body mimics the grip of the icy-cold sheets, of lying alone, shaking, bound up in the hallway. How many shock treatments? Ten years of holding the memories wrapped up tightly just under my skin has worn me out. Once I begin to speak, it all starts to unravel, and I want to finish almost as much as I had wanted to leave that place, all those years ago.

My arms wrap around my long tan legs. *Hold it together.* My jaw clenches so tight it's difficult to form the words. Such a relief when I get to the end of the story. And finally, the tears, warm and salty, stream down my face.

"And here I am, so many years later, baby and all. A miracle." I can picture my infant daughter, her angel face, asleep in the adjacent cabin; even from here, sensing her soft even breathing somehow calms me. My legs slacken, finally let down, let go. Later, as I lie on the warm waterbed in our little cabin, the crescent moon peers at me through redwood tips. *A light in my dark.* At last, I have told the story, uttered the words out loud for the first time. The silence is broken.

I

When I Was a Small Child

1942–1955

Mom and Dad, 1942

Tumbling hard into the snow bank, Charlotte's face turns bright red, scrubbed by the sharp ice crystals. She feels fully alive. Aware of Cliff's arms firmly holding her, she begins to thaw from a long decade of loneliness and a job going nowhere. The Cheerio sledding party at Mickle Hollow is just the thing. In 1930, she was forced to return home directly after college to help out, and when Pops got sick, she learned to run the business. Somehow, Stanley Sonn's Outdoor Advertising Company had to keep going. Evenings, Charlotte composed articles for the *Cobleskill Journal,* the town's weekly newspaper. She mostly enjoyed writing editorials, or news stories with a personal aspect. Now and then, they would let her publish poetry on the obituary page, or for a holiday. She regularly sent off epic poems, longer, classical in form with more depth, to magazines like *The New Yorker.* Typed copies of these, and notebooks of first drafts, handwritten in her graceful script, piled up on a high shelf in her room's small closet. A fat folder sat there too, filled with rejection letters. The politely penned disappointments seemed encouraging, but no one offered what she was looking for — acceptance.

Her poems of later years, written in perfect iambic pentameter, and even a script for a play, were corny, and contained tragic lines about love and broken dreams. In college Henry was her boyfriend. In a red candy box, she saved keepsakes, like dance cards; some had "Henry" written on every line. At no time since she lost Henry to the war had she felt her heart so touched, and for no particular reason, except the passage of time, she was open and vulnerable. Cliff slipped in like a soft breeze when she wasn't looking.

Five months later, on the fifth of May 1942, they married. No long engagements or extended courtships. Straight ahead. After all, she was thirty-three and he thirty-six. Too old to be practical and wait, and so ready to be in love. The wedding was in the Methodist Church, where they both had recently become members. It was their compromise, she from a Baptist family, his parents Mennonites. The long white satin dress, tulle veil, armful of yellow roses and baby's breath were proof that it was real. The smile on her face in the photos, through showers of rice, showed that she was finally happy.

Farm life meant isolation from friends and family. Charlotte was clearly not cut out to be a farmer's wife. Out of respect for Cliff, who loved the farm, she'd been willing to try it, swallow her pride and move into the two-story white farmhouse on Lawyersville Hill. The lambs were so cute on bottles, 5:00 a.m. milking. In the evenings she taught herself to knit, making his-and-hers matching pullover vests, and argyle socks for Cliff. The sock design — four colors in diamond shapes — and the bunch of short double-point needles boggled her mind but kept her occupied during a nervous pregnancy. Thank goodness for the telephone! Ten o'clock would come along, after breakfast and the morning farm chores were finished. At last she could sit down to relieve her swollen ankles and dial her mother's number. They talked every day but Sundays for about an hour. Each in her own way was alone, would look forward to this special time together. Charlotte counted on her mother's advice and calming voice to assuage her worries. Their bond was close, deep even beyond their genetic links, back to the Revolution.

And so, when Charlotte, Cliff, and one-year-old Judy moved back to Cobleskill, just two blocks away from Grandma, everyone was happy and breathing easier. Grandma could see her little darling regularly, hold her on her lap, and press her own cheeks to the plump rosy ones of her granddaughter. The daily phone calls continued almost until the day Grandma died fifteen years later. Even after that, Mom claimed, periodically, that she had "heard" from Grandma. Not hard to believe. I too sense her, know she's there somewhere, and sees us.

Bridge Club Night, 1949

The light comes in rosy-orange slivers through the half-closed venetian blinds of my tiny bedroom just off the kitchen. The door stands partly open and I can see Mom moving back and forth, swaying nervously in place as she opens a can of Planters Mixed Nuts and some candied fruit to set out. Disappearing into the warm living room, she distributes the glass dishes among three bridge tables that I helped her set up right after my nap. I feel proud, being five and old enough now to help, especially when Mom's tired.

Following her into the kitchen, I notice she's rubbing her temples, her face pasty white with no smile. She stares out the window, lost. Then she spins around and marches to the corner cupboard. Reaching up, she twirls the shelf, looking at the various little bottles. She picks one of the short brown ones, pops off the top, shakes out two of her headache pills, and swallows them. When Mom turns around, she glares at me as I'm caught staring at her. My weak smile seems to relieve her. With a sigh, she checks, making sure the macaroni will be done for our dinner at the same time as the three pork chops sizzling in the electric fry pan.

I can't wait until after dinner. Dad will be home, cleaning up from work while I watch Mom get dressed. My favorite part comes when she sits on the bed, curls up the sheer nylons into neat little wads, and slowly pulls them over her toes and delicate feet (size AAA!). She eases them all the way up her legs to hitch onto garters, which hang off her girdle. Clip-clip, clip-clip, and they're stretched over her winter-white legs, giving them a golden sheen. She shimmies the white half-slip over her head, careful not to muss up her hair. Finally, she slips into the straight tweed skirt and my favorite gold silk blouse. I like finding it for her in the closet, feeling for its softness, the three-quarter sleeves with ruffles, and rub it gently across my cheek.

The doorbell's piercing ring sounds all the way back to the bedroom. Mom jumps, then recomposes herself and nervously puts on the finishing touch, Roman Red lips. She stands tall, so beautiful. Checking her seams quickly in the long mirror, she hurries to welcome the guests. The Dumonds arrive first. I'm allowed to come into the living room to greet our old family friends. They are always so nice to me. Soon the house fills with voices and laughter as everyone settles in for the evening. The dealer at each table of players shuffles, and I hear the familiar fast flutter of cards flipping past each other. My hands are too small. Someday I'll be able to shuffle that way, bending the cards and letting them go at just the right moment to fall into a perfect pile. I love that sound.

On Bridge Club nights, I have no babysitter. I stay in the back of the house. Later on, when there's a break, Mom will serve dessert: a warm apple crisp with vanilla ice cream. She'll let me help her. She scoops the ice cream and I carry the cut-glass bowls, one at a time, out to the bridge tables. Right after that I have to go to bed. It's very boring back here, looking at books, and I've already put Patrina, my best doll, to bed in her cradle, bundling her up and kissing the top of her curly head. Maybe some orange juice would taste good! I mustn't bother them to get it for me. They get mad if I interrupt while they are playing bridge. They act so serious, staring at their cards and eyeing their partners. I can just quietly get it myself. Mom would yell at me for hopping up on the counter, but she's not here. She won't even know about it.

Jumping up, I swing my bare leg over the edge and pull myself up. There, see, I can do it myself. Satisfied, I reach into the refrigerator and pull out the half-full pitcher of orange juice. I set it carefully on the counter, feeling the icy glass on my leg. Next, I open the cupboard and grab my favorite Fiesta juice glass, the sunny yellow one. Now the tricky part: getting down. One leg goes straight back, hands clutching the counter's edge, and I push off backwards toward the floor. But my knee catches, or maybe it's my clumsiness again. Somehow I whack my head on the edge and land on the floor with a thud, legs splayed out. My right hand flies up to my forehead. Oh, no! Blood covers my hand, dripping onto my seersucker pajamas, and it hurts a lot, like those Popsicle headaches, throbbing, throbbing, and making a mess all over my clothes and the floor. I want to get up but every time I try, my eyes go funny and I'm dizzy, so dizzy. I can't call out. They'll be so mad when they find me, even worse if I mess up their game. My head pounds. I press my sleeve against it to catch the blood.

When she finds me, Mom screams, first from seeing the blood and then to call Dad. People staring at me as I sit on the floor causes quite a hustle-bustle in the kitchen. At Dr. Wadsworth's office, I learn that the cut over my eye went very deep and he will have to sew five stitches to close it. The scar will be my reminder. I feel rather fond of that scar right above my eye: my small badge of independence.

PATSY

The day I find out about Patsy being sick, I feel a little scared, but I believe she'll get better, like maybe she has measles, or chicken pox, or a broken arm. I'm not sure, but I think she might have polio. I don't know anyone who's had polio, just hear that word whispered in hallways, in the school nurse's office, and by my parents. After all, I'm only five. Mostly I go to school, come home for lunch, learn my numbers and letters, take naps, and have recess.

I miss Patsy. We stood close for our class picture of Miss Storm's kindergarten. I think she's so pretty, with soft light brown hair, wavy past her shoulders, liquid dark brown eyes, and she wants to be my best friend. For two months we sit together, play swings on the playground, jump rope, even manage to pull our little cots close to each other for naptime. One day she's here, bright and smiling, and the next she's gone. I can't imagine that Patsy won't come back.

My parents call hers to see how she is doing. After a couple of weeks, we learn she's in the hospital. I just keep picturing Patsy showing up in her crisp white blouse with the puffy sleeves, pleated plaid skirt, shoulder straps crisscrossed in the back, black patent leathers polished to a "T." She's that kind of girl. I hear that Patsy is not doing well. My parents explain that the doctors are trying to help her.

One week, I notice in *Life* magazine a giant double-page photo of a girl in an iron lung. A mirror sits above her head, tipped, as she lies trapped in the machine. Her parents sit close by, hopeful, half-smiles flitting across their lips. I cry when I see that picture, black and white and shades of gray, the color drained forever from their lives.

I wonder about my friend in the hospital. Does she have polio? Will she be all right? After a while I kind of forget about her; I mean I don't think of her twenty times a day. I remember the feeling of us skipping on the asphalt playground, perfectly in rhythm, our hands squeezed tight. One cold day when I get home from school, Mom is crying. She sits me down and tells me that Patsy won't be coming back, ever. She's gone to heaven. I cry too, for Patsy and for me.

DRIVING

That's me, posing for my dad in our backyard near our spanking clean blue-like-midnight Plymouth. He must have just washed it on Saturday. It looks so shiny and pretty. Maybe we're getting ready for a trip. Otherwise he wouldn't have time to wash it because he'd be out all day painting signs and putting up posters.

I'm about six in the photo, the summer I want to learn to drive that shiny new car. Usually Dad parks it facing toward East Main so we can just get in and go. One day I pretend I'm driving us all to the store, being older now, going into first grade. Climbing into the driver's side feels really important. I grab a couple of pillows and a car blanket from the back, stack them up in the driver's seat, and I'm set to go. I shimmy down to push the pedals, give it some gas, happily turning the wheel side to side and imagining the passing scenery.

Soon I am moving, really moving down the driveway, wheels crunching over bumpy gravel. I toot the horn as I approach the street, hoping someone will save me. The Plymouth shoots down the final steep part, out into the street, across two lanes of surprised-looking drivers, and comes to a full stop in front of the big auto garage. Terrified, I also feel quite pleased with myself, having done a good job of steering and not having hit anything or crashed the car.

My mother is not so proud of me. Screaming, she comes down the driveway and yanks me out of the car with a "What-do-you-think-you're-doing, young lady?" My driving ends for quite some time. It will be at least ten more years before I sit alone behind a steering wheel, dreaming of far-off places I could go.

TINKELPAUGH BROTHERS

My uncles? Well, great-uncles actually, Grandma's brothers. The day we stop by Uncle Earl's old car repair shop, the one he partly owns, I find out about and meet Uncle George. Grandma and I are out doing errands. She's wearing one of her weekday flower-print rayon dresses, swishing near her ankles, straw hat shading her blue eyes. I'm in a cotton playsuit and Keds. I guess Grandma needs to talk to one of her brothers. She said we'd stop by the shop. I feel excited because I don't know anything about a shop; there will be cars there, and Uncle Jimmy, the quiet, kind uncle from Summit Lake.

We have to circle around in back of the bank and Karker's

Market, through the Hotel Augustan parking lot, to end up on the backside of the A&P and Selkirk's Hardware. I love it back there, and have snuck around a few times, but never noticed the grimy little hole-in-the-wall shop with the yellow and blue sign: TINKELPAUGH BROTHERS GARAGE. I peek in the door. The shop is made up of one small room with a big glass window; the walls are lined with shelves of car parts. A single bare light bulb dangles over the high counter. In the other half of the building is the garage where they work on cars, one at a time.

Out front sit a couple of beat-up chairs, and in one rests a skinny old man with a huge bushy moustache. I can't figure out how he could possibly eat supper without making a mess of it. Uncle George. Grandma says, "Good morning" to George, then finds Jimmy under a car and steps around to talk to him. Uncle George just sits there sucking on his pipe, tipping in his chair.

I've never been this close to a real garage. The smells remind me a little of Dad's shop in the basement, like turpentine, paint, thinners, mixed with something like dirt. I'm dying to go inside and look around. Uncle George says, "Sure, go ahead, no harm in that."

Slipping past Uncle George, I enter the cave. My eyes adjust and begin to take in all the objects inside this hideaway. The shelves are full of little boxes, dark metal shapes, some shiny, some dull like the lead in my pencil, all in a mess. Eventually I turn around, and there behind the counter, at grown-ups' eye level, are about six calendars, each one with a picture of a woman in a teeny bathing suit, and on some, the top piece has fallen off! Needless to say, I am shocked. Somehow, I know this is wrong, that the uncles are hiding these pictures of partially undressed women, and I don't know why Uncle Earl would allow it. After all, a customer might see them. It must be Uncle George's doing. He looks dirty, smoking that pipe and all.

I want to get away and stop looking at those naked breasts. I realize that no one knows I'm in here and I just keep staring, thinking about how huge they are, how round and smooth. It makes me feel funny, so I leave, walk out into the parking lot, and go look for Grandma. She doesn't know about the calendars, so she doesn't know about me looking at them either. I just can't figure out what they're doing there, those half-dressed girls hiding in the dark of Tinkelpaugh Brothers Garage.

SEVEN

I'm lonely, wishing for a sister to walk home with after school, to share my room, whisper secrets after dark. Mom is lonely too, I can tell. Day after day she lies on the couch, eating filled chocolates from her box of Whitman's as she watches the afternoon soaps, *The Guiding Light* her favorite. When I get home from school, telling stories from my day, she perks up, comes out to the kitchen and sits while I have a snack: Skippy on Ritz crackers with milk. Usually, she pours herself another cup of coffee.

I feel sorry for Mom, home all day with no one but the TV to keep her company. She's an only child and so am I. She often reminds me of this, like a secret we share, a special bond. I just think I missed out. I'm sure there will be no sister, though. I've asked that question before, too many times, and I know not to ask ever again. There was something about Mom's "operation" when I was three. Grandma took care of me while Mom was away, made our breakfast and dinner, slept in the back bedroom. Dad was gone too. All of Mom's friends sent her get-well cards at the hospital. Some were sad and beautiful, some funny, and she saved every one, kept them in her desk drawer in a stationery box. I imagine her hospital room filled with flowers, because of the tiny cards I saw: "Thinking of you" or "Get Well Soon!" After she came home and was sick in bed for a few weeks, nobody would talk about what happened, just that she had an operation.

For years I wondered about it. "Mommy's sick. You have to be quiet, so she can rest and get better." Then, one day, Grandma told me they took out her "female parts," where babies grow, and she can't ever have more children. Personally, I don't think she could handle more kids because she's sick so often, has a headache, or is just too tired to make dinner. Poor Mom. I think the operation didn't really fix anything.

COMING HOME

Dad carefully opens the kitchen door, scrapes his muddy feet on the hard rubber mat and steps inside. The delicious smell of paint and turpentine cling to his worn blue shirt and overalls. Drips of dark green paint have spattered over the old brown wing tips, his painter's shoes. I saw him downtown today on his ladder at the Hotel Augustan, touching up their big sign. Now he seems tired from the day. His two-note whistle carries throughout the house, high-low, high-low, announcing his return gently, so as not to frighten Mom. She sits up abruptly, extinguishing her half-smoked cigarette, answering, "I'm in here, Cliff, on the couch."

Dad hangs his brown work jacket inside the door at the top of the cellar stairs, removes and places his shoes on the top step, and ducks into the tiny bathroom to wash up. From there he goes directly to greet her. "Hello, darling." (He always calls her that.) "How was your day?"

Mom wears a plain wool skirt and aqua-blue long-sleeved blouse, tucked in but beginning to wrinkle and pop out. Her slightly matted hair and lack of make-up tell him she hasn't been out today. He leans down to give her a kiss on her high forehead right next to her lock of white hair.

"Can I get you anything?"

"No."

The sound hangs in the air, like a hawk suspended by the wind. It's a punishing silence, and he knows he should have been home earlier. Just needed to finish touching up the letters on the big hotel sign, soak and clean the brushes. Tears spring up and reabsorb almost as quickly, giving a brief sparkle to his deep brown eyes behind gold-rimmed glasses. How he wishes he could have done better.

BACK DOOR

Mom is singing this morning, and I'm so glad. No headache! She rinses our turquoise Fiesta breakfast dishes, hand-scrubs the sticky yolk from inside my eggcup that looks like a chicken. I sit at the kitchen table practicing my new cursive, even though school's out for the summer. Mom says if I write even ten lines every day, I'll have beautiful handwriting for third grade this fall. I believe her too, because she has the prettiest writing in the world. When I look over her shoulder, the deep blue ink flows like a river from her fountain pen. The words must be locked up in her perfect lily-white hand, just waiting for the afternoon when she feels well enough to sit at her desk and answer letters.

It promises to be a hot day. I can feel the air, thick and wet, filled with the high-pitched songs of those hot-weather bugs, katydids. The back door stands open, the dark green-painted screen lets in a faint movement of air. As soon as I finish my work, I'll roller skate down to Barby's house. Maybe we can play Katie Keene paper dolls or go for Popsicles later. My yellow play outfit is brand new and already I'm worried I'll drip grape all over it. I love those purple ones, the doubles you can hold with two hands, or break apart and share with a friend.

I get up from the table and offer to help clean up, but Mom's all finished and making a fresh pot of percolated coffee. She says I may go out to play now. Later we'll shop for fresh string beans and ripe tomatoes at Barber's roadside vegetable stand. I always love this little adventure, our short drive in the country. Mr. Barber gives me treats, like cherries or red plums, soft and juicy. "Okay, Mom, I'm going now," I say, skates in hand, skate key on a string around my neck. "I'll be at Barby's and home for lunch." Out the door I go, and BAM! The old wooden screen door slips out of my hand and slams shut. Oh, no! I want to run, but I hear her screaming. I freeze, that old feeling of dread rolls in like a big black thundercloud, and I know without a doubt that I'll have to go back. Already she's crying, shaking, and falling apart.

"Why can't you be more careful?" she yells, out of control.

How could I be so careless? Dropping my skates, I go back in to see what I can do. I feel so sad. Any little thing sets her off. She's seated at the table, head down and sobbing. I go to her, kneel down, touch her shoulder. She shrugs me off, can't stand to be touched. Nothing helps and I feel helpless. She'll probably get a headache, one of her bad migraines. My playtime's over for today. And poor Mom — her day is ruined too.

DAD

I love how it feels in the house on winter mornings. Outside it's all quiet, sounds muffled by snowfall, but inside, the kitchen radio chirps along, even when Mom's still upstairs. Dad's world centers on the basement — down the narrow stairs into the warm and fragrant depths of the house — his workshop and haven. The big oil furnace labors down there, pumping its heat magically through all the radiators. It seems so friendly, powerful, and beyond my understanding.

The smells of that place draw me down; I like to sit on the stairs, watch Dad, and figure out what's happening. Turpentine and linseed oil mingle as background smells — the way he turns old chairs and tables, with multiple coats of paint, into antique furniture. The cherry, pine, and maple glow with a deep luster showing their hidden beauty. Magic. Yes, Dad is the magician of the house, the keeper of our dreams, the one who can turn the old lean-to shed and office into a kitchen. He and Mom plan it together, and somehow he makes it happen.

Every tool, substance, potion, and glue needed for any job in the world lives in that basement. The old painted pie cupboard — with small bottles of bright paints, brushes, turpentine, canning jars, gold and silver leaf—holds the mystery of future projects. I move down a step or two. Several bare bulbs give a soft glow and make the entire scene feel inviting. I want to leave the clean and orderly kitchen and come down into that warmth.

"Can I help?" I ask.

"No, not really. You'd probably get dirty. But you can watch."

You invite me and I creep down closer to get a look. I approach the bench where you scrape and rub an old tabletop. The smell intoxicates as I breathe it in, savor each breath of that delicious magic. You smile warmly at me and ask simply about the lunch plan. Our talk is a delicate mist between us, like some of the smells; it takes the essence of our bond and spreads it out thinly, like diluted glue. We feel comfortable with this way of connecting with each other.

Oil and grime films on your summer-tan hands, and solvent-soaked rags rest on every surface. I remain clean, still in my play clothes, afraid to touch anything but happy just to be here in this place with you.

"Juu... dee," Mom's demanding voice cuts into my dreamy mood. "It's time to help make lunch."

Why does she need me now? Oh, how I hate to leave this place! Can't she fix it herself? I want to stay here in this safe and special haven with you—I want to be by your side. I could help you clean up, soak the brushes. Then we'd wash up with that squishy stuff in the can and go upstairs together for lunch—a team—but of course I go up the stairs alone to make sandwiches.

Later, on Saturday afternoon, you lift me onto the passenger seat of your old Ford pickup and I sit there like your little princess. We drive right down Main Street. Everyone sees us together. I'm proud of you too. People know us, nod to themselves, seeming to take in the whole story of our lives.

The trip to the dump is fun. We turn left at the light by the bank onto South Grand, under the railroad overpass, left again at the tracks, and drive right past the fairgrounds. After backing up to an enormous pile of junk, you swing me up into the bed of the truck. From there I heave the garbage—old bundles of posters, empty paint buckets, scrap wood, stiff dried-up rags and other interesting objects—as far as my skinny arms can propel it. This act of flinging trash gives me great satisfaction, something about the energy of things sailing through space, crashing onto the heap. I secretly pretend I'm angry, find my target and then let fly. When the stuff crashes into the target, I'm not mad anymore.

On the ride home, the old push broom bounces in the bed of the truck along with empty galvanized metal garbage cans. I always feel sleepy and content. Then you reach over and squeeze my hand to thank me for helping you today—for being your little girl.

GRANDMA AND THE PEAS, 1953

The first time Mom goes away, not counting her operation, I walk to school in the morning, and when I come home after the last recess bell she's gone. I know this because when I walk around to the back door, I see that the old Plymouth isn't parked in the driveway. That means Grandma's inside, not Mom. I skip across the flagstone patio, excited to see Grandma. She waits in the kitchen, and I can smell, and then see, the small batch of warm brown gingersnaps cooling on two cake racks near the stove.

"Hello, precious." Her warm soft arms enfold my skinny shoulders as I inhale the cinnamon ginger of the cookies and the delicate rose powder that is hers. She pours glasses of milk and we go out the screen door to the back porch and sit at the picnic table. I'm so happy Grandma's here, and as we chat about the spelling test and the new book I brought home to read, I forget about my mom.

"Where is she, anyway?" I finally remember.

"Well, sweetie, she's very sick, and your dad took her to the hospital. She'll probably stay there for a few days, a week, or more... we don't really know."

Now I feel really upset because I didn't know about Mom being sick. Is it her headaches? Her nerves? What does that mean?

"What's wrong with her," I ask. "Will she be all right?"

Silence. I watch her softly wrinkled face as she lowers her head and blinks back tears from her eyes before she can pull out the handkerchief hidden in her dress and wipe them away. She has only cried in front of me a couple of times before.

"Yes, we hope so. They'll give her some special treatments so she'll feel better, not so nervous."

She doesn't say any more. As she disappears into the kitchen, screen door closing quietly, I stare into the branches of the backyard cherry tree, smiling at its new pink blossoms and old craggy limbs where I love to climb and observe from halfway up. Very soon Grandma reappears with a large basket of bright green peas. We rock on the loveseat and shell peas for dinner, comforted by the gentle motion and the busy working of our fingers. Before we finish, I am bored.

"Can I go swing, Grandma?"

"Sure you can, sweetheart. Go ahead, I'll finish up."

Not long and I've pumped up to a good rhythm, air whizzing past my ears, hair streaking back as I fly forward, feet straight out in front. The pumping soothes me, lets me lose myself as I breathe in warm sun and smell the cherry blossoms. After a good workout, the swing slows down. Then I'm just leaning back and forth, no pumps, getting ready to jump off. I let go and land solidly, feet planted on the lawn.

Lost in a daydream, I feel the wooden seat hit the back of my head. WHACK! My hand reaches up, grabbing the spot. Next I walk slowly toward the porch. Grandma, absorbed by the dish of peas in her lap, hums softly to herself. Looking up, she knows right away something's wrong — probably sees the ruby-red smear on my hand. My blonde hair soaks up some of the sticky blood and becomes matted and wet. She carefully examines the wound. Next thing I know, I'm lying on my side on the loveseat, head in Grandma's lap, wet icepack on the back of my head, swaying ever so slightly.

Since Grandma doesn't drive, she calls Dr. Wadsworth and he comes right over. He stitches up my head in the kitchen where I sit at the table, head down, just like taking a nap at school. When it's over and he leaves, I cry a little, my head in Grandma's lap again as she strokes my hair while she cleans off some of the blood caked around my neck. I wonder what Mom would say if she were here, and feel relieved that she's not. Maybe my gash will be all healed when she gets back and she'll never have to know how I messed up and got hurt.

Our macaroni and cheese casserole, my favorite, is nearly hot. Grandma tosses the fresh peas into boiling water with a pinch of salt and a pinch of sugar. The toasty cheese crust is a beautiful nutmeg brown; the peas so pretty in blue Fiesta bowls, tiny butter pats melting down through the shiny green jewels. As we say our grace, Grandma smiles at me across the table. "We have a lot to be thankful for," she reminds me. And especially now, I know she is right.

SUNDAYS

The morning sun makes brilliant dancing diamonds on the turquoise-blue walls of my bedroom; they float there, keeping me company.

"Judy, you'd better get up now or you won't make it to Sunday school," Dad half-whispers at my door. After a rough night, Mom still sleeps in her drape-darkened bedroom next door. I tiptoe to the bathroom, careful to avoid three separate places where the old floorboards creak, like small animals announcing themselves. Seated on the toilet, I pray not to wake her with my peeing. I remember not to flush, then pick out my clothes and slip downstairs without a hitch.

"Good morning. How's my girl?" Dad cracks a three-minute egg into my favorite eggcup, the white milk-glass chicken with red eyes and a beak.

"I'm good, Dad. Didn't even wake Mom up. Maybe she'll sleep till church." Sitting there, having breakfast with my Dad — orange juice, soft-boiled egg just right, and peanut butter toast — I feel safe. By church time Mom will be better, smiling and happy to see me. Dad fastens my top two buttons in the back, hands me my church offering envelope sealed with my dime in it, and gives me a quick peck on the cheek as I leave to walk the two and a half blocks to Sunday school. The air, sweet and soft, surrounds me like cotton candy. Later, I hope to see one or both of my parents, spot them as I walk down the aisle in my choir gown, and much later we'll meet at Grandma's house for Sunday dinner, the best part of the week.

From church I can get to Grandma's by cutting through the driveway of Bundy's Funeral Home and half a block of backyards. I wish I could go to the edge of town and run all afternoon. Instead, I arrive at Grandma's back door. I smell three fresh pies cooling on the pantry shelf next to the window. "Hello, precious," she beams, as she folds me in her strong arms and kisses me, soft cheek against my hot face. All my worries disappear, and I enter her world. I climb the almost-too-steep back stairs to the only bathroom. Twinkling sunlight reflects off the tiny square white floor tiles. I can edge myself up on the seat now, without help, so Grandma doesn't have to make that extra trip upstairs.

Is Aunt Nellie ready to come down for dinner? I knock carefully on her door, and peek through the large brass keyhole. Her swaying blue rayon dress appears, draping over her wide hips, and I quickly stand up as she opens the door.

"Come in, Judy." She smiles sweetly, reaches down to touch my shoulder. Her back window, which overlooks the pink climbing rosebush, is open. I sit in the huge wicker rocker while she sits at her vanity, tucking a few more hairpins above each ear.

"Can we do the Ouija board today? Do we have time before

dinner?" I ask. She nods and produces it from the bottom dresser drawer. Then I join her on the bed, careful not to wiggle too much or change what's happening. I can ask any question. We place three fingers lightly on the pointer, like a tiny three-legged table with a round window. It moves, stopping briefly on a letter or number, yes or no. It's eerie how it actually spells out words like "beware" or "visitor," or pulls strongly in a direction giving definite answers. Sometimes the movement happens with our eyes closed! I really like getting answers. If only the Ouija would say that Mom will get well for good.

CRAYOLA SUN

"I want to be an artist when I grow up," I say confidently at the breakfast table on Sunday morning. Mom had just opened the Mother's Day card I made for her: pastel-colored tulips bloom in a row, pink, lavender, and yellow; spiky green leaves reach for the radiant face of a bright Crayola sun.

"Honey, your picture is beautiful," she replies. "This is really a special card."

I feel so proud my spirit swells. I had thought it was the perfect time to announce my plan. At eight years old, I see my life stretch out before me — a magic carpet of colors, purple and turquoise, sky blue, cloud pink — carrying me into a grown-up life as an artist. I'd be well known, but not famous. After all, I still want lots of kids. I could paint and draw while they're in school, be there when they got home, a good mom.

"Oh, I hope you won't do that. You're smart enough to be better than just an artist. Be somebody important." Her words hit me like a slap. Suddenly my tulips seem pale and dull. At this moment, I can think of nothing that is special about me. I quietly retreat as my magic carpet fades, becomes the well-worn Persian stair runner in the hallway. Colors muddy to dull maroon and dark blue. I trudge upstairs to dress for Sunday school. By then, clouds have blown in and the hall darkens. When I reach my room, cold rain blows across the sills, and I hurry to close the windows against the chill storm.

Slowly, despondently, I dress: Carters' cotton undies and a nylon slip, white piqué blouse with dark blue piping, navy pleated skirt from my Sunday suit, white fold-over socks. I buckle the thin straps of my black patent leather shoes. All I can feel is the bleak cold rain sweeping across my Sunday. One step at a time, my dreams fade; like tulip petals dropping off, they lose their color and blow away in the wind.

SUNDAY PICNICS

Kitchen work done, all cleaned up, the family relaxes together in the living room. I climb into the overstuffed rocker to look at Grandma's picture album. I always ask questions about the photographs and especially love hearing stories about when Mom was a little girl. "Sonny," they called her, her last name was Sonn. She always looked happiest when the family stayed at their camp on Summit Lake. Usually Grandma went up there with Uncle Jimmy on Fridays. Mom and her best friend, Lillian, would go along. By Saturday, when Grandpa could get away from work, the girls had already rowed across the lake and back, gone swimming a couple of times, and caught some trout for dinner that night.

In the blue cloth-covered album, some pictures show winter scenes with shoulder-high snowdrifts. Mom and her friends stand arm in arm, bundled up in thick fur coats like polar bears. No smiles here, totally serious except for the photos of the sledding parties. Then, they're laughing so hard I'll bet it warmed them up. Most snapshots portray summer, with views of the lake and the family's camp from different years. When Mom attended college they still went to Summit. She and a few friends would sit on the dock or stone wall and pose in their long funny bathing suits that went over the knees. Their feet, all in a row, dangle in the lake, and their smiles beam bright enough to dazzle the whitecaps.

Then too, there are photos of places the family went for Sunday picnics when they weren't at camp. A whole series catches my eye: beautiful flat rocks, a stream, and waterfalls — Canajoharie Gorge. I recognize it right away, as we went there too, and it was my favorite summer place. In one particular photo, some of the family sits at the edge of a flat rock, like it's a bench. They must be spending the day. Grandma and Aunt Nellie look pleased, but serious, posing for the camera. Uncle Earl looks so handsome and young, just back from the war, I suppose, happy to be with Myra, his " little sweetheart," again. It was so hard for them to be apart. Aunt Myra's thrilled to have him back.

I can see that it's hot. Grandma has rolled her stockings down around her ankles, and Nellie has hers off, bare feet cooling in a shallow pool. My mom, "Sonny," sits stiffly with a big frown on her face, peeking out from under a wide straw hat. I think Sonny was alone with the grownups that day.

I remember going to the gorge with Mom, Dad and Grandma. I was running ahead, lured by the distant roar of water crashing down, swirling in the eddies. Mom yelled to me, "Slow down! Wait! Be careful… don't fall… it's slippery." But I can't wait, never do, and so around the bend I go, lickety-split. In minutes, I can see ahead the bright rainbow colors of bathing suits, all the kids at the falls. One at a time they climb, monkey-like, up the side rocks to the top, give a little jump, and off they go with whoops and screams of excitement. Standing where I can watch is almost as good as the next part. Just when I see Mom and Grandma come round the bend, traipsing along with the large picnic basket, I wave madly and take off, heading for the top of the falls. My skinny body launches into the rushing water and I'm carried away, all the way to the deep cold pool at the bottom. I can't imagine going to the gorge without feeling that rush — the pressure on my back, flooding over my head and shoulders — immersing my soul and taking me away.

AUNT NELLIE

It seems like Aunt Nellie has always lived in the upstairs back bedroom of Grandma's house. Sunday dinners, she sits opposite me, her sweet face and silver curls framed by the tiny pink roses that climb up the window trellis beyond. After some delicious dinner, like juicy roast beef, new potatoes, and gravy and peas with baby pearl onions, we clear the table. I help while Grandma makes tea and slices pie. Aunt Nellie reads the tea leaves right after pie. I sip a little tea from a delicate china cup just so she'll read my fortune. She takes pride in her readings, tipping the cup and draining the last drops so the leaves come to rest revealing a message from "beyond." As I look over her shoulder, she points out what she sees. "Look there, a little boat — that means you'll be going on a trip soon." And she usually has it right. I watch very closely, wanting to learn to see things in the clumped brown leaves. I love the way she gazes off for a second, over her spectacles. Something jumps into her head, like a spark. Then she softly speaks the message.

Aunt Nellie moved from Chicago to live with Grandma in 1947, after Uncle Herman died. She keeps Grandma company. The two sisters, who had lost their husbands in their mid-fifties, could share the house. Other people rented rooms upstairs too, like Marion Boyce, my first grade teacher, and her sister Helen. On occasion, a student from the state college would rent Mom's old bedroom. But Aunt Nellie has the best one; her room overlooks the backyard and adjoins the bathroom. She always liked talking about her darkly elegant home back in Chicago: velvet drapes, mahogany carved doorways, richly patterned carpets, Morris chairs, and stained glass windows. From photographs and the stories she tells, I learn that she advised people about their futures, and in particular could put them in touch with "departed" family members. Once she helped a stage actress who gave her a sterling silver medallion that she wears over her heart. I love holding it, feeling its raised Roman profile and the coins that dangle from the bottom. Sarah Bernhardt, she says, was a famous actress. She especially treasures this gift.

The summer I'm nine, Aunt Nellie dies suddenly. This happens right after Mom suffers another "nervous breakdown," and stays at the hospital for a while. I've never seen a dead person laid out. Bundy's Funeral Home feels very cold, and I shiver despite the hot day right outside the door. Dad leads me up front to look inside the coffin. Aunt Nellie looks strange, like they put make-up on her, which she never wore. Asleep, peaceful. I can't forget that day.

I visit her empty room. The bed is neatly made. Patterned and plain silky dresses hang in the closet; lily-of-the-valley talcum powder faintly tints the stale air in her closed-up room. Her Ouija board could be mine someday. The Sarah Bernhardt brooch goes to Mom, stashed in her drawer with old dance cards, sequined gloves, and evening purses from her college days. Aunt Nellie's journals and letters are packed away in boxes, stored in Mom's bottom desk drawer.

Years later, when I ask to read the journals, they're missing. "Gone? What do you mean? Where did they go?"

"You have to understand, Judy. They had to be destroyed. We couldn't let anyone ever find them," my mother tries to explain. "People might get the wrong idea."

No, I don't understand. All I know is that something valuable was taken from me, and lost forever. It just isn't right.

GRANDMA

I skip on the sidewalk, then up two steps to the porch, its railing freshly painted, and spin the doorbell a few times. I just like the feel of it, with the sound in my hand. Grandma will know it's me. I go right in, stop for a minute, feel the warm sun on my face stream through the front door windows. It's often like this on my way home from school. I'm ten and love to stop and visit her.

The entry hall feels like church, all quiet and lit up with patterned rays of gold on the carpet. When I open the inside door, the one with twelve panes of glass and a lace curtain, the smell hits me like being inside a gingerbread cookie. The cinnamon-ginger is everywhere, even inside my mouth before I've taken a bite. In the back kitchen they're laid out carefully on cake racks, stacked and staggered like the stone wall in the garden.

I run up behind Grandma. She sits at her treadle sewing machine, sways back and forth, rocks steadily like the train just pulling in at Center Street Station. I hug her soft sloping shoulders and smell her rose-scented powder, feel the smooth rayon of her dress on my arms, and know her love for me is forever. She turns and hugs me back.

"Here you are, precious. Are you hungry? Let's have some cookies and a glass of milk."

She gets up slowly, kisses me on the forehead, and goes to pour the milk. I sit at the table with my books piled up; my gaze drifts past the black and gold Singer and lace curtains to the tiny pink roses that cluster around the window and spill down the sides. Beyond sits the old well pump, the barn, and Petey, the aging cat, perched on the broken-out windowsill of the milk shed to sun his golden fur. His little snub nose lifts up ever so slightly to catch any movement of air, free to leap and run away at a moment's notice.

I'm scared. Mom's in the hospital again, Cooperstown this time, so Grandma will stay with us all week. We'll walk home after a while; stop at Morlang's Meat Market and Johnny Karker's store on the way. I'll help her shop and make dinners, as Dad will be home late every day this week. We're so lucky that Grandma can come over. I have no idea how long Mom will be gone this time, only know she's having another round of "treatments" to make her feel better. This will be her third hospital stay this year. I sure hope it works.

DEAR MOTHER

February 21, 1955

Dear Mother,
You are a very beautiful and wonderful
Mother.
I Love You Very Much.
I hope you get better.

Love,
Judy

I typed this on Dad's old Remington typewriter, even used the red ribbon for the "I Love You" part. Mom just got home from the hospital, so this is like my Valentine since she wasn't home then. I even made a white lace paper heart with tiny red hearts all over it. When I give it to her, though, she looks at me with a question. I don't think she knows it was Valentine's Day last week. Do treatments make her forget? She goes back again next week. Dad says after more treatments she'll see a special doctor in Albany.

I see Mom's not so sad lately, just tired all the time. Maybe she won't be so jumpy. When she came in the back door, she looked all dreamy eyed, stared at me, half-smiled, but no hug. Dad led her in to the couch, where she practically lives. I notice that she doesn't remember stuff, like where she keeps her purse, the cigarettes, her pills, or the week's grocery money. No driving. Dad says we'll take care of shopping and the errands. She needs to rest for a few days.

Grandma calls the next morning, as usual. Mom doesn't pick up the phone right away, so I get to talk to her. She's worried, I can tell. After all, my mom is her little girl. I'm worried too.

* * *

Decades later I would find Mom's little red notebook, everything of importance noted in her flowing blue handwriting:

June 5, 1953 — Charlotte,
hospital — Cooperstown — nervous breakdown.

September 1953 — Bought chair and lamp.

September 20, 1953 — Aunt Nellie died.

October 3, 1953 — Charlotte, hospital.

October 28, 1953 — Got television.

November 3, 1953 — Judy — Booster shot, diphtheria, etc.

December 9, 1954 — Week in Cooperstown hospital, then to Ellis. Got Cliff to bring me home after 3 days, but went back for shock treatments (16).

II

Growing Up

1956–1961

Junior High

"Pssst, Judy!" Barby's sharp hiss cuts through the hushed classroom. She catches my eye, passes me a note folded in quarters. Mr. Saxton, "Dougy," looks our way but misses the pass. I keep the note on my lap for a minute, then carefully unfold it and sneak it into my propped-up math book. "Jimmy likes you." Three little words. My face seems hot and I'm sure it flushes bright red. I take a quick peek at Jimmy, and he's looking at me! Smiles like he knows about the note. I feel embarrassed, excited, and clumsy, like I might fall off the chair or dash out the door.

Mr. Saxton calls on me and asks for a simple description of a trapezoid. Although the shape dances clearly in my mind's eye, the words won't come out in orderly fashion. Jumbled. The class giggles and he moves on. At home, Mom focuses on our kitchen remodel project. Dad tears down walls, rips out our old cabinets. My playroom will become our spiffy new kitchen. Mom imagines herself an interior decorator. In fact, she's taking a correspondence course from the New York School of Interior Design. Packages arrive in the mail: books, outlines, floor plans, drawings, and tests. Her studies consume her, which makes both of us happy. Still, she nags me to practice the piano.

"What about all that money we spent on piano lessons since second grade? You wouldn't waste that, would you? And then you wanted to play the cello. Soon you'll join the orchestra if you practice." So I stick with both. The new cabinets arrive all the way from Nappanee, Indiana. They have a satiny natural cherry finish with hammered black wrought-iron hinges and pulls. Gorgeous! My mom is brilliant and has designed the coolest kitchen ever. Black and tan linoleum squares make up the floor, which Dad installs over one long weekend. I help by handing him tools as he applies the black tar-like glue in a combed pattern, then lays the tiles one square at a time. In the corner he builds a brick enclosure for the new GE oven, a scrumptious shade of turquoise. The matching refrigerator has a freezer in the bottom and opens with a foot pedal. Mom chooses an unusual dining set to accent the room: black lacquered round table and four matching captain's chairs — the total effect, our dream kitchen.

Finally we move in. From the old kitchen, we carry stacks of Fiestaware to our new cabinets. The colors, fiery red, cobalt blue, sunshine yellow, and grass green, look like jewels on the counter before lining up on the new shelves.

The following month, Coppes Nappanee, the cabinet company, sends photographers to take pictures of our kitchen from all angles. Mom's design has won the competition! The prize: A spot in their prestigious catalogue. Now she'll work harder on her interior decorating to achieve her goal.

For me, the highlight of the winter comes when I win a contest on the *S.S. Glendora* TV show. My prize is a trip to New York City and a visit to the set of the *Sid Caesar Show*. My parents drive me to Albany at 5:00 a.m. to meet my chaperone and the train. I love the railroad station: the rocking motion of the heavy viewing car, the frozen landscapes outside, humming along beside the Hudson River. Then we arrive at Grand Central Station, like photos of world-famous places in travel books. The high-domed ceiling sparkles with hundreds of leaded glass panes, like prisms. Sophisticated, well-dressed people hustle in every direction. The smells of warm pastries, exotic teas, fresh flowers, and perfume enchant me, and I love the way my patent leather shoes, with little flat heels, click on the endless marble floors. Outside we hail a taxi. Next, we show up inside the TV studio: Cameras on cranes, huge floodlights, men and women bustle around, make final adjustments, touch up make-up. I meet Sid Caesar, who smiles, greets me with a handshake, and repeats my name. The rehearsal is boring; however, I enjoy all the activity and am anxious to get back and explore Grand Central. Fortunately, enough time remains for a hot turkey sandwich at Schrafft's. I feel quite grown-up being in New York without my parents. I can hardly believe they let me go.

April blows in with a harrowing blizzard. Huge stalactite icicles hang outside my bedroom window. They melt and slide from the roof's edge into treacherous piles, luckily disappearing in time for my family's big spring vacation, six whole days in New York. We pull up to the canopied entrance of the Algonquin Hotel. A handsome man in a purple jacket and cap opens the car door for Mom, like she's the queen; then he helps me out of the back seat. After getting the luggage from the trunk, we pack into a shiny elevator with wrought-iron lacework for walls. This is my first time in a fancy elevator; it smells like dressing-table powder, rose perfume, and ladies' dress shops. The nice man sets up a rollaway bed for me; even so, the room's not crowded. We must be quite high up because from our window the cars and buses appear like Tonka toys, and people like busy ants. Beeping horns and trolley bells float up from the street below, sneaking in the window, which is cracked for fresh air. Our porter lets a little steam out of the radiator. "There. Now, sir, is everything to your liking?"

Dad says, "Thank you," and hands him a quarter. The porter tips his hat and disappears.

"Wow!" I think. "I have arrived!" Mom flits around the room, hangs up her black wool dress, silk blouses, and coordinating straight skirts. Several pairs of shoes line up in the closet, smartly matching the outfits above them. Due to the dirty slush in the streets, she'll wear fur-cuffed boots that pull on over her shoes. I love the special way her inch-and-a-half heels slip into the heel pockets of the boots, fitting close like leather gloves. Once we settle in, it's time for lunch. We can walk to the famous Automat restaurant only two blocks away; I can hardly wait.

The streets are slick, wet with snow thawed and melted by sun and salt. I remember the skyscrapers from my trip in December. Clouds partially obscured them then, but today they soar into a clear, perfect sky. Glints of sunlight sparkle from each tiny square of glass near the tops of buildings. Giant fluffy Easter bunnies crowd the windows of F.A.O. Schwartz, and I beg to go in. "Maybe after lunch," they say, and we continue crossing noisy streets at crosswalks. Streetcars clamor by, taxi drivers lean on their horns. Exciting chaos.

In glistening window displays, waxy mannequins wink at me, acknowledging my gaze. I can't stop staring at their glossy fingernails, pastel silk blouses, soft kid gloves, and matching purses, short veils falling from their pillbox hats. Mom and I always try to achieve this look for Sunday school and church. Since I sing in the choir I don't often get to show off my outfits, hidden under a maroon robe. Mostly I dress to please Mom and look nice for my junior high Sunday school class. Mom promises me a new spring coat this trip. And because it's the week after Easter, there will be great sales at B. Altman's. Finally we reach the Automat. Inside I hesitate, puzzled, expecting something shiny and special looking. What I see is a large plain room, long lines of bundled-up shoppers and lots of Formica tables. It reminds me of an oversized cafeteria. "Come along," Dad says. "You'll be surprised. I think you'll like it." As we stand in line waiting our turn he reaches into his pocket, jingles the change, and hands me a few nickels, dimes, and two quarters. I've been staring at a wall of small windows and am beginning to figure it out. No servers stand behind a counter dishing out steaming bowls of soup, casseroles, and sloppy joes. Instead I see a wall of small glass doors like mailboxes. Behind each door sits a plate or dish of food with Saran Wrap stretched over it. Labels explain the contents: Ham & Cheese on Rye, Potato Salad, Hot Macaroni & Cheese, Jell-O & Fruit Cocktail, Ambrosia, Turkey Club. There's a whole separate section of desserts: cream pies, fruit pies, cobblers, and puddings.

"Go ahead." he says softly, "Have whatever you want." I plunk in my quarter and the door pops open. I retrieve my club sandwich, complete with potato chips and a pickle. So cool! A cup of cream-of-mushroom soup sounds good, to warm me up, and a root beer for a nickel. I eat every bite but am too full for dessert. We'll definitely be back.

At the hotel, Mom takes two Cafergot pills for her migraine and lies down to rest with a cold washcloth on her forehead. The curtains are closed and I can't see out. Mom needs total quiet, so Dad lets me go down to the hotel's ground-floor shops by myself and gives me $1. I spend most of my time riding up and down in the elevator, just catching a ride to see what happens. Each floor looks slightly different. As I peek out, I see myself reflected in mirrors with gold frames over small curving tables, dishes of mints, and vases of fragrant daffodils. The seventeenth floor has its own parlor, velvet-covered chairs for reading, and a settee by the window. The couple I meet getting off the elevator must be rich. She's wearing a full-length mink coat; his overcoat is black wool, soft as a kitten when I brush up against him by mistake. I hope they'll invite me in for cookies, but I get a glare from the elevator operator that tells me I wouldn't be welcome. Later that evening Dad and I eat downstairs in the hotel dining room. Mom's headache took a turn for the worse so she stays in the room.

By morning Mom feels better, thank goodness. The pills must have worked. For the next two days we live her dream. Now that she's a licensed decorator, she can do business with wholesale furniture stores and places like Scalamandre Silks. Mom and Dad saved money from her first decorating job and came here to buy new furniture for a client and for us. The elevator walls at Anderson's Furniture Company are made of glass; we ride up and down viewing four floors of dining sets, sofas, beds, dressers, coffee tables, and lamps. My favorite piece is the tall wing chair Mom's having covered in "red poppy" brocade for us. For each end of our sofa she chooses gold French toile lamps with creamy silk shades. She picks out celery-green silk for new living room drapes, and a gilt ceramic box, just right to hold her cigarettes and lighter on the coffee table.

Next month when Dad finishes the wallpapering, our house will finally be done and beautiful. I love to watch Mom pick out the colors and fabrics, see it all come together in her mind. She dresses so smartly today. Dad holds her black wool coat over his arm as she strolls from one room to the next. Mom talks intimately to the well-dressed manager who treats her with respect, jotting down notes and descriptions of the items she orders. They meet at a big desk to fill out papers. Mom sits tall, auburn hair curled under just below her black velvet hat, tipped to the side like a beret. They must imagine she's an important decorator.

Mom lights a cigarette, sets it down after a long inhale, and signs more papers. I know she's nervous from the way her silky crossed leg keeps a rhythm, her toe leading in fast circles like a polka. Everything will be delivered in three weeks. They shake hands, smooth ivory fingers pressing together, making her very happy.

The next evening we attend a play billed as a comedy staring David Niven: *Hotel Paradiso.* I absolutely love it and laugh loudly at the antics of couples switching partners and rooms, jumping on big satin-covered beds, hiding out, getting caught. My mother seems embarrassed by my behavior. She later tells me that she didn't realize it was a "bedroom farce," that there would be "dirty jokes," and that I am much too young to be exposed to that. The next two plays we see are very boring. Still, it's fun being perched way up high in the top balcony of the tall, narrow velvet theaters. I feel special dressing up for dinner at the Brass Rail. It's my favorite restaurant in New York. They pour water into cut crystal glasses, like prisms catching the light. Deep reds of the thick velvet curtains remind me of Arabian Nights. We sit in curved leather booths while soft music plays and voices float like tinkling silver bells. Dad lets me order what I want, so of course I have duck with orange sauce, my favorite. Never have I eaten a meal so perfect.

I'm in love with New York, almost in eighth grade, and things are going well. I think Mom's new decorating business will be her cure.

The Fitting

Ninth grade and everything changes. Physical Education. Instead of practicing the jitterbug and shooting baskets in gym class we go directly to the girls' locker room, stash our books, purses, and clothing, and dress in our gym clothes. It's not a uniform exactly, but some version of it: shorts, tee shirt, and white Keds. As we change into our outfits, we unintentionally expose ourselves in our underwear, and again later when we dress after showers. The whole affair both excites and frightens me — being in high school, that is.

It's the fall of my freshman year, a coming of age ritual, time to purchase my first bra. Mom insists on accompanying me to Olsen's Department Store on Main Street. She promises to let me pick out my own bra. I have visited the ladies' underwear department many times, feigning interest in a slip or nightgown as a gift for Mom or Grandma. Once I even purchased a few items for myself: Light tan Berkshire nylons with seams and a garter belt for Sundays. Most recently I was urged to buy a panty girdle, an obnoxious contraption, so my tummy will be completely flat and nothing will jiggle under straight skirts.

"Hello, Judy, and Mrs. Fisher. How nice to see you." Mrs. Alder smiles from behind the glass counter, recognizing me from church. I smile back weakly, say hello, and let my eyes return to wandering from one display to another. "Playtex: the Living Bra" and "Cross your Heart" by Maidenform. How embarrassing! I'm fourteen years old and was sure we'd be looking at junior bras, not the real thing. After all, my budding breasts hardly qualify for a bra at all. I just can't face the gym locker room without one. "We're here to buy a bra for Judy," my mother announces. I quickly scan to see if anyone has heard. Luckily not. "Fine. Well, let's see," Mrs. Alder begins, coming around the counter to where we stand and eyeing my blouse. "Let's look at a couple of styles and then we'll take your measurements."

I cringe inside at the thought of measurements, imagining how that will go. She pulls out a small clear plastic drawer from behind the counter for my inspection. "Here, dear. I'm sorry there isn't much of a selection in 'juniors.' We don't have too much call for them. And of course we don't know your size yet." I carefully finger the two piles of bras, all cotton, with adjustable straps.

"Let's do the fitting now." She leads the way, behind the counter into a tiny fitting room with a peach-colored curtain. Once inside she directs me to remove my blouse. "Go ahead, dear. And take off the undershirt too. Let's see what we have." Very little that matters! Blushing, unbearably shy, I unbutton my blouse slowly and clutch the skinny white cotton undershirt in front of me.

"Now stand up straight and we'll measure underneath." The cloth tape measure feels cold on my skin as she pulls it tightly around my ribs. "That's for the number. Thirty-two will do it. Now the cup size." She stretches the tape right over my tender nipples and I think I might die on the spot. No one except Mom and Grandma has ever even seen me naked.

"Triple A. Okay, I'll be right back with a couple to try on." Soon she appears with two bras in hand. The cups are almost flat, very much like me, and sewn in concentric circles mounting slightly to little points. How will they look under my new sky-blue sweater set? Some of my girlfriends have more on top and look terrific. Mostly I'm hoping that no one notices anything different about me. Mom purchases the bras; she decides that two would be right, always a spare. She comes into the dressing room to give her approval. I want to be excited by this landmark shopping trip, but mostly I'm worried. What will happen Friday at gym class when everyone sees it? Will anyone know it's my very first bra?

Locker doors slam, voices giggle and laugh as the girls from third period run into the locker room. I'm here early, hoping to change into my gym clothes before Sal, Arlene, and the others show up; however, no such luck. As if they can sense my embarrassment, several girls, attracted like flies to a picnic, notice my new bra and feel compelled to mention it. Bad as this is, I know I'd be worse off in my undershirt.

THE PIT

When is the exact moment? A trapdoor drops quickly like the platform of the condemned; lights dim and a counterclockwise motion draws me down, the force like the suck of a riptide, relentless, not letting go, as I struggle against it. I feel my chest caving in. My arms wrap around, trying to hold me. They end up feeling like a python's grip, and with each shallow breath, held longer on the inhale, I become smaller and more rigid. My thoughts cast about, seeking "the incident" — what was it? — that triggered my descent. Where did I mess up this time?

On this particular day no outward signs appear, just a sinking feeling as, home from school, I enter the house. The glass in the front door rattles, and I notice long dusty slants of light filtering into the living room. Mom sits on the couch, smooth stockinged legs crossed, cigarette in hand. Her sharp glare tells me everything. I already feel guilty and wonder how bad it will be this time.

"Hi, Mom. Sorry I'm late, just stopped at Linda's for a minute to check on an assignment. And we walked the long way home — oh, and had a little cheerleaders' meeting for tryouts after school." Now I'm backpedaling. I can't mention the vanilla cokes we had at The Spa (strictly off limits — too low class, she says) or the Spring cigarette we passed around at Linda's as we shared the all-important happenings of our day.

"It's nearly five o'clock! Where have you been? Who were you with? That Arlene? I hope you didn't walk home with her. I've been worried sick, (one of her favorite phrases) sitting here waiting. Now I've got a migraine coming on."

"But Mom, remember I told you I'd be late today because of cheerleading, and — "

"You should have called." Her voice edges up.

"Gee, Mom, I'm really sorry. I didn't mean to make you feel bad. Time just got away from me. I'll do better next time...."

"That's what you always say!" She's yelling now. "And then here you are, late again. How can you do this to me?" She rams the filter butt into the ashtray, stands up, pushes past me, and stomps up the stairs.

I can really feel it now. My head buzzes and a sense of panic settles around me like a shroud of ground fog. I want to shake it off, but the molecules of mist have already congealed into a familiar position. The chill of being without hope sets in and begins to drag me down. Though I recognize the feeling, I have no memory of what happened the last time, or why, and no ability to stop it.

Mom's bedroom door slams, final evidence that "the play" is in motion. As I climb the stairs with my head down, I'm almost sleepwalking. At the top, her door is next to mine. I stand between them and listen for a sound, a signal. I knock softly... "Mom?"

The heavy silence tells me I won't be admitted, so I enter my own room, quietly close the door so as not to disturb her, and lie down to wait for Dad to come home. On my bed, knees pulled up, I wrap my arms tightly around my legs, feeling the hopelessness of the situation. Mom has gone into her dark hole and I am in mine. Once she said she hated me. Was that today, or just a different time? I can't quite remember. But those stinging words are stuck in my head. No matter how much I think I should be able to hang around with my friends, I often get slammed with the reality of Mom: that she needs me; that she needs to control me, that I make her ill.

Feeling sick, I begin to shake, my body contracting with a deep pain. Each breath hurts so much that I contemplate stopping. This is the worst pain I've ever experienced, and though I haven't thought much about death, right now it seems like a good option — just don't take another breath, kind of like fainting or falling asleep. Peaceful. A relief. A respite from this place without hope and full of pain. My pain. Mom's. If I can just hold that next breath....

I gasp. Air slams into my lungs and I can't refuse it. Just then Dad's truck crunches over the gravel outside my bedroom. His footsteps swish through the accumulation of yellow birch and red maple leaves. He has no idea what's inside. I hear the kitchen door downstairs open, then shut. I hear when he sets his metal lunchbox down on the Formica counter. He whistles his two-note hello as he takes off his work boots and hangs his jacket. The house is dead quiet. No TV. No talking. No dinner in progress. He might as well come right upstairs, and after he checks around, he does. I picture him standing outside our rooms, doors closed, wondering, guessing at what's going on. All too familiar. He raps and enters their bedroom. As usual I silently wait to hear what comes next. There are words, mostly hers, as he coaxes the story out of her.

After a while he knocks on my door and I hear myself say, "Come in." Dad sits on my bed, clutching his hands in his lap, and reaches out for me, first with his voice. "Your mom is kind of upset with you," he begins, "and she needs you to apologize for what happened today."

"Yes, I know," I say, so quietly. "And I did apologize." I mention this realizing it's pointless.

We both know what comes next. Best to get it over with. I must convince Mom that I am really, really sorry, that I won't do it again; ask her to forgive me. That's it, the drill. And until that happens life stands still, hushed, my breath held. Do it now.

I will myself up and off the bed. Dad will wait for me in case it goes terribly wrong. In her room the thick drapes are pulled closed and the radiator in the corner thunders, emanating the evening's heat. Mom slumps, propped up on two pillows, staring straight ahead as if I'm invisible. Then she turns and glares straight at me. Her dark hollow eyes blame me. I come with sadness and promises, and on my knees, I beg her forgiveness.

"Mom," I whisper, not wanting to make her headache worse, "I'm so sorry. I won't let it happen again." Please, please can we make this better? Can we fix it? Go back a few hours and I'll come right home.

Underneath, I am hidden away; the girl who tells crazy jokes to her girlfriends, juts out her jaw and talks pig Latin, loves being with them, and wants desperately to be a cheerleader. In my fantasy life Mom would be well, would let me have slumber parties and invite friends over for dinner. Things would go wrong, of course, but wounds would heal. In that other world, mistakes could fade to dim memory, a page in the story of a normal teenage girl growing up.

"I don't believe you," she says. And I know she's probably right. What's wrong with me anyway? I'll surely mess up again and hurt her.

"I'll try harder," I say, trying to convince us both, all the while silencing the other me, the defensive one who's screaming, *But I didn't do anything wrong! I was just late. Is that a crime? Can't I have fun with my friends? Can't you leave me alone?*

It is so quiet in the room and we both feel bad. I start to cry. After a bit, her mood thaws and we make a truce. I think I can do better, control myself, figure out a way to make it work.

"Thanks, Mom," I hear myself say, relieved that for the moment we'll have peace in the house.

"I'm going downstairs to help Dad make dinner. Will you come down soon?"

She draws out the silence with her sigh. The darkness of the room suffocates. I open the door for some air, and to leave. I wait for her answer.

"You go ahead. I don't know if I can eat. But before you go, bring me another Cafergot. They're on the bathroom counter. And some water. It's probably too late to stop the headache, but maybe it will help."

She always says that. Once her migraines start, the Cafergot doesn't help much, but she takes them anyway. I think her headaches must be hell and I feel really sorry for her. When she's in the living room on the couch I draw the moss-green silk drapes, bring her a cold washcloth for her forehead, and massage her nylon-stockinged feet. If the headache isn't too bad she keeps smoking her Parliaments and watching the news. Then, some loud commercial might set her off and I silence the TV. Eventually, either her medicine works and she doesn't get a full-blown migraine or she orders up some hot milk and the little yellow sleeping pills and goes to bed. Always the same. I can see it coming, hopeless, and for the life of me, I don't know how to change any of it.

TUNING UP

Missing the school bus that morning, the first warm day in April, sends me into a tizzy. I don't dare go back home and walk into a scene with Mom that I just escaped. Best alternative is to hoist my cello across my hip, its wide carrying strap slicing my chest, and start down Lark Street at a fast clip. Every so often a car pulls up behind me and I turn, hoping to recognize someone and hitch a ride.

The only people on the street at that hour are the old folks heading to the A&P for their Wonder Bread, milk, and groceries, or walking their cocker spaniels. Most students have already arrived at school on the hill, disembarked the bus, stowed jackets and extra books in lockers, dressed for track, or unpacked their various musical instruments.

I cut across the field out back of Bundy's Funeral Home and pass the Methodist Church, its front door ajar. The organ sounds ring out. Miss Meriness practices early, and the way she pounces on each chord makes me pick up my pace, focus my effort to make it on time. Three and a half blocks to go — north on Grand Street, west on Elm — I'll only be a tad late.

When I reach the Catholic Church at the bottom of High School hill, their door is open too, but not a sound comes out. I follow my impulse, quickly duck down the church driveway, and go around back to the little chapel to visit Mary and her candles. There are always several red glass holders with votives lit by early visitors making their prayers. So little time, but I light one anyway and cross myself, the way I've seen others do. I secretly wish I were Catholic. The forbidden rituals, confession, and the fact that three of my best friends are Catholic — all this pulls on me. When I mentioned to my mom that I'd like to attend their church, just see what it's like, she practically had a cow! Like it was some evil thing. Why does she get so mad? I don't get it. Silently, I promise Mary I'll be back. Fortunately, no one sees me here.

Heading up the steep path, I'm in the home stretch. I push myself, willing my legs to keep pace and not give in to the burning messages from my thighs to slow down, stop, or ditch my cello. Finally, I crest the hill and puff up four steps to the heavy front door, grab the fat brass handle, and pull the plate glass door toward me.

Inside, the long hall is weirdly empty and still. Slanted alabaster light glares off the polished granite floor. Absolute silence. I miss the laughter, babbling voices, and bells, the shuffle and clatter of morning lockers opening and closing. As I pass quickly down the corridor, all I hear is my own breath, the pounding of my heart, relentless, tapping out its rhythmic reminder of my lateness.

And then, knowing it had been there all along, I begin to hear the sound of the orchestra tuning up. Faintly at first, I hear the violins, each open string plucked gently for accuracy, its clear fourth needing to harmonize precisely with the other instruments: bass, cellos, and violas. The closer I get, the more dense and complex the sounds. Cacophony. Reeds and horns override the strings. Clarinets, oboes, and saxophones claim the midrange, practicing trills and riffs. Flutes, bassoons, and a tuba fill in the top and bottom. A drummer nervously taps out a sexy rhythm on his snare. No one will hear me sneak in.

Miss Wilcox stays busy with the violins. They need a lot of extra attention to be in perfect accord with each other, or the entire orchestra will sound out of tune. She has turned away from the cellos; enough time, I hope, for me to get seated. Standing behind one of the stage curtains, I extract my bow from its pocket and awkwardly slip the stiff cloth case over the top of my cello. Done! I fold and stash the case on the floor, wait for the right moment, and move stealthily toward my place in the back row, right behind Claudia and Carolyn, already tuning up their cellos. As I sit, the chair slides a bit, making a skidding sound, hard rubber on wood, a sound definitely not part of the orchestra. Miss Wilcox hears it right away, turns just in time to catch the guilty flush on my face and spot my music floating to the floor. She glares, the "Where have you been?!" glare. I can do nothing but adjust the cello between my knees and quietly pluck the four strings, tune my instrument, and hope she doesn't make a scene. After the morning I had at home, I don't think I could take another drama.

CAMP, 1959

Summer camp, alive with days of privilege and nights of secret plans to jostle the smooth schedule of our senior unit — Cherry Point. Evenings provide a silken balm, relief from my agitated home life. Just to be away for two whole weeks, shortly after school closed! I hadn't thought my folks would let me go. And thank goodness for Senior Girl Scouts, the anchor of my stormy little ship, a harbor where I'm always welcome. The after-school weekly troop meetings at Carolyn's, and occasional weekend campouts, mean that for one day I'm not expected home until 4:30, maybe even 5:00.

Collecting dry sticks and mossy limbs fallen from the previous winter's heavy snows, we giggle and chatter in the woods. The shore of Lake Otsego spreads out close by; the water lapping softly through tumbled stones creates a sweet rhythm. We drag tree fragments to a spot near the fire pit where we chop and break up the wood and stack it. Then we build a twig teepee over thin shavings of birch bark; larger pieces crisscross the whole thing. Our night's fire takes off. We share these tasks in order to hone our outdoor skills. Badges and levels of proficiency are involved, but at camp, it's all about feeling good.

These friendships feel natural to me, and quietly soothe my spirit. We gather in a circle; form small baskets, like nests, from pine needles and twigs, write secret messages on birch bark with charcoal, drum in rhythm with sticks on rocks and logs. I warm to these new friends like chocolate and marshmallows softening between graham crackers over the coals — "S-mores."

The previous year, my first time at Girl Scout camp, I stepped on a rusty nail that punctured my foot. A number of tetanus shots went directly into my foot — fourteen, I think, like my age; and though I insisted on staying at camp, negotiating the narrow footpaths on crutches, my activities were severely limited. I watched the girls from shore during canoe and swim lessons, and had to stay back in camp with the younger ones when my unit went on their overnight. Nonetheless, I had an amazing time and felt sad when my parents picked me up.

This year, as the campfire blazes each night, my heart expands with the gorgeous harmonies of "hang your head over, hear the wind blow, hear the wind blow, dear, hear the wind blow," and *Kumbaya.* Our faces light up, golden-amber, and flicker like the flames, reflecting back the feelings I have for my new friends.

Make new friends, but keep the old,
One is silver and the other gold.

This familiar round dives in and out of itself like silverfish trout playing in the cattails at the edge of a stream, sun glinting off their backs. Each part perfectly complements the other, weaving the whole, just like our unit. Life is perfect in these star-crossed nights on the edge of the lake. I feel happy for the first time in a long time. Holly and Sandy have become my mentors, the understanding counselors who truly listen to me. I feel at home here, where my heart can rest, be safe, and learn. At the end of summer, I trust them to be friends forever, as they have touched me so deeply.

When the final day comes, I cry bitterly with my tent-mates as we pack up our bedrolls and canvas duffels, neatly rearrange the four cots on the wide-planked platform floor, sweep, and promise to write. We exchange tiny wallet photos of shining faces, records of the sweetest summer of my fifteen years. My world is dissolving. Sweet voices still croon in my head: "M – I – N ... N – E – T... O... S – K – A...Minnetoska, Cherry Point."

Minnetoska: Land of dreams, where tribal elders care — their wisdom does not die with the red-orange glowing embers — children laugh and run and play and are kind to each other, truth and loyalty guide the days like the sun that sheds its ever-present light and blankets our world in its welcome embrace. Will I ever come home again — my heart's true home? Sadness creeps over me as I realize, in the depths of my being, that it could be a long, long time.

After Camp

Soon it will be over. Tonight, my bedside reading lamp shines all too brightly, illuminating a book I don't intend to read. Two clicks reduce the light to a dim glow, one that matches my mood. In my clean rosebud shorty pajamas, propped up by two feather pillows, I feel ready to say goodbye.

Two weeks at Camp Minnetoska confirmed for me that kindness and understanding aren't just abstract concepts — they mean something. As our voices blended in song around the campfire, we grew close, bonded in a way my heart remembers. The lake in which we daily immersed our bodies felt like an icy baptism — all so magical. The tribal bonds fed my soul. We shared so much. I was happier than I can ever recall.

With no previous history, we came together easily; personality problems sorted themselves out. Our counselors guided us with steadfast brilliance, like the North Star on the clearest night. And in those sharp cold evenings, my frozen heart began to thaw. Perhaps it was the turning point I had hoped for, one that would change the way I'd been meeting challenges and dealing with my mother: create a veneer of protection, a shield to carry over my heart. But now I'm ready to lay it down.

When my parents picked me up, they didn't understand my tears. Mom missed me and was anxious; glad to have me back, she expected a warm reunion. Dad gave me a quick hug and the usual peck on the cheek. Tense emotions flooded our meeting, as I showed up absorbed in my grief at leaving the life I'd grown to love. Each goodbye hug and promise to write tore me up. As we loaded my duffel bag full of smoky laundry into the back of the Chevy, I felt the pulls of camp and home toss me around, swirl me in an eddy, ready to dump me out, coughing and spitting, to compose myself and swim. A survivor, I thought I could make it, but my heart was ill prepared for the return trip to my old life. Mom pulled the car door shut, withdrawn and disappointed; I slouched in the back seat, holding my heaving chest.

We went home the back way, heavy station wagon lumbering over velvet fields strewn with horses, cows, fat wheat ready for its final summer cut. Later, Mom said we'd visit Grandma because she was sick in bed, maybe a hernia. The doctor would go by that afternoon. I sat up tall as we passed her house on Grand Street, to glimpse any sign of her — a door cracked open, a letter sticking out of the mailbox. The shades were pulled against the afternoon heat and I could imagine her inside, lying there in the cool stillness. I noticed the worry in Mom's voice and let go a little of my own dark mood. Grandma has to be all right.

Back home, I sorted my dirty laundry — whites, lights, and khakis, dark greens with denim — enjoying the musky smoke it had absorbed. Dark piney resin spots glared from the seats of most shorts and pants, remnants of hours and days spent sitting on the forest floor or on logs around the campfire.

"Those stains won't come out. Your clothes are ruined," Mom whined.

"What about that turpentine stuff you use on Dad's work pants? That might work."

"It'll take the color out. No, you've wrecked them." She shot me one of her you've-done-it-again looks. I had no reply.

"Maybe next time you'll be more careful. We're not buying you any more summer clothes. You'll have to make do with what you have."

Next time. But I knew I wouldn't be more careful, was likely to mess up again, continue to displease her, never get it right. The washer slogged away at the clothes, spinning out of balance and threatening to shake loose the small painting on the wall. Stop. Rebalance. Start again, and maybe the fresh, clear water would rinse it all away.

Once the water heater had recovered from two loads of laundry, a hot bath with its privacy called out to me after dinner. I added a little packet of bath salts to the thick stream that filled the tub. The mugginess of August pressed into my lungs. I needed to feel special.

Even at 90 degrees outside, the ancient electric heater still sat in the upstairs bathroom, its ugly gray body about the size of a suitcase, its innards composed of long spiral coils that zigzagged back and forth. When the temperature last winter dropped below 32 degrees, the room's tiny radiator couldn't keep the room warm, so when preparing a bath, I was allowed to plug in the old heater, carefully avoiding its black-and-white cloth cord, to bask in the radiant heat.

"And don't ever touch it with your wet hands! And don't unplug it until you're bone dry. You'll be electrocuted and die!"

Winter baths had always included these dire warnings, and I grew petrified of electricity, cords, and plugs. I feared that hot intensity, the fire, even as I warmed my wet self as close as I dared.

With the window open and the door cracked to encourage a breeze, I stepped lightly into my summer bath. The heat elated me, penetrated deep, and brought me into myself. As I eased into the water, the feel of its contact all over my body held me like Grandma's hugs — soft, secure, and accepting. I soaked and slid all the way underwater to wet my hair, paused to hold my breath and let out the bubbles one by one. My fingers combed my long hair, splayed out like a floating halo. The golden thick foam of my Breck shampoo felt delicious, and I scrubbed extra hard. Then, cool water spilled over my head, full-on pressure from the faucet, like a waterfall. And even through the noise of it, Mom's sharp voice pierced the thick air.

"Why are you taking so long? You've been in there long enough. It's almost bedtime. You still have to dry you hair and roll it. Otherwise it'll be all matted by morning." (This was a look she often referred to as "drowned rat".)

"Okay, just rinsing, be out in a minute."

"And don't forget to scrub the tub ring. Turn the faucet tight so it doesn't drip. And hang up your wet towel."

I knew these things, cross my heart, and she reminded me every single time I took a bath. I heaved a big sigh and realized I had no energy left for a response beyond "okay." Her reminders and criticisms left me weary, with little hope of change. My head throbbed and I understood how tension could bring on a headache.

Mom's evening ritual had already started: One sleeping pill around nine with a little snack. Given that a headache was hovering, Cafergot was also on the round tray. In an hour, if a certain drowsy feeling didn't accompany the *Ten O'clock News,* she'd take another pentobarbital and Cafergot with hot milk, prepared by Dad. At 11:00 or so, leaning heavily on his strong bony frame, she'd stagger up the stairs, and, lying flat on her back, allow him to pull off her stockings and tight girdle, unbutton the blouse, awkwardly prop her up to pull the Barbizon nightgown over her head, and lay her down again. Sometimes I just watch, or help him, silently folding her silky stockings over the back of the rocker. She looks so peaceful then, asleep like an angel baby lost in her dreams, almost smiling. Then last week, unintentionally, it happened. The idea just came to me.

I'm in the bathroom, holding an aspirin bottle in my hand, and I notice Mom's amber pill bottles. The small one, pentobarbital, stays right there in the top drawer of the bathroom vanity, as she often needs more sleeping pills in the middle of the night. When I rock the bottle back and forth between fingers and thumb, the small yellow capsules rattle. The bottle is three-quarters full, and in a second I flip off the top and slip four into my bathrobe pocket, like I know what I'm doing, as if I'd planned it. Back in my room, the capsules fit perfectly in a little butterfly tin, and I hide them in my safest stash, the secret compartment under the plaid upholstered rocker, along with my locked diary. I pray Mom will never again find and read my private thoughts.

Each of the next three nights, after brushing my teeth, I remove another four pills from her bottle and add them to my tin. I feel calm and oddly numb, confident that a plan is emerging. The hot days linger, unspoken hostilities hang heavy in the air like soggy laundry. September and the start of school are still a long month away; time away from home, maybe cheerleading, basketball games, Scouts, and friends. Then too, there will be Latin II and Miss Hamel's World History — dreaded subjects that will cause me to work harder than ever to make good grades. Even that looks pretty good, just so far away. I can't wait.

A thin sheet covers my lap. The brisk night wind feels cool; it ripples the café curtains and passes over me with a hint of rain, maybe thunder and lightning. Finally, a promise of relief from the long day's buildup of pressure and humidity. I pour a cool glass of water and sip slowly; I swallow each pill separately — sixteen in all. I reread my letter, composed earlier on college-ruled paper, and feel satisfied with its message. There is little more to say. All the details leading up to this moment have tumbled through my head a million times and are wrung out and spent.

I have conveyed, to the best of my ability, the essential meaning. They will have to deal with it from here. It's over for me — a good choice, I think. I will be free and in a better place.

A sweet sleepiness begins to seep into my body, like the time I had my tonsils out in Dr. Becker's office, only without the sharp ether smell. They had promised I'd wake up and get to have ice cream. Dr. Becker gave me a Russian painted wooden doll with a fierce face. Inside was a woman, and inside that, a small child, which I lost. I came to think of him as my guardian. I hope, as I lie here, that someone will help me on this journey. I know I won't be waking up or having ice cream. I know things will be better, and whatever happens, it will be an improvement over the present circumstance. As I slip into a dream, I see the note flutter to the floor with a little puff of wind, like a leaf on its final journey.

The words lie on the floor, the message facing up, waiting till morning. They will read it in a panic, once through, the words searing their minds with the girl's truth: that they did not love her. And call the hospital.

August 6, 1959

Dear Mom and Dad,
I am going to take some of your pills and kill myself. This is no joke.
I love both of you so much, but you don't love me, so there is no point in living.
I'll always love you, though.
Judy
PS: Please write Sandy and Holly and send them my love.

LIFE GOES ON

Why am I here? And alive? They say I'll go home after a week in the hospital. I remember vaguely hearing a nurse say they pumped my stomach, that I'm so lucky my parents found me in time. I try hard to put the pieces together, but it seems more like a dream that happened to some other girl trying to escape her life. When Mom visits, she looks worried, stares at me, but doesn't even get mad.

As I lie propped up in the steel hospital bed, I can see most of Cobleskill from my window, spread out below, nestled in the valley like a bird's-eye view. I know right where our house sits — under the thick maple foliage just three doors west of the tallest steeple in town, the Lutheran church. When the wind blows just right, I hear its hourly chimes, reminding me that I am still here.

Three weeks later school begins, and no one knows what happened to me. At home everything is different. I have a hard time knowing what to do or how to act. I feel exhausted and watch TV a lot, don't call my friends or return their calls. Mom is on her good behavior. She doesn't criticize, nag, or get angry. When she gets a headache, she slips quietly away to her room without much fuss. Dad treats me like I'm sick, gives me extra attention. None of us mentions what happened, how I nearly died or why. I'm not sure if Grandma knows — if she does, she doesn't show it. We all silently agree: just forget it ever happened and move on.

Sophomore year brings more homework than I ever imagined. Miss Hammel, notorious for being the strictest, works us hard in world history. The room goes dead still when she enters. Best to be wide-awake, especially if she calls on you. She rewards complacent attitudes and dreamy looks with detention and extra essays. As if our load weren't heavy enough, but no pity, that one. Next comes Latin II: "*Gallia est omnis divisa in partes tres*" (a translation from the Gallic Wars). This is the sleeper class. If not for Claudia and Carolyn and our unique version of speaking Latin, I'd never make it. In the evening, Claudia and I call each other — homework calls — and laugh hysterically over fumbled conjugations and rhyming pig Latin.

Slumber parties at Sandy's are the most fun, when I can convince Mom to let me go. Shorty pajamas and sleeping bags, laughing till our bellies ache, doing impersonations; up till midnight or 2:00 a.m. Next morning, Sandy's mom fixes us the primo breakfast: pancakes with real whipped cream from the squirty can, and hot chocolate. With all of us seated around the table in our PJs, rumpled hair, munching and giggling, I feel completely at home, one of the gang. I'm in heaven.

In October, the three of us, in Dad's Chevy station wagon, drive over to Massachusetts, near Boston, to visit and interview at Northfield School for Girls. My parents have decided I need a change next year. Mostly I don't care. Life feels complicated. Sometimes I don't seem to fit in, like at weekend necking parties, where slow dance music and dim lights encourage steadies and singles to explore their passions. I wish. With no boyfriend and no prospects, I feel left out. Going away to school sounds like a relief.

Cheerleading tryouts are after school on a Thursday. I feel anxious about the whole thing. All month I practice for hours trying to get my timing just right, my moves smooth but energetic like a dancer, my arch high enough with the perfect curve when I peer sideways in Dot's mirror. Dot, the cheerleading coach. We call her that behind her back. She'd probably kill us, or worse. She can get really annoyed, her ocean-blue eyes giving us "the look." But it's great to be on her good side too. Dot Hudson is the first adult to be straight with us about our periods, which we call "having our friend." As the girls' gym teacher, she deals with it all the time, being the only one who can excuse us from P.E. She keeps track, and she knows when someone's faking. The first time I had to talk about it, my cramps were so bad that she let me lie down in her office. Then she told me about Tampax.

I was really scared to stick that thing "up there," and didn't try for ages, but once I got the hang of it, a lot of problems were solved — like overflow and accidents. I bleed profusely and use the biggest, thickest Kotex pad made. So bulky, and so embarrassing, but it works.

I'm pretty sure I know who will make the squad, and they all deserve to. Some of my friends were cheerleaders last year, practiced and worked really hard. Each one has extra-special magic: Great looks, perfect hair, the coordination and grace of gazelles, top grades, too — qualities that I lack. My hair hangs straight down and is too fine to hold a flip. I feel awkward at dance, P.E., and even cheerleading sometimes. And with boys. In a slow dance I'm afraid of tripping, lost in some *Moon River* dream. I'm kind of plain looking, nothing special, and at five feet seven inches, too tall. I might as well admit it — I probably won't make it.

Someone has the bright idea to create song leaders to back up the cheerleaders. Carolyn, Mary Ann, and I form this new group. A little status goes along with the position and helps with my social life, freedom, and self-esteem. We are required to attend games. Basketball is the biggest thing going on throughout the long winter. No other sport in our school carries the same team spirit. I especially love going to the away games in Schoharie or Middleburg, even Cooperstown. The bus ride, with loud singing, the tired excitement on the way home after we've won, voices hoarse from screaming, even the quiet gloom and depression following a game lost but well played. The feeling of belonging on that bus — thick, warm, and delicious like dark chocolate syrup — fills all the lonely nooks and holes in my spirit. Exhausted, arriving back in town near midnight on a Friday night, I creep up the stairs at home, trying to avoid each creak in the wooden steps. I fall into bed half dressed, teeth not brushed, so happy that tomorrow is Saturday.

BIKE HIKES

The sharp nip in the morning air wakes me way too early, right about the time I hear the rattle and clink of thick bottles dropping into our galvanized milk box on the porch. Today, besides tall bottles of milk with an inch of cream, we will get a short bottle of the heavy stuff to whip for chocolate pudding. Later, I'll make our dessert from a Jell-O pudding mix, adding a bit of fresh cream, then pouring the runny chocolate mixture into footed glass dishes. In the icebox, they will chill and thicken by dinnertime.

After the milkman leaves, Dad starts the lawnmower and passes it back and forth across the yard. I can picture the blades flashing in the sunlight, the cut grass piling up in little furrows for me to rake. He times it just right so the lawn is dry, but still it's not too hot out. I just want to sleep in. The world is against me. I can pull the sheet over my head, but I can't hide from my life.

Saturdays. Chores, and then I'm free! Around 10:30 I crawl out of bed and immediately begin to wad up the sheets and drag them from my room to the hamper. Might as well get it over with. Freshly ironed sheets sit in a small stack in the linen closet. I dash downstairs for a shot of O.J. in a Fiesta juice glass, just to get through the morning.

Before I meet the girls for a bike-hike, I must clean my room, my parents' room, and the bathroom: change beds, dust mop, vacuum, dust and polish furniture with Lemon Pledge, scrub the bathtub, swish the toilet, and mop floors. These are my Saturday jobs. If Mom's sick, she'll try to make it down to the couch so I can clean the upstairs. If she feels really bad, I'll have to do it later so she can pull the thick drapes closed and try to sleep in her darkened bedroom. Then there can be no noise. I must unplug the phone in her room. Tiptoeing everywhere, we try to keep watch so no one will sneak up and ring the front doorbell. So shrill! Dad stuffed cardboard in the ringer to muffle it. I wish

Mom could get over her migraines. According to the doctor, there's no cure. Cafergot offers the only help, that and her sleeping pills. And then, in the morning, pep pills.

Bike-hikes offer my great escape. Three or four of us usually meet near the Park Theater before noon, with peanut butter sandwiches, chips, and cold bottles of Coke or root beer in our bike baskets. Today it's Ginny, Sandy, Claudia, and me. We take off down South Grand, under the railroad bridge, past the fairgrounds, and across the creek, its spring-green willows billowing gently. The landscape changes abruptly, town ends, and we're free. I love to pedal fast and hard on the straight stretch, and at Mineral Springs Road we hardly stop, just hang a left. A couple of miles later, we turn up a dirt road for the real adventure. The slight incline and bumpy, dusty surface make it a sweaty job.

The air is pungent, alive with the smells of farms and hayfields. We turn into the dirt driveway of the ramshackle farmhouse we discovered weeks ago, throw down our bikes, and climb up to the rickety porch bathed in sharp sunlight to eat our lunch. We practically inhale our sandwiches, wash them down with cokes, still chilled, and we're off to explore. Voyeurs and vandals.

We start in the kitchen. Leaks and broken windows have let in the rain and snow, leaving water stains on windowsills. Most have failed caulking and loose panes of glass. We help them along, busting out a few more panes. Cupboard doors hang askew, hinges rusted, linoleum peeling upward from rotted floorboards. How long since anyone lived here? Dented aluminum pans, pots scarred black; thick chipped white mugs left unwanted on grimy shelves; fingerprints, baby ones down low; an old wooden pull-cart shoved in the corner. I imagine a family living here, happy in their out-of-the-way existence. They would have fixed the broken squares of glass, reworked the glazing to perfection.

Up the narrow worn-edged steps we find two bedrooms and the house's only bathroom. The beds are stripped, mattresses stained, askew as if someone had started to steal them, drag them downstairs, then thought better of it. In the dresser lie clothes that smell of mold and mouse pee; and in the closet hang three dresses. One, on a cloth-covered hanger, is fashioned of finely crocheted ivory silk or rayon; intricate patterns border the hem and wrists, fancy collar made separately, then attached. I see that it's my size, and I must have it. If Grandma ever dressed up, this would have been so beautiful for her. I stuff it in my knapsack before anyone sees.

Time to go. We four race down the road; low-slanted sunrays warn us that we're out of time. Every weekend, the day's end surprises me; the light runs away, dives toward the western hills. By 5:00 Mom fusses, if it's 5:15 there will be the looks and lectures: "Where were you? I was so worried" and "Just look at you, all streaked with dirt." I never get home early, occasionally on time, but often a little late. But worth it? Every minute feeds my soul, I think, as I deposit my dirty Bermudas, shirt, and socks in the yellow hamper. Next Saturday, the time change. Darkness descends. Winter closes in. No more bike-hikes this year. How will I escape?

Sleeping In

Saturday morning sleep-in. The sun's blazed into my bedroom window for hours already. I simply roll to the wall and pull the old feather pillow over my head. The mantel clock continues to chime loudly each quarter-hour. First the coffee aroma, then the soft padding of my father's slippers rouses me from my slumber. Saturday, my day to clean, and I wake with a dull headache and a tremendous desire to pee my brains out. Following five minutes of splashing my face with icy water, I down two Excedrin, pull on my bathrobe, and head downstairs. Surely Mom's awake by now, has had her pep pills, coffee, and toast, and hopefully is in a good mood.

She sits close up to the table in her tall-backed Windsor chair, a deck of cards stacked for her to spread out seven piles, turn them over, and begin. A steaming cup of coffee beside her, she stares out the window, watching the goldfinches twitter around the bird feeder.

"Good morning, Mom."

Like a movie in slow motion, her face turns toward me. Dark circles ring her eyes, and I know she hasn't slept much. I shudder, cringe at what will come next.

"Where were you last night? I know you didn't go bowling, because I checked — they hadn't seen you girls all night. You were late, quarter of eleven at least. I heard you sneak upstairs. Had a headache by then, of course, so I didn't get up."

Silence.

"Answer me! And don't lie about it!"

Her angry words jolt me like a clap of thunder and leave me drained.

"Well," I begin, "when we got there, to the bowling alley, I mean, all the lanes were full, leagues, you know. We decided not to wait all night. Linda said we could go to her house — "

"So," she interrupts, her voice sharp, full of accusation, "why didn't you call?"

She has me there and we both know it.

"The pay phone was busy," I croon lamely.

* * *

We'd been laughing, nearly peeing our pants in the parking lot, as we watched the older league bowlers with their serious looks and beer bellies hanging out of shiny polyester team shirts. Six of us hopped into Sandy's parents' turquoise-and-white station wagon. A brief guilty thought crossed my mind: *Call home,* but it was over when someone passed me a freshly lit Spring cigarette. The menthol cooled my mouth on the slow inhale, like the breeze the car made cruising out of town, windows half-down, picking up speed as we veered toward Warnerville. It was still light out, and plans were emerging. We would drive past the Palace skating rink and see who was there, maybe stop and look in, or if we dared, actually go in! There wouldn't be much time, not enough to rent skates and take a few spins around.

The easy rhythmic music already played in my mind as I laid my head back on the seat and dreamed of Matt, who would see me walk in, and with a breathless little catch in his throat, ask me to skate with him on the next slow one. As the lights dim, the mirrored ball flashing red, blue, and gold, Matt would get on his knees to tie my skates, then he'd reach for my hand and we'd be off like a summer breeze.

The car skidded into the gravel parking lot, breaking into my fantasy. Our laughter wove a delicious melody, tone over tone, one note beginning where the last trailed off. We were oblivious to the approach of three guys until they stood right next to our open windows.

"Hi, girls," drawled Mike. "Guess you all are too busy to notice us."

A bit embarrassed, but feeling the comfort of our numbers, we collected ourselves and, cool as we could, began to chat with them.

"You guys been here long? Have you been inside? Rented skates, or are you saving up for a six-pack?"

We giggled, knowing not one of them was eighteen or had much chance of buying beer. They were cute, though, and Matt seemed particularly handsome that night, his black leather jacket slung over one shoulder, the sleeves of his clean white tee shirt rolled up to expose gorgeous biceps. His jet-black hair, though a little too glossy, was long enough to be neatly slicked back and fall casually to one side of his forehead.

The cool, shiny black BMW glistened behind him, low-slung and inviting. Sometimes we talked, me standing by the handle-bars, just touching the cold chrome.

"Hi, Judy," he said shyly. " Got time for a quick ride?"

Boy, did I! I was out of the car, following him to his motorcycle in no time.

"Back in thirty minutes, boys, don't worry about us. Warner-ville Hill — thirty minutes flat — you can time us."

The little buttons on my sweater never got fastened all the way, and my hair was a tangled mess as my ponytail flew straight out behind me, but I didn't care. My arms clutched Matt's warm body as we eased into a turn and flew up the windy road. The evening felt balmy, and the full moon was so bright it seemed like daylight. Soft tree shadows danced on the road, brilliant halos outlining backlit clouds. In ten minutes we stood at the edge of a pasture overlooking the valley and surrounding hills from the most romantic spot I had ever visited. Matt scooted his arm around my waist, gently pulled me to him. My heart never quite stopped pounding from the ride. Now it fluttered and danced beneath my sweater like a fast jitterbug. He kissed me softly, and then again, like it really mattered.

"Hey, I knew I liked you," he murmured. "Just had to get away from those guys. You know what they'd say about us, don't you?"

Yeah, I sure did. I just didn't care. I knew that everything was perfect, with the moonlight blessing us. This moment might never come again, and we both felt its fragile bliss, like a sparkling spider web, stretched taut, trembling with the slightest breath of air.

Then we just held each other without speaking, for the longest time, let go in sync, a perfect dance step. We re-mounted the bike and headed downhill as fast as he dared. The tires left a gash in the gravel as we skidded up next to the car.

"That was a really long thirty minutes," Mike laughed as I gingerly climbed off the bike, steadying myself on Matt's arm. "Where'd you go? Sleepy Hollow?"

My face was red-hot. "Thanks, and goodbye, see you," I whispered to Matt.

"Yeah, see you again," he said back. The girls were shocked and curious. "What did he say? Did he try anything? Do you like him?"

I tried to laugh it off, be cool. "Oh, just a fun ride, no big deal."

"Matt's not your type at all," they whispered. Cute though, they agreed and nice, very nice. Just hangs out with the wrong crowd. And the motorcycle! Best to stay away, not be seen with him. People would talk, get the wrong idea. Nervous giggles, and the subject was dropped.

The conversation turned to weekend basketball games and summer plans. We sped home, took the back way, Mineral Springs Road, eased into town by the park. It was after 10:30 when Sandy dropped me off at the bottom of my steep drive-way. The house lights were off, except for the porch and hall. A quiet dread began to seep in, replacing the pure joy of just an hour ago. I had learned how to turn the front door's brass knob slowly, then push hard and quick, turn gently and release, like holding my breath and letting it out. That way the door wouldn't rattle or squeak. Clicking off both lights downstairs sounded like gunshots in the dark, but no one stirred. I paused, still as a man-nequin. The stairs of the 120-year-old house creaked randomly. I had to pee, bad. Somehow I managed to do so without waking my folks, or so I thought.

After replaying the night's events, and letting myself feel that dream kiss over and over, I fell into a fitful sleep.

* * *

Mom's sharp accusations jolt me from my daydreams.

"Still, you could have called," she pouts. "You are so inconsider-ate. Don't tell me excuses." Then louder, "There is no good excuse!"

She stands up, slams down the pack of cards in her hand, spills coffee, and heads upstairs. The bedroom door shuts with a bang, then nothing. I move numbly around the kitchen; Cheerios in a bowl with milk, small glass of orange juice. The sun burns high by now. Its sharp white brilliance pierces the kitchen in steep shards over the sink. I can hear Dad out near the garage loading his truck for the dump.

He won't be in again till lunchtime. The day stretches ahead endlessly, with little to soothe me. All I have today are my moonlit dreams.

NORTHFIELD JUNIOR

September, seven months to the day after receiving my acceptance letter, we inch up the narrow ribbon of driveway to my new dorm, West Marquand. The imposing four-story brick structure sits on a knoll that overlooks a gently rolling meadow and the Connecticut River. Just below, the Headmaster's House, with its two large chimneys and black shutters, looks nearly pastoral. I dreamed of this day all summer, and while sad to leave my friends in Cobleskill, I need to get away from home. It's best this way. I believe my teenage self is just too much for Mom to deal with — the reason why they're sending me away.

In June I began to prepare for the move. Once I'd shopped and acquired all the proper clothing, I sewed miniature laundry labels into each item, including underwear and a set of white damask napkins. I like sewing in the living room, Mom close by on the couch. She smokes her cigarettes and nibbles chocolates while I focus on the tiny, even hemstitches.

As the World Turns drones on, and the stack of pressed and labeled clothes grows. My life turns around too, imagining what I'll do at school when I put on the turquoise dummy smock ("dummy" stands for domestic duty). Swab toilets? Scrub floors on my hands and knees? Kitchen chores? I'll save the white cotton/poly shirtwaist dress for special occasions like May Day, Christmas Vespers, and Sacred Concert. For everyday classes, I'll wear pleated dark skirts, thick wool leggings, pullover sweaters, cardigans, button-down oxford shirts, and a navy blazer. The required "sturdies," ugly comfortable oxfords, are good for daily activities except church and sports. The absence of formal uniforms and fancy clothes makes everyone feel equal.

Summer days in upstate New York drag on, intolerably long and stifling hot. And what with Grandma having died just a month ago, I feel lost. An ache lingers in my throat and chest whenever I think of her, like all the time. In our living room, her photograph sits on the oval marble-top table, the one she gave us for Christmas. The redwood picnic table and matching benches grace the flagstone patio. Her wedding ring and gold brooch rest in a dish on Mom's dresser. Grandma's house remains all locked up. There's talk of a sale or auction later this fall. I can't bear to think of it, her whole life dismantled, sold off. She got sick; then after just two weeks in the hospital, she was gone.

Life at Northfield takes my mind off Grandma. I feel excited and scared at the same time, afraid I won't be able to make good grades, fit in or know how to act. My roommate, Lee, is a senior. I sense right away that we'll get along, though we're quite different. Across the hall live our floor's "cop," (student officer) Kris, and her roommate Liz. They're seniors too, just about the nicest people I've ever met. Before and after study hall they open their room for us to visit, hang out, talk, and listen to jazz on the record player. Before bed, a bell rings for "funny time," a school tradition of letting off steam. Twenty minutes with no noise control. Shouts, hoots, and laughter warble down the hall mixed with nonstop talk. Then, another bell, a warning, and the volume tones down. Yet another, and the halls fall quiet. Our sweet cop makes rounds, checks in, says goodnight. All is well.

A new and positive aspect shows up in my life. I don't mind the structure and making time for serious study, particularly when we all do it at the same time. Studying feels so different from my home experience, where the litany of "do your homework, practice the piano/cello/flute, clean your room," felt so negative. And, I was alone. Here at Northfield, hardworking students surround me; inspire me with their good study habits and serious approach to academics. But the subjects are difficult. At home I was used to getting A's and B's, an occasional slip to a C+, like in Miss Hammel's World History. Even Latin, I could pull off a B.

And now? Those C's look great! Every waking hour of study hall and all day most Sundays are crammed with writing papers, studying for quizzes, memorizing Biblical dates, Algebra II, and reading, reading, reading. I especially covet any extra time I can squeeze in for French Lab and time with my favorite teacher, Miss Wilkins. Her lilting accent takes me to Paris, where I think she lived and studied. I sit in my little cubicle, headset snug around my ears; I listen, repeat, and take pride in perfecting my accent. After sophomore year's dry Latin, this is *le bon temps.* I'm cut out for dorm life. Living with women feeds me in the place where I was lonely before and didn't know it, reminds me of camp, but lasts all year. Lee is what you'd call a good egg. She studies hard and is very serious, with a dry, edgy sense of humor. Our late-night talks range from politics to religion to philosophy. Her beautiful clear voice won her a place in the esteemed "Estey" Choir. My fondest hope is to at least make Chancel next year, the only extracurricular activity I really care about. At Christmas Vespers I weep, feeling the rich strains of the organ and choirs open my heart:

Dost thou remember the prophet of old,
Who that most wondrous story told,
How of a Virgin, pure and mild,
Should be born a perfect child.
The seer spake true, the virgin so fair,
A son from heaven doth declare,
Sing we Noel, Noel, Noel!

Music stirs me in the deepest place, a connection that has always been my link to Spirit. When I was five or six, I joined the children's choir at our Methodist church. I loved it all: The starched white angelic robes; walking down the aisle, pacing out the hymns, sitting right next to the altar with my friend Ginny. I took part in every choir from then on, church, junior high, and high school, just to be around the music. And sing.

On Sundays, the first muted strains of the organ prelude set the mood. Families filed into the main sanctuary, found their accustomed seats, whispered hushed greetings to neighbors. Then the choirs would sing, a cappella, the opening prayer from the next room. A magic spell blanketed the church like the pure white snow just outside. The organ would burst forth with the first hymn, and the children's choir would lead the procession to the front, clutching hymnals, singing and walking in rhythm.

By 11:00 a.m. the church was often filled with slanting colored light. At Easter time, intense rays struck the altar's stained-glass windows, and the church took on a warmth as if creating its own heat, becoming the sun. Just before Christmas, at the darkest time of the year, hanging lamps and candles created a soft glow in the sanctuary. Christmas Eve Candlelight Service was the best. Each child carried a lighted candle, wrapped at the bottom in foil to catch the drips. We walked slowly, careful that the flames didn't go out, then placed them in the tiered holders up front. Of course, we knew *The First Noel* by heart. The dimly lit room came alive with candlelight and the smell of freshly cut spruce boughs, thick with magic. My heart and soul bonded to these memories, in this place where I could let down and be present. We won't talk about long boring sermons, the twitching, wandering thoughts, and a hidden desire to run outside. Church was the place I learned patience.

By my first spring at Northfield, with classes more familiar and grades improved, I try out for Chancel Choir and am accepted! I've been looking for my niche for next year, some special role. I didn't get elected to dorm council, though I wanted to be — someone smarter or more experienced won the position, so when Emily, one of our dorm's new cops, invites me to room with her, everything falls into place. I will serve as her helper, friend, and confidante. This is what I had hoped, to feel needed. Emily is bright, perceptive, compassionate — the perfect cop and roommate. Next year, when I come back as a senior, I'll have my place.

We shed many tears as we say our good-byes, and the graduating seniors pass the torch to us. My special friends, who have guided me through this difficult year, are hardest to part with: Kris, my beloved cop; Liz, always there for heart-to-heart talks; Susie, my jewel of a senior, from Colombia; and Lee, my moody, goodhearted roommate. Most likely I'll never see any of them again. The part that makes it okay: amazing friends who'll return next year. In the midst of finals, graduation, and packing, we laugh and lay out our plans. We made it. Seniors!

DREAM, THE GIFT

Grandma says I can have something of hers when she's gone. *Where would she go?* I wonder, disturbed at the notion of her absence. "What do you like?" she wants to know. My mind dances through her house like a Sugar Plum ballerina, looking here and there at all the things I love.

Would it be the Maxfield Parrish painting that hangs over the player piano, naked beauties by the cool water at sunset, inviting me to bathe with them in the healing waters, apricot and cobalt blue? Perhaps I might choose the round ink-blue Chinese rug with ducks floating at odd angles, or the shiny black-and-gold treadle Singer, which rocked me to sleep while Grandma sewed napkins and doll clothes.

But the Fairies! That would be the thing. Two live at her house, like shadows, living by fire and water. The Inside One hovers near the hearth, all sleek and glowing, dancing before the flames, always taking extra curtain calls as the fire cools to embers. She is lovely, tall and alive with the Fire.

The other, her sister, lives outside and stands guard at the well. Mossy-green waves ripple across her breasts and the backs of her upheld arms and hands. The Guardian, she pirouettes around and around the well, twirls in liquid spirals to the unseen music of its holy waters.

"Yes," I tell her, "that is what I want — the Fairy Spirits." I feel certain.

"Then they will be yours," she says. "You shall have them both — my gift to you, precious one. And with this gift, you know I will never leave you."

Dear Grandma

I saw you the other morning, in a rare dream. How I long now to touch your face, feel your smile; your words falling on me like tropical rain, teasing from me the pale orchid hidden in my heart. Most days my mind touches some treasured memory of you from the bosom of your house, 13 Grand Street, under the broad shading elms.

I often stopped there on my way home from school to surprise you and find you just arising from your nap, stoking coals in the black kitchen stove. If only I had known you were lonely, I would have come every day to hug your softness as you clasped my fragile soul in your arms. And now, I miss you so.

Sometimes I found you in the kitchen, swaying to the rhythm of your Singer treadle. In June, the pink climbing roses outside the window would clamor for our attention. We had to stop, pick some, bring them in, and scatter them around the house in little vases. You often surprised me with handmade doll clothes: a new chintz blouse and fur-trimmed coat for Alice, my favorite doll. Once, you even made us matching pale-yellow eyelet dresses, mine for my first piano recital.

I thought you'd always be there, making Sunday dinner for us, heavenly smells of pot roast and potatoes, pies cooling on wooden racks in the pantry window. Best of all, you, greeting us with your warmth. I never imagined I'd be given your rocking chair, the one you always sat in by the fire after dinner; the comb-back rocker you nursed your darling daughter in. So much love rested in that chair.

I remember seeing you at home in your bed, your belly so bloated. The doctor came, and Dad took you to the hospital. Only one time after that did they let me visit you in the hospital, and I could not believe it was you; there were so many tubes attached going every which way. Then you were gone. You died, they told me. I saw you one last time at your funeral. My heart was seizing and I thought I couldn't stand to have you missing from my life. Every day became a blur. Never would I touch the rose-petal-soft wrinkles on your face and arms again, feel your embrace holding me together.

It was then I began to unravel.

Slowly, and bit by bit, I realized that the strong silken web wrapping the fragments of my soul was gone. My cocoon vanished. That warm place embracing my child-heart had fallen away, and I was lost between my safety net and an unknown future.

Your house was still there, but never the same. Iron chairs replaced wicker porch furniture; drapes and lace curtains gone, the place spiffed up with coats of paint and a new roof. A newish car was parked in the driveway, where grass and English daisies used to grow because you never learned to drive. They tore down the old barn to make a garage with a roll-up door.

Once I sneaked up the driveway to see if anything remained of our old life. The roses were gone, even the tall trellis that tried to hold them, so wild and spreading up and over the side porch roof. I missed the old well's pump, too. We used to pump it together, priming the flow until pure crystal water rushed into our pail. Inside, we'd dip, fill a pitcher, then pour two glassfuls and drink the delicious nectar. Nothing ever tasted that good.

After a while, I stopped walking past your house — it became too painful. Slowly the memory of you ebbs away from my daily thoughts, like the tide receding from wet sand, leaving a thin trace of where it had been. Even so, your love sustains me and will forever be imprinted on my heart.

MY SUMMER

Not much to look forward to this summer. I'll probably help my folks fix up the carriage house out back; they're turning it into an antique shop. Mom wants me to paint a mural on one wall: Pennsylvania Dutch design of two birds and a loopy heart of vines. Good. Something to do. And I can help run the shop: label, make lists of wholesale/retail prices, arrange, organize, and display.

It turns out to be fun. Dad lets me wait on customers. I walk out with them, open the padlock, turn on the lights. Voila! Later, I may have to go find Dad so he can offer dealer prices or answer specific questions — like the exact periods when molded glass decanters were made, what flint glass is, the date and origin of the early American corner cupboard, and a million others. I'm just learning.

Antiques, and their special names, catch my interest, especially when I connect them to their three-dimensional shapes. Patterned glass used to seem boring, until I begin picking up and holding goblets; I touch the indentations and observe how light catches in the chiseled grooves, like prisms. Names enchant me: Thumb Print, Honeycomb, Bell Flower, Quilted Diamond, and Curtain Tie-back. Fascinating! Who came up with these names? My work becomes a treasure hunt when Dad comes home with new acquisitions. We research, name, discover values, polish, price, and put them out for sale.

Dad especially loves old tools and implements: butter paddles and rug beaters, saddle planes, scythes, locks and keys. Many objects hang from iron hooks and pine pegboards up and down the stair rail, their shapes and textures revealing clues about how they were used.

Over the summer, the shop fills up, and I get to sort through each and every box. Our old kitchen counter, ripped from the house remodel, provides a place for research, sales lists, and the cash box. And I'm proud of my mural, which is nearly finished, with its lovebirds hovering over a small secretary desk next to the grandfather clock.

Chairs hang from the high walls; some even tuck under the stairs: ladder backs, rockers, Windsors, Shakers. The corner cupboard is my favorite piece of furniture, NOT FOR SALE. On its shelves sit our most special curios and china: copper luster teapot and pitchers, flow blue cups and saucers, snuffboxes, candlesnuffers — STRANGE AND WONDERFUL OBJECTS. These implements of another era recall activities and rituals of daily life. For the first time, I have a real connection to history. Dad immerses himself in this new business of antiques and I feel glad for him. Mom shares his interest, and when she feels well enough, she burrows into reference books, like Ruth Webb Lee's volumes on glass, searching for dates and mold marks and rare finds.

Mom needs something to focus on, to take her mind off of being sick and off of me. The shop provides a healthy diversion, a way for her to occasionally interact with people. If she feels up to it and is dressed, without a headache, she grabs the keys and accompanies interested travelers to the shop. Her tolerance for such excursions runs short if she suspects they're just looking, with no intention of buying; she gets annoyed, says they're "looky-loos," wasting her time.

I hold a completely different perspective, welcoming the distraction from required summer reading or housecleaning. At least I can meet new people, hear stories about their travel and interest in antiques — not bad for a small-town summer.

III

Seven Months

1961–1962

Dummy Duty/Betrayal

"Mashed potatoes, today," she announces. "Ever done them?" "No!" I cringe when I spot the giant steel mixer in the corner of my dorm's kitchen, its relentless blades turning, maybe catching the edge of my kerchief as I bend over, or a random finger.

Doing my domestic kitchen assignment (called dummy duty) in the middle of the day gives me a break, time to be alone in my room, catch up on laundry. At 11:00 sharp, after chapel, I report to the large commercial kitchen on the backside of Marquand Hall. The smell of boiling potatoes sweetens and slightly thickens the air. I enter the brightly lit space, do up the top buttons on my turquoise dummy smock, and grab a clean white scarf for my head. I fold it into a triangle and quickly wrap my hair as Miss Johnson explains the day's task.

"Now, you've got to be real careful of Big Mama," she warns, patting the huge silver-gray machine in the corner. "She's strong and the milk is *hot*, just scalded. You don't look strong enough to lift the pots. Nancy, help her, would you? The poor thing looks scared. Show her what to do."

We struggle to first drain the huge pots of boiled potatoes and dump them into the cavernous bowl, like a silver pit toilet. Next, we measure the hot milk, a quart at a time. We pour it in slowly, as the giant paddles swirl to break up the potatoes. As I stare into the pot, I'm reminded of slush at the sides of roads, melting after days of plowing. A certain graininess develops, then a yellowing, like leaked oil or pee. Ah, it's the butter! Potatoes look prettier than snow as they start to turn into soft peaks tinged with sunlight. At the proper moment, we slow the mixer, and then it stops. Now the perfect potatoes sit covered, waiting for the girls to clamor into the dining room, chattering like chipmunks, until the final bell rings. Stillness blankets the room like new snow. One clear note rings out, and then a quiet song of thanks before the girls heap potatoes in drifts into large steaming bowls, and set them on the tables.

The welcome sun streams through the narrow south windows of the dining hall; low slants of light catch prisms in fine dust, evidence of the girls scurrying to find their places at the tables. For the next half hour or so, the familiar chorus harmonizes the tinkling of forks on china with animated voices and little bursts of laughter. I sit surrounded, and savor the warm creamy potatoes, tomato-ey meatloaf, and the sense of belonging.

I love this time of day. With my dummy chores over, I'm free until 3:30 Bible class, can do some laundry, homework, even catch a nap. As a senior, my time is less monitored and that little bit of freedom feels precious. Emily, my student-cop roommate, attends classes all afternoon. Life with her — so sweet. I cherish sharing the intimate moments in our room as some girl works through the anguish of a breakup, problem grades, or depression. But today I'll enjoy the room to myself. I can lie on my tightly sprung bed, quilt tucked up around my shoulders, stare at the funny odd angles in the dormer ceiling of the tiny room that used to be the maid's quarters, drift off for a while.

I hang up my dummy smock, grab my bag of laundry, and head to the basement to start a load. The dorm empties out after lunch; most everyone has left for 1:30 classes. I feel rather smug, like I've stolen the time, having already completed my French lab for the week.

The basement feels cold and dank; only bare light bulbs illuminate the space where two machines already spin, one slightly off balance. I'm in luck: a third sits empty, waiting. I won't have to haul my dirty clothes back upstairs. Soon, my mixed load agitates gently in a bath of Tide. Now, back to my little nest for a nap. Just down the hall from the washers, I get the urge to pee. I set down my box of detergent, push open the door into a three-stall shower and bathroom, and there, two of my good friends, Pam and Margie, sit on the floor side by side, backs against the rough wall, passing a lit cigarette.

"Wow. What are you doing here?" I can't quite believe what I see.

Startled, they stare at me, clearly upset.

"Sorry, just doing my laundry, came in to pee. Gee, I'm really sorry."

Silence hangs heavy, like it's dripping down the ancient cellar walls, filling my throat so I can't speak.

"You're not going to tell on us, are you? Tell Emily? Mrs. Luther? You know we'll be in deep shit if you do."

Slowly I back out the door, scared and confused. How could I tell on them? With the honor code, however, how can I not? What should I do? I need to talk to someone, now! Questions swirl through my mind like floodwaters rising out of control. I drag myself up the back stairs. The afternoon I so looked forward to feels like the light has been sucked right out of it. If only I could start over, back up just ten minutes, pass by that bathroom door and pee upstairs. That one little turn changed everything.

In the days that follow I can't sleep; I brood day and night over what to do. The honor system, foundation piece of the school rules, clearly states that if one student discovers another breaking a rule, she is honor-bound to report the incident to a student officer or faculty member. And if the offence is not reported but later found out, she stands guilty too, possibly subject to the same punishment. My two friends glare at me through Sunday night dorm meeting, corner me in the hall and beg me not to tell. I weigh the possibility of forgetting I was ever there against my guilty conscience and my oath as a cop's roommate. I can't do it. I withdraw, show up late for dinners, and feign sleep to avoid talking to my dear roommate Emily.

My inner climate turns dark; a fierce storm brews inside me with nowhere to find cover. For some peace of mind, I decide to talk with the chaplain, Mr. Campbell. At least I can speak out loud, describe my inner turmoil, and hear his counsel without betraying my friends. He's the one person I can trust to keep my secret.

Within the week, Judicial Committee calls me in. They strip away my senior privileges. Emily remains upset at my breach of the rules, and Margie and Pam are in deep trouble. How could the chaplain betray me?

"You do know that you broke the honor code, right?"

"Yes, I realize that." My voice sounds muffled and faraway. I can't look at my friends without feeling their judgment — hating me for telling. There's nothing more I can say, having blown it in every way. I breathe softly, pull myself in as small and invisible as possible. Back at the dorm, I feel Emily's disappointment and know that my friends may be suspended. I swallow four aspirin and turn myself to the wall, covers over my head. I want to stay here forever. Skip classes, lie in bed, stare blankly out the north window... hope this will all pass over. I wait in limbo, swaddled tightly in my sadness, no tears, and feel the darkening sky. How will it end?

Then the nightmare: I try to kill myself, slash my wrists. In the morning, as I make my bed, I discover a razor blade among the sheets. Where did it come from? Now I feel totally frightened. I need help.

The following day I go to the infirmary. They give me a single bed in an open room by a window, where I look out across rolling lawns to Marquand Hall, my dorm. I watch the girls as they rush off to classes and Chapel, clutching stacks of books, walking in twos and threes. Their far-off laughter cuts through the crisp fall New England air. My life has broken off from theirs, from uniforms and dummy duty, parlor dates, homework, and choir practice, the ordinary days of my senior year: the prize I've waited for. How did I get here? How will I find my way back to some clearly better times?

Dr. Mueller, the school physician, asks me a few questions: "Are you happy at school? Do you like your roommate? What do you think you did wrong? Do you think about suicide? What about the razor blade?"

I mumble my answers, sure that they don't matter. I want to

tell him, tell *someone,* how much I hurt inside, how lonely and guilty I feel. "Are you depressed?" he asks.

"Well, yes, I guess so."

"Do you want to stay in school?"

My shoulders shrug involuntarily, as I wish I were anywhere but at school.

"How about going home early for winter break?"

I could make up the work, of course, come back when I feel better. I look down, the lump in my throat threatens to let loose. I just stare out the window at the gray sky when he tells me he's already called my parents, and they'll pick me up tomorrow.

The next morning I pack my black leather suitcase with winter clothes: cable-knit sweaters, wool and corduroy pants and skirts, turtlenecks, knee socks. I leave my uniforms, dummy smocks, books, and bedding in a steamer trunk in my little room, for my return. Emily cries as she reaches up and hugs me tight, saying it will all work out and I should just get better. I leave midmorning after a brief meeting with the headmaster and a quick goodbye hug from Mrs. Luther, my dorm mother.

I will probably never see any of them again.

The ride home is bleak. Landscapes of narrow slushy roads match my mood as I slouch into the back seat. Not much to say. Apparently I'll have extra time away and go back to school after Christmas, on probation. Maybe it could turn out all right.

Our old Chevy pulls in at Albany Hospital, where my dad explains that I'm to spend a few days here, for tests. "We'll be seeing a doctor, to be sure you're okay." Though surprised and a bit bewildered, I feel little resistance, and comply as I check into the "open" psychiatric ward.

A few days stretch into several weeks of tests and talks and waiting. Long days in the patient lounge fill up with TV game shows and talks with my new friend and confidant, a young priest named Andrew. We converse for hours at a time. Since everyone there smokes, I begin to smoke and am soon up to a pack a day.

Andrew's thin face and deep-set brown eyes convey a sadness that reflects my own. He trembles when his fine-boned fingers hold a match to my cigarette. I do the same for him, to pass the time, to feel connection to his frail and vulnerable heart. Slowly I begin to feel things again. Our fears back off like scared dogs when we walk the grounds, crunching on the frozen crust of old snow, in the sharp sunlight, bundled up against the cold, our breath a mix of smoke and steam.

Over and over the story churns in my head like the blades of Big Mama, repeating, relentless. What should I have done? If only I had kept quiet... no, couldn't do that... honor bound to tell. I failed... but what about honor? Loyalty? I should do the right thing, but what is that? I don't know anymore. Could I please just have my life back, the one before the day that screwed up everything?

School seems so far off, like a cotton-candy daydream that belongs to someone else now. My future looks cloudy and uncertain in a way that frightens me, keeps me awake at night staring out black windows, going over options. Talking with Andrew makes me feel better. I think I can trust him and he understands me. I'll get out soon, they say, go home and maybe back to school. A few more days and it will be over. It never occurs to me I could spend the next seven months locked up, wondering if it would ever be over.

THINGS GET WORSE

With little contact from Mom and Dad, I become bored, feel flat and isolated except for my talks with Andrew. He's even more depressed, feels bad about maybe not wanting the priesthood, caught between two worlds. I think he's sweet. Sometimes we play double solitaire in the solarium and never read the stupid magazines they leave around: *Better Homes and Gardens, Women's Day;* no good ones like *Look* or *Life.* What do they think we do in here in the open psych ward, redecorate breakfast nooks or plant pansies in window boxes?

After some initial tests, like Rorschach (kind of interesting), there's nothing going on. Andrew's the only person I can relate to, and he's not much fun. Too serious, but that's me too. I haven't laughed or found anything amusing for a very long time.

The doctor says he suggested that my parents stay away so the staff can observe me without their influence. Fine by me. I feel relieved, actually, don't have to put up my guard, and since I know I'm not crazy, it's just a matter of time till they release me. Maybe I'll go back to Northfield, though I can't imagine how that could possibly work. More likely I'll return to good old Cobleskill High, which seems okay with me, but a letdown for my folks. December, almost Christmas, and I should be home by now. Why am I still here?

One evening, after a tedious hour of Lawrence Welk and the champagne bubbles from hell, I'm really wishing I could leave. The usual 9:30 bedtime meds; fifteen minutes later, the go-to-bed warning, then two orderlies begin to escort the dawdlers and drowsy ones who can't stagger to bed on their own. A black orderly, the creepy one with bad vibes, taps my shoulder. I cringe. I don't want him to touch me, and quickly get up, trying to avoid him. He grasps my wrist with his thick hand and chunky muscled forearm. I twist away, but he has me in his grip and steers me down the hall to my room.

I'm without a roommate this weekend, which usually works okay, but tonight a bad feeling hangs over me. We enter my room and next thing, quick as lightning, the orderly shuts the door as if he'd planned it the whole time. I feel like a cornered animal. I know I'm in trouble now, start to shake all over. His big hands grab me, pull at my clothes, his thick, dank breath hot against my neck. I push back, hard. He's hurting me, sticking his fat hands under my pajamas.

Now I'm screaming, and he hisses, "Shut up, shut up!" He shoves his whole arm over my face and pushes me down on the bed. I've never had to fight for my life before; it feels like I'm trapped in a snare, exploding in every direction, flailing about, burning up inside.

Finally, someone has heard the ruckus and bursts into the room. Thank God! I can stop fighting now. But something is wrong, terribly wrong. They grab me! Why? What is going on? I struggle as two nurses push me, hard, down onto the bed. They don't understand! He's yelling that I attacked him, tried to grab his keys, and then became hysterical when he tried to subdue me. They believe him! I am pinned facedown, sobbing, trying to explain what really happened. Out of nowhere they pull down my pants and I feel the jab of a fat hypodermic needle shoved straight into my butt, like a crazed hornet. The sting of it makes me collapse; my body goes slack and, as they drag me up onto the bed, everything goes black.

I feel so tired behind my closed eyes and must have been asleep for eons. Am I hung-over? Do I dare push open my crusty eyelids and see where I am? My thoughts won't stay in one place long enough to catch even one, examine it, put something together. I long to press my cold fingers to my eyes, just to feel the pressure. I try to move, but my arms won't obey my silent command. My heart races with this new and frightening information. What's wrong?

My eyes open in a flash as I struggle to move, anywhere, but I discover that I'm tied up in bed, lanced tight like a fresh wound, in a straightjacket. I feel sick. I'm drowning in thick black mud and it's taking me down.

THREATS

Sequestered on the locked ward. No walks outside. No Andrew. They keep the real crazies here. Soon, I hope, I can talk to my doctor or parents and get the whole thing straightened out. I really want to be out by Christmas.

Because the Librium didn't work, they say, the doctor has prescribed electroshock. Monday morning, in the predawn darkness of my room, a light comes on, followed by the quick stick of a needle as they are prep me for my first treatment. Soon I feel too sleepy to care about it. Two weeks pass in a blur, ten treatments in all. I hardly remember anything, and then it's over.

I must have improved, because they let me get up and watch TV, walk around the ward — and no more treatments. This is what I get for Christmas? Slowly, slowly I begin to remember myself. The pieces don't quite fall into place but float around like fleecy clouds with indistinct edges; one melds into another before an image forms. I feel more out of control than ever.

At least I'm safe from that orderly. And then one day, in the small patient lounge with no one else around, he shows up. He's pissed off. I'm freaked out at seeing him, but feel somewhat protected as we're within sight of the nurses' station. He glowers at me, says he's been questioned about what happened and could lose his job.

"You better shut up about it. If I get fired, you'll be real sorry."

I stare back at him, wanting to feel brave. Just then, he reaches into his pocket, pulls out and shows me his knife. When he flashes it open, I recognize it as a switchblade, even though I've never seen one. I get the message.

In the next few days, I hit a new low point. I guess I'll have to keep the story of what happened that night to myself. What do my parents think about this, my being restrained, then locked up, claiming an attack? Do they even know? Can I still go home, or does this change everything? What can I say without the orderly coming after me? How can I get the hell out of here? Now I am truly depressed, and my future looks grimmer than ever. This cannot end well.

COMING APART

D istant screams interrupt the spinning *Wheel of Fortune* of my dull TV reality. The lounge sits empty this afternoon while some patients visit with families. A few aren't back from their "treatments" yet. Only a huge disturbance could break into my mood today. I feel stuck, like glue that dried too fast, and the pieces don't fit — that's me, always in the wrong place.

I hear distant banging, shouting, and then the blue light at the nurses' station lights up. Orderlies and nurses race down the hallway, away from the lounge, to deal with an emergency. Someone is "going off." I see this a lot on the ward, where we are locked up tight. The more extreme patients live here. I need to get out, especially with the image of a polished knife blade dancing in my nightmares. And where will I go? They say I'm going home any day now, but what kind of relief will that be?

The nurses' station is now abandoned. This intrigues me, so I stand up and wander over to its imposing counter. On the other side, charts and papers lie in neat piles on the desk; clipboards hang from a row of hooks, file drawers are locked up tight with all their sad stories hidden inside. Most intriguing, someone has left a fat ring of shiny keys on the desk, arousing fantasies of escape and freedom. I look carefully around and find myself alone. As I reach in and pick up the keys, it's like a strange dream begins. All turns silent around me, muffled, like the first snowfall. Faraway sounds, from another dream, have nothing to do with me, so I ignore them.

The smallest flat key on the ring fits the door of the medicine cabinet. I've seen them taking down bottles, measuring out doses for our evening tray of meds. I am drawn, like moth to flame, to a large amber bottle, with a handwritten red label marked

SLEEPING DROPS, I guess so they won't mix it up with the tran-quilizers. Slowly, deliberately, I reach for the bottle and take it down, cradle the precious liquid in the crook of my arm. With the magic keys, I've captured freedom within my world, and without much thought or effort I locate the bathroom key and let myself in. For the first time in many days, I am truly alone. I feel safe.

The tension in my neck and chest begins to yield, like soft putty, and I let out a long slow breath. Not much time. I drink it down. Bitter, bittersweet, liquid eases down my throat, promising me a kind of peace, relief without regret. Now I'm on my way to my true home. I slide down to the floor in a corner by the sink. I will go where no one can get to me. Even as I hear muted pounding on the door, tiny pleading voices, I feel free and begin to lift off, seeking my way back....

Dark hallway... on my back ... bumpy ride, like a night train... shouting ... layers of blowing veils ... wads of cotton candy ... flashing lights, red and gold, seen through closed eyelids ... sinking, slipping between layers of liquid glass .... Then nothing. Blessed sleep.

When I wake up, the nurse by my bed explains to me that I drank half a bottle of chloral hydrate, and that they barely got to me in time, saved my life by pumping my stomach. I'm in the Moser Unit of Albany Psychiatric Hospital. I clearly won't be going anywhere.

"What about my parents? Do they know? Are they here?"

"They're speaking with your doctor today, discussing the next step."

"Do I have to see them now?" I'm sobbing. I dread facing Mom. She will cry, and I'll be so sorry for everything. And Dad, poor Dad. I hate making him sad. He bears such a load.

"No, Dr. Abbott thinks it best you don't see them."

"Do they know what happened? About the orderly... you know, how he came after me...."

"I'm not sure what you're referring to. You'll have to speak with the doctor. I'm just on C.O. duty, here to watch you."

"Constant Observation." This lowly status, with a nurse

watching every move, means I'm never alone. Eat, pee, sleep, dress, and shower — all the same. One thing runs into the next, like saturated dark pigment, staining, blurring the brush strokes, till it's all muddy brown. I wait through the weekend for the doctor who never comes.

Soon I'll be going home, they say, and that scares me. What is home, anyway? I can't seem to remember, hold on to a clear picture. The shock treatments have scrambled my thoughts, my memory. Jumbled snippets come and go, like bits of dreams: room painted turquoise blue... cold wind blowing snow onto a comforter as I struggle, shivering, to close the window... huge clumps of luminous icicles crash to a sidewalk below... shrill sirens and strobing red lights, fire engines roar out from their midnight slumber... dark hallway, door shut tight... soft sobbing escapes through a wide crack under the door... trays of hot milk, pills of every color... Dad cooking pork chops in an electric fry pan. Like snapshots, but I can't catch any of them, put them in order. How will I be able to put my life back together?

ALBANY TO NEW YORK

Fleeting images from the previous three weeks swirl in my head — doctors, tests, restraints, the flash of a switchblade — dreamlike, strung together like Pop-It beads with tenuous connections. The day starts out bitter cold and dismal, sidewalks frozen solid with slush, then salted and melted for safety. Inside the ward, my mind is cloudy as I wait in the lounge, my small bag, packed, beside me. I'm slightly hopeful, since my parents will come soon, get me out of this hellhole, and somehow I'll return to my life, whatever that means.

I feel frightened, on guard; I hover close to the nurses' station for its questionable protection. Around the backside of the protruding prism window, I can see the sharp edges of the locked medicine cabinet — the one I broke into and complicated this whole mess. No, something happened before that... why am I here anyway? Questions float in like jellyfish, transparent, appear and disappear. Ten shock treatments have really screwed with my mind. I stare at my bag, then down the long corridor, trying to figure it all out.

Dad steps out of the elevator, far away, in his charcoal-gray storm coat. Mom follows in her best soft black wool coat with the fur collar, carries a black patent-leather purse. My parents look so small, confused, like children, almost, as they walk toward me. I am nervous and shaking, but glad they have come.

"Please take me home," I beg, softly sobbing into the cold dampness of their winter coats.

Dad signs papers, receives instructions. Soon he carries my bag to the Chevy, and I climb into the familiar back seat as the heater's blower whines into high. When we turn onto the thruway, I notice that we are driving past the Route 20 turnoff, then past the next exit leading to Cobleskill and home. We make a less-familiar turn south, toward Poughkeepsie and New York City.

"Where are we going?" I ask.

Mom sort of snuffles and turns away.

Dad answers, "We thought that since you've been in the hospital, we'd all take a break, a little visit to New York. You know, like we used to. We'll see a couple of plays, shop at Best's, have dinner at the Brass Rail, window shop. For Christmas. It'll be fun... and we want you to see a doctor there."

I slump back in my seat, relieved not to be going home right away, to have a distraction from all that has happened. I need to sort some things out. At least I'm out of that place. Maybe I'll be okay after all.

It's one or two o'clock when we pull into Howard Johnson's, late for lunch, but we didn't spot any good places earlier. The cozy warmth inside comforts me as we slide into a leatherette-upholstered booth, and I scan the menu for my favorites: club sandwich with potato chips and pickles, or their classic, macaroni and cheddar cheese. It surprises me when Mom starts to cry. I ask her what's wrong, which is a stupid question, given that everything is wrong. She goes to the ladies' room while I sit quietly with Dad, feeling guilty and confused. Mom comes back, a little puffy, having washed her face and reapplied the Roman Red color to her lips and blotted it on a napkin.

Back in the car, tension hums under the surface. "Just a little farther," Dad says, then turns right and cruises up a long driveway. He parks near the entrance of a very large and beautiful building that looks like a mansion.

It doesn't look like a hospital, thank goodness. Its curved driveway suggests turn-of-the-century elegance. Perhaps some Arabian horses once grazed here, the dream of a teenage girl galloping across the open fields. I look up at the large second-story windows and see metal grates, reflecting shades of gray in the stormy afternoon sky. Curious. What kind of place is this? Maybe a private school like the one I left only a month ago.

"What is this, Dad?"

"It's a very nice place," he says. "Not at all like Albany. We want you to see a specialist here." Then he's silent.

I'm nervous now, wondering when we'll go to the hotel and start our little break, the vacation he said we all needed. I ask, but he won't say any more, just that we're here to consult with a doctor.

The three of us walk toward the entrance. Stone columns rise on either side of a large wood-paneled door, giving the place a very formal look without revealing anything. I lean forward to read the small brass plaque to the right of the door: New York Hospital, Westchester Division. I suck in a deep breath and feel like holding it for a long time to prevent the next thing from happening.

"Come on, Judy," Dad says gently, holding the door open. Slowly, I cross the threshold, and find myself in a large room, like a hotel lobby. There are groupings of upholstered chairs, handsome carpets, small polished end tables; I catch the scent of Lemon Pledge as I steady myself, holding onto the wing of a tall chair.

Dad steps up to a window-counter and talks to a smartly dressed woman with a name badge pinned to her blue cardigan. After a few minutes I see him filling out papers. He glances back at me, then quickly away. Mom finds a comfortable chair, fumbles nervously for her Parliaments. She fingers the silver foil, pulls out a cigarette, and lights it with her monogrammed lighter.

No one talks to me, and I feel like I'm in a dream or a movie. I want to sprint out of there, but my feet feel stuck to the polished floor. Sadness creeps through me like a seasonal flu. I fear they might leave me here, and I want to scream, beg them to take me to the hotel like they promised. Have our little vacation. Even go home. But I'm so tired. It seems I will have nothing to say about what happens next.

> Patient was accompanied to admission room by parents. She was quiet, withdrawn and almost mute, but fully cooperative to admission on a Voluntary Minor application, and accompanied nurse to Hall 4 without question.

Hospital record, January 1, 1962

DR. BURNES

The oatmeal this morning looks gray, a bit like the day outside the dining room window. I dab with my spoon, watch the crystals of white sugar dissolve as milk creeps up the sides of the bowl. I know today is special: After four long days here, I will finally get to meet my doctor.

Following a.m. meds, a nurse escorts me through long anonymous hallways, past wards without character, just names or numbers like the more open Hall Eight. We pass through numerous sets of double-locked doors to a wing in the main building. The doctor's name stands out on a brass placard next to the door: Dr. S. Burnes, M.D. My mind plays with his name: I have a shrink and his name is Doctor Burnes.

My nurse knocks on the door and we enter the simple office, nicely appointed with bookcases that line the wall. Behind him, a window overlooks the gray-black landscape of half-melted snowdrifts and silhouetted bare maples and elms. He sits, then stands from his dark brown leather chair; shakes my hand, clasps it lightly — the briefest of greetings.

"Sit down, please, Miss Fisher. I'm Dr. Burnes. I'll be your doctor. We'll have a little talk to get things started."

He proceeds to interview me, taking down my physical, then family history; he asks a lot of questions about Mom, her illness and depression. Do I currently have thoughts of suicide? How do I think I am doing? How about anger toward my parents? The thing that pisses me off — I could do my own interview better. Dr. Burnes seems arrogant and incompetent. By the end of his questioning, he knows very little of the real me, so how can he help me with my problems? This is depressing. My dream was to have a really cool therapist, someone I could learn to trust and confide in, who would listen to me, who could help me. I'm sorely disappointed. I should have known.

During the hour, Burnes takes notes, occasionally looking up to stare at me with his dull brown eyes, straight mouth, and no smile. He's completely humorless. Wonder if he has a wife and kids. Probably not, I decide, because there's nobody home. I find it difficult to imagine a helpful relationship with this man, talking to him every week or two for an hour, revealing my heart, my thoughts, and emotions. Instead, another idea forms in my mind: Shield. I will veil everything I tell him, and he will think he sees into me. All he'll get will be blurred traces of reality, a frosted glass over my soul. No, I can't risk showing my true self to him.

" — And so, Miss Fisher," he breaks into my thoughts, "I hope we can delve more deeply into your hatred of your mother next time. I'm prescribing a medication to calm you down. We'll monitor you for about a month or so, then reevaluate how you're feeling. I'll see you again then, Miss Fisher. Good day."

MISS STERN

Watching Miss Stern through the plate-glass window, set at an angle across one corner of the "Nichols Cottage" lounge, I feel both fascinated and repulsed. The steely-eyed head nurse shoots me a glance, sensing, I'm sure, my intense interest in her. I smile weakly. Her stare doesn't waver. I turn back to my gin rummy game with Maggie and suppress my feelings. Par for the course — one doesn't dare reveal much of anything if one hopes ever to leave. Daydreams of evenings at home in our cozy living room, playing three-handed seven-card rummy with Mom and Dad, drift through my mind. "Gin!" Maggie's won again, caught me in my fantasy of a loving family.

Rattling keys announce pre-lunch meds, and we see Miss Stern, poised for action: she balances her small tray of potions in one hand, unlocks and re-locks the heavy glass door with the other. The lounge seems like a fishbowl: thick plate-glass windows in a long arc look to the nurses' station, hall, and dining room. A long row of tall windows face south, over undulating lawns covered with crusty snow. Miss Stern barks out our names as she approaches, like taking aim with a gun; making sure you know you're the target.

"Miss Fisher," she says. Her eyes bore into me, needing to capture all my attention.

"Drink it all now," she croons, or " Don't hide any pills in your cheek or under you tongue," depending on the day or week and the medication. "Open up, let's see." She inspects for held bits of pills. Satisfied, she moves on to her next victim.

A sly smile flickers across my lips as I flip the pill from its hiding place above my front teeth, tucked against my dry gums, into the ashtray where I can later stuff it into a cigarette butt. This will allow me a day to think about my dilemma, to contemplate escape, and to let my hatred of Stern smolder beneath the surface. Of course I don't let on to anyone, just quietly play cards, smoke, smile wanly, and sit in a heap like everyone else in the room, wishing to hell I was anywhere but here.

MAGGIE

After morning meds, Maggie shuffles even more slowly than at night. I suspect they've restarted her Thorazine.

"Seven-card rummy or gin?" she asks dully.

"Seven-card, of course, since you're giving me the choice." I played this game with my parents for years, every Sunday night, and I'm good.

"I hate that I'm back here — thought I could make it out this time."

"So what happened?" I ask. Maggie hasn't been on Nichols Cottage for about three months, had advanced to Hall Eight. I thought she was gone for sure.

"Really missed our card games — and our talks," I add.

"Yeah, me too. So, for my sixteenth birthday I was out for the day with my folks — lunch, shopping — and they kind of freaked out on me. I got really mad about being locked up, and was yelling at them in the restaurant, then crying. It's been over a year and a half since they committed me. Their cocktail parties and dinners go a lot more smoothly without me at home."

I remember her stories of running away from home; real serious, ready to hitchhike to California or as far as she could make it. Maggie's a big girl for sixteen, large bones, could probably pass for older, and pretty. A kind of sweetness dances across her face as she pauses for a minute, lost in a fog.

"Anyway," she continues, dealing the cards, "my parents figured — again — they couldn't handle me at home, so they gave the doctor some cockamamie story. I hate being here, but at least I'm not home."

What a choice.

RITA

Rita's eyes blaze with anger as she glares at me across the solarium. She holds my gaze as she ambles through the room and extends her cigarette to the student nurse for a light.

"Good morning, Rita. How are you today?" Miss Riley says sweetly. "Can I give you a light?"

Rita's stare never falters as she jabs the cigarette toward Miss Riley.

"Come on, Rita, you could at least be nice about it," I say. "What did she ever do to you?"

If looks could kill, I'd be dead. Obviously, I said the wrong thing. Rita stalks across the room, sticks her face right up close to mine, exhales deep fiery breaths, hissing like a dragon. I shudder, wishing I'd kept my mouth shut, hadn't acted so self-righteous this morning, like I could walk right out of here whenever I wanted.

"Miss Riley," I plead, "I need to go to the bathroom right now. Please, can I go? Rita, excuse me, I've got to go."

She lifts her arms up over her head like a mime, like she never even thought to touch me. Turning, she strides off to the window table, puffing away, and doesn't look back.

"Look, Rita, I'm sorry. I just want us all to have a nice day, not get in trouble, you know?"

And she does know. Periodically she looks up from her solitaire layout and checks me out, checks us all out. It's before breakfast and all too quiet on the ward.

Miss Stern glares at us through the large window from her station as she assembles the tray of meds, mostly little paper cups with tablets or syrupy liquids, names written on the sides in black pen. Rita's eyes are dark brown, liquid, and seething, but I hate the look Miss Stern gives me even more: steely blue, hard, and cold as a glacier. That woman has no heart.

The air in the room bristles this morning as Stern balances the meds tray in one hand and unlocks her station door, locks it behind her, then the solarium door. We all know something's about to give — it's the static. Makes the tiny hairs at the nape of my neck itch, stand straight up. She gives us her look, as if to say, "Don't mess with me," but it's too late.

Stern passes out a couple of easy meds, then heads straight for Rita and hands her the cup, accompanied by her usual cold stare.

Rita looks up, smiles pleasantly, and takes the small cup.

The Thorazine tablet stays in her mouth for a few seconds, then flies about ten feet, hitting old Stern in the ankle as she crosses the room. Mayhem! Stern heads out of there, keys flashing. Two orderlies show up and haul Rita off. A string of foul language and rage fills the room long after she's gone.

We can relate.

Shock Days

On shock days, they separate us out early by denying breakfast. Once we're corralled in the lounge of our ward, special meds and then cigarettes are passed out. A nurse reads the call list for breakfast, and if you're not on that list, you're on the shit list and must wait, nervously, until they call you for prep.

Shock treatments happen three days a week, Monday, Wednesday, and Friday, which gives us time — a day in between — to recover and reassemble ourselves before the next treatment.

Monday seems the worst. We know there will be three hits by Friday. I particularly hate the preparation, but there's no use fighting it. One at a time we get up when Stern calls out our name: "Miss Fisher," she says, as if my table at the Brass Rail were ready. I slowly put out my cigarette and a student nurse leads me to the hydrotherapy room. Out we go, heavy doors unlocking and locking behind us, into the central hallway where Miss Stern can watch from her brightly lit nurses' station. Unlock into the treatment-wing hallway, lock behind, into hydrotherapy, relock.

My table, on wheels, cowers here waiting for me, nearby, the iced sheets. It takes two nurses to do me up, not because I resist but because I might. They always seem so nice, almost apologetic, only two or three years older than I am.

The room feels cool; early morning light glints off the steel table legs; sheets swim freely in a tub of ice water; bars on the windows.

I have been here before.

"Okay, now it's time to take off your clothes." Silence. "Shall we help you?"

A simple shake of my head as my fingers move to the top button of my blouse lets them know I will comply. Soon I stand naked, trembling. They wring out the first sheet, fold it, and lay it across the gurney. The second icy sheet in hand, the nurses begin to wrap me. I hold my arms out straight while they swaddle my torso like a mummy. Then they help me sit and lie down on the table, a towel beneath my head.

"I'm sooo cold." I always say this. My jaw shakes, then clenches, as the pointless words escape my lips.

"You'll be warm soon," they remind me, always the same response, like a litany.

Another sheet wraps around my chest and arms, binding me, and they roll me back and forth like they're changing a bed. A cold sheet across the top secures me to the gurney where I'm trapped for several hours. Only the crook of my left arm remains exposed, where they will soon insert a needle and slow-drip Sodium Pentothal into my pitiful thinning vein. Finally, a dry white flannel blanket over all. "There," the blanket assures, "you'll soon be warmed up!"

They wheel my gurney into the hallway and park it in line to wait my turn. It seems I usually stay back a ways, sometimes last, maybe better than being first. In the hours that follow, waiting for the shock treatment, I lie listening to the moans and pleas, requests, soft sobs, and screams of those ahead of me. After a while, as promised, the sheets do warm up, my shaking stops, and a kind of peace comes over my body, like the numbing of Novocain before the drill. My mouth becomes cotton-ball dry, relieved only by dabs of water from the nurses, which never reach my throat.

Often, tears run down into my ears as I survey my sorry plight. Nothing to do, nowhere to go, just wait for the inevitable. I hear a man's voice, husky, vulnerable, asking how long now, how's it going. I wonder if the voice belongs to that nice boy I danced with last week, or last month; so familiar, but I just can't remember. Someone up ahead screams. All I know is that today is Monday, it's winter, and the doctor has scheduled me for another series of ten electroshock treatments.

I hear Rita going off two or three tables ahead, screaming and swearing, though she promised to be good today. "God damn you doctors!" she wails. "Sons of bitches!"

Always mad, that one, a fire burning deep inside her. I kind of admire her outbursts, as I never get angry myself. I just hate to see her get into so much trouble. They'll probably take her next, out of turn if they have to, just to shut her up. I don't make noise because I don't want too much Sodium Pentothal, except when I do want more, and then I protest a bit. That's the game. I can't help but cry sometimes, then space out, try to think of something good, like getting out. Without fail, my bladder fills to capacity, even without drinks of water, and the urge to pee becomes intense. I always ask the nurse, fantasizing the day they might say, "Sure, Miss Fisher, no problem," unwrap the wet sheets, help me off the table into a soft chenille robe, and guide me to my private pastel bathroom.

"Just pee in the sheets. Everyone does." And so, ashamed, I do.

The anxious wait for my shock treatment, and the feeling of being in this place, bring on a desire to be anywhere but here, where I await the disintegration of anything I can still call me. I know when I wake up I will be less of myself. Pieces of my memory and known world will be gone. They repeat, over and over, that the treatments are meant to help me, but I never understand that part.

A patient is wheeled past me from "that room," our final destination. She appears silent, peaceful, asleep. Finally, it's my turn. My visual landscape is moving; the gurney rolls as we turn a corner and the door closes behind me. I take in the room: overhead fluorescent lights, nurses, the doctor, who greets me and reminds me right away that the treatment will not hurt.

I know how this goes. I'll just count backwards from one hundred, go to sleep, and wake up later back on the ward. I feel a little sleepier as they increase the Sodium Pentothal. The nurse above my head twirls strands of my hair and begins to dab on some goo, stuff that makes the electrodes stick to my head, transmit the current. I don't know how many there are, maybe ten, but I feel ugly, like an alien space mummy.

Once they're all attached, the doctor and nurses talk quietly among themselves, getting everything checked out and ready. When they loosen the top sheet that ties me to the gurney, I know it's almost time. They put a "bit" in my mouth, several tongue depressors stacked and wrapped together with cloth adhesive tape, "So you won't bite or swallow your tongue," says one of the nurses.

After that, at their request, I begin to count slowly, backwards: 100, 99, 98 — nice and easy — 97, 96, 95.... I thought all morning about how I always count, fall asleep, and later wonder what happened. It occurs to me to fake it, the counting, and just once stay awake to see what the shock feels like. So far, I've been too scared.

Today is different, seems just right... 94... 93... stop. Silence. My eyelids droop, nearly closed, tiny slits allowing only a small slice of artificial light; my body lies limp from medication saturation. Then it happens.

I feel assaulted, heat in every cell down the front of my body, a blanket of liquid fire explodes, goes off again and again. Electric currents arch my body in convulsions, then slam me down against the gurney, still tied up in sheets that bind me. I hear my own voice, disembodied, screaming through my clamped jaw. It's like a detonation inside my spine. Total insult, outrage! Time suspends in moments of white heat, shock, and pain. Then nothing.

I awake in a dream, initially remember nothing. I shuffle down a corridor, leaning on a nurse's arm for support, sit on a toilet. I am a small child being dressed by not-my-mother. She leads me through a hallway to a chair. Shyly, I look around and see a few people who look familiar. A nice lady puts a plate in front of me with food on it. Lunch? My nurse sits beside me, hands me a spoon. I stare at it because I can't quite remember what to do next. She places the spoon in my hand, her warm palm covering mine; she speaks softly, encourages me to eat, though I am not hungry.

After lunch I sit for a while, then lie down and sleep. When I wake up, unfortunately I remember where I am. By Wednesday, I start to function again, but it's of no use, because today is shock day.

Later, in the hall, shivering, I remember what happened on Monday, and I vow that I will count out loud every single number until I disappear.

BIRTHDAY DATE

The second series of shock treatments is over just in time for my eighteenth birthday. Since I've behaved, I gain more privileges, and get transferred to a new ward, Hall Eight. Lighting up a Marlboro — we light our own these days — with my new friend, Sandy, the subject of Saturday's dance arises.

"I'm kind of excited," I say, "Like nervous. I haven't seen a real guy in months, not counting the orderlies around here. The last guy I danced with at school tried to feel me up on the walk across campus. I don't know if I'm ready...."

"Oh, come on, don't be a baby about it," Sandy chides. "You probably just need to get laid! Not likely to happen here, though. They watch us like hawks, and nowhere to do it. The dance happens in one big room. Too bad."

"What's it like? Girls on one side, boys on the other, like junior high?"

"Yeah, kind of like that. But a few of us know each other by now. On this floor, they let us get together once a month, something to look forward to, you know."

As I get dressed after dinner, I have the jitters. I haven't worn a skirt since I arrived three months ago. The pain in my belly is worse today, nerves I guess, or cramps. I don't dare complain or I might be in trouble. I choose a dark blue pleated skirt with a powder blue V-neck sweater and black flats. No pins allowed, but they've agreed to let me wear my silver heart locket. I pull my straight hair back into a ponytail with a rubber band and pale pink ribbon, and seek out the only mirror on the floor — the one made of highly polished steel in the common bathroom. *Not bad,* I muse, checking my reflection.

The long trek to the community room is fun, sparked with spirited conversations about who might be there, what could happen. The energy borders on rowdy, sizzles just under the acceptable level. No one wants to cross that line, and most of us can control our behavior. Soft music emanates from the room ahead.

"Hey, kid," Sandy says, with a quick slap to my butt. "Smile! This is not a funeral."

As soon as we enter the room, she lights up and offers me one. Then she points at various guys.

"Joe over there by the table of Cokes: real cute, great dancer. Stay away, though. He's big trouble. He beat up a gal real bad last winter, broke her front teeth out before they could take him down. Unpredictable, yeah, that describes him, but oh-so-sexy."

" Now Bobby, the blond, he's kind of sweet, nice, too nice. Nobody home, though; he's been here too long. Then there's the new guy over there, Maurice. Watch out. Nobody's got him yet."

A Johnny Mathis song, *The Twelfth of Never,* sinks into my ears and I soak it up. I wish someone would ask me to dance. Couples drift past in the dim light; they clutch each other as close as they dare.

I feel a gentle tap on my shoulder. Maurice appears at my side: liquid, almost black eyes, thick curly brown hair, and surprisingly taller than he had appeared across the room.

"Want to dance?"

"Sure, that would be nice."

We float to the middle of the floor, bury ourselves in the crowd. His arms pull me gently to his chest and the last four months fall away like shedding a skin. After all, tomorrow I will "celebrate" my eighteenth birthday. Everything seems suddenly right. Even the dull pain in my side has receded. A dreamy love song infuses my being, if only for this moment. And I sink into the safety of the warmth enfolding me.

Where could this ever go? I wonder, and then, what the hell — I feel happy, relieved, and hopeful. The music and smooth dance moves soothe my aching body. I let the night take me as its prisoner and guest. By morning I'm hot and sick, my fever burns over 103 degrees.

Nurses pack me into an ambulance, which speeds away from the hospital on my first trip out in three months. What a way to spend my birthday, I think, dreamy from the fever, excited to be going somewhere. When they open me up, my appendix has burst and I'm a shade shy of disaster. A week passes, with a visit from my parents in the regular hospital. Pumped full of antibiotics, I'm back in the slammer. But I had a taste of freedom. If I can just manage to stay clear of trouble and convince the doctors I'm cured, maybe they'll let me out.

RUNNING AWAY

The first thaw comes in late April, a month after the equinox, when daylight and nighttime are equal. It brings a reprieve after months of winter; it shows up like a light in a dream, calling me back from the blackness, the darkest time I've ever lived through in my eighteen years.

I see the snow shrink, acquire a crusty glaze on top, not unlike my Grandma's best apple crisp, chunks of dirty gravelly ice like brown sugar clumps. I long to touch it, stomp around the estate grounds, run through the slush. On Thursdays, some of us, who have earned the privilege, walk outside to a crafts class like a herd of kindergarteners. In the meantime, I'll have to stay content to gaze out the window at the changing light that reflects off the melting snow.

The brown stubble of last year's well-tended lawns pokes through what patches of graying snow remain. Today is cloudy, angry, a storm brewing from being cooped up too long behind brilliant thunderheads. Miss Riley, my favorite student nurse, will escort us after breakfast and meds. She keeps the Occupational Therapy list in her pocket and calls out names. I feel elated when my name is finally called, like an afterthought, and hurry through the door so I won't be left behind. Our own little group, seven or eight women, acts nervous and quiet as we traipse down the well-lit hallway to the double glass doors. Out two more doors and we're free!

The joy I feel at being outside is dampened only by walking in formation, and having Miss Stern join the group to keep us together. I want to skip down the sidewalk, roll in the snow, pick the new yellow and purple crocuses I see poking up around the base of a giant old elm. Instead, I walk along and chat with a couple of the girls, just like we're out for a midday stroll.

The class, as usual, proves boring, but at least it's a change of pace. The teacher tries to interest me in a knitting project with enormous fat blunt needles, but I decline; I prefer twisting some raffia and willow to form a loose nesting basket.

On the way back to our ward, just before lunchtime, the mood is quiet, spent. We all anticipate having to go back: step inside and feel the loss of freedom; hear the key in the lock, the bolt drop in place behind us, the long walk down two hallways.

Suddenly I'm not walking anymore. I run across that patch of crusty brown and white, feel the spongy earth under my feet. Air pumps through my lungs, streams past my face and through my long hair, tangled up behind me. I reach my stride now, my chest exploding. It fills me with hope, and drives me closer and closer to the chain-link fence in front of me.

With a surge of energy, I scamper up the fence like a panther, bent on escape. Already I dream of catching a ride and getting away, of having luck on my side, finding a new life. Instead, I feel Riley's hands close tight around my ankles, pin my shoes into the diamonds of the fence, and prevent me from swinging over the top. She is crying, begs me to let go and come down. I know I'm defeated, with nowhere to go. I climb back down and collapse, sobbing, into her arms. On the walk back to Nichols, she has an iron grip on my arm so I can't get away again. Already I dread the punishment that most surely awaits me.

Applied Self-Control

I lie flat on my back and watch the late afternoon sun turn the new maple leaf tips to rosy blush. I know that something has to change. I'll have plenty of time to think about it now: the next long hours stretch into night, as my "treatment" lasts at least twenty-four hours. That's what Stern said when Riley dragged me in from my morning breakaway. Stupid! How could I let myself take off like that, not think about getting caught, about Riley running after me, catching hold of my foot as I scaled the steel fence. She wouldn't let go and I knew she was right; I wouldn't get far and then it would be much worse.

So now I've landed back in Hydrotherapy, and the ice has done its work: I shiver till the wrapped sheets warm up, their bindings trap my body like a swaddled mummy. I feel alive and desperate to get out, but I lie serene, exhausted, and begin to contemplate my true escape. I am just realizing how I must act to achieve my goal. In the beginning it was so bad I gave up on myself, became hidden away so far that I was lost, separated from anything and anyone who cared for me, including the girl who now lies tightly bound in wet sheets, on a gurney in a cold room. Alone. I have considered many things, but now I think of a new plan. I will find her, that lost girl, and together we will defeat the system, win our prize: freedom. The rest we can figure out later. And the price of freedom? Applied self-control.

The sun has gone now. Darkness infuses the room. After a while, Stern comes in to check on me, turn on some lights.

"So, thought about what you did today, Miss Fisher?"

"Yeah. I really messed up, didn't I?" I fight the urge to cry, will the tears not to run down into my ears. "I sure won't try that again."

"Really... and why not?"

"Well, I learned a hard lesson today and I'm actually feeling better, more calm...."

"Hmm... is that so?" She sounds disappointed. "Still, you're not getting out of here tonight. And you'll be on my watch for a while, until you straighten up."

It's all I can do not to scream in agony, but I'm learning. I see a tiny light, just enough to get my attention, show me the way out of here. Its golden presence warms my heart, gives me courage as I forge my battle plan.

I'll have to be good, follow all their rules, do exactly what they say. The difficult part? Going through each day as if I care — about something. I am desperate, seeing my last chances of freedom disappear with each wrong move, like sand running out of the hourglass. Another round of shock treatments would surely do me in, and more meds could loosen my will power. Being back on "Constant Observation" for the coming weeks is a depressing thought, and I steel myself for my tomorrows as they stretch before me, the lengthening days of the spring of my eighteenth year.

Weeks pass. I play double solitaire and rummy with Maggie; smoke endless cigarettes lit by nice student nurses in pale blue-checkered uniforms with starched white caps. We talk, Maggie and I, about being here, about how she ran away from home at thirteen and landed here two and a half years ago; went home, ran away again, and now is back. Whenever she moves up a floor, something always brings her back to Nichols. The return is an inevitability she depends on, like our periods, and I wonder if she'll ever go out on her own. She's the only girl close to my age on the ward, so we've become friends. Besides, she's nice to me, smart, and not at all crazy.

My last day on Nichols, Maggie gives me her grandfather's playing cards, a vintage set of two decks: one, silver elephants on blue; the other, gold on red, in an oxblood monogrammed leather case. I cry, tell her of course I will see her again, that she'll be moving up soon, not to worry. I figure I'll never return to Miss Stern and Nichols, so this might be goodbye. I know I must try to save myself now and not look back.

I move up to Hall Eight and begin to get a taste of freedom.

Student nurses let us light our own cigarettes; pick out our clothes, shower and dress unobserved. I know my roommate, Sandy, from last month, a tall lanky blond, strong like a wrestler, with a foul mouth and dirty mind that makes me anxious. She just won't shut up, but for some reason she seems to like me, takes me under her wing, shows me the ropes. It's hard to stay out of trouble around her, but my resolve stays strong and each day I move closer to my goal. Dr. Burnes tells me that the board considers releasing me by summer. With twenty-seven shock treatments and a clean record for two months, things look good.

I think I can make it. I picture myself out there. Maybe, just maybe, I'll get another chance at my life.

Bittersweet

"Riley." We all affectionately call her that behind her back. Only in front of Miss Stern does she become Miss Riley. She hails from Mt. Sinai Hospital. For Maggie and me, she offers a connection to sanity. When she is assigned "Constant Observation" duty, I have someone to talk to, someone I'm not afraid of. She can't be much more than twenty, a second-year student nurse doing psych rotation. Her red pageboy stays neatly pinned under a curved white starched cap, and freckles dance across her nose and cheeks. The blue-and-white-checked dress and white pinafore identify her hospital. Riley, secretly my only friend except for Maggie, has a warm smile, a sign that all is not lost.

Unfortunately, student rotations last only two or three months. Riley has been my personal C.O. nurse at Nichols Cottage. During this time, I've been quiet, distrustful, and often groggy from drugs or shock treatments. Confiding in anyone seems out of the question, but Riley seems different: She shows genuine interest in me, questions why I'm here. I think she really wants to help me, but how can she? Miss Stern rules Nichols Cottage and there's no getting around that. I know Riley puts in a good word for me. I believe she keeps my carefully edited secrets, shared in moments of utter darkness and frustration — secrets that will never be heard by the coldhearted bitch Stern, sitting in her glass cage, who determines everything.

One morning, when her time is up on Nichols, Riley comes to say goodbye, Stern's day off, thank God. Riley hugs me and I cry for the first time in maybe months. She promises she'll keep track of me, but I know I won't see her again. Another loss. This time, bittersweet.

MAY DAY

After two months on Hall Eight, they send me back to Nichols, like a punishment. I definitely feel better, but somehow my plans and resolve keep being sabotaged — by me. Hanging around Sandy, my roommate, and her vile-mouthed friends made me so angry. One day, three of them congregated in our room, talked like sluts and drew pictures of naked people having sex in weird positions. I couldn't stand it, hauled off and hit Sandy in the head, started a fight. So unlike me! Dr. Burnes says this proves I'm making progress and can finally express my hostility toward my mother.

Little accidents happen all the time, especially playing badminton. Don't they understand how clumsy I am? It's not a good game for me. I've suffered two sprained ankles, a sprained wrist, whacked myself in the head, leg, and foot. It seems like I hurt myself on purpose, yet I never consciously think about it. It just happens, like running away. There's no plan, other than I want out.

My parents are extremely unhappy with how things are going. Mom started to send me crazy poems about the hospital and my doctor, with cartoon illustrations mocking them. Staff reads all our mail first, so Dr. Burnes shows the poems to me and asks me what I think. Seems like Mom has lost it. After that the doctors won't let my parents visit — they think it's damaging. I agree, except how will I ever get out of here? And then, go home with them? Not many options really. I try to stay out of trouble, to show that I'm better. I'm scared that they could keep me here for a long time, like Maggie. My folks claim they don't have the money for that, which is a good sign. Maybe when the money runs out, I'll have to go home.

June proves difficult. All my close friends, both at Northfield and Cobleskill, graduate and make plans to go off to college. I feel sad, missing out on everything. When I ask about the plan, when I can go home, the doctors act evasive — no direct answers, just more questions.

"Do you think you're well enough to go home? Do you feel prepared to live with your parents? What are your plans? What about school? With many things to consider, you still demonstrate that you are ill and need to be here."

This does not look good.

On June 30, my parents visit for a scheduled appointment with my doctors and me. I assume we'll discuss my status. We meet in a visitor's room off my ward, and to my great surprise, I learn that I will leave the hospital today. Dad says the release papers have been signed. Dr. Burnes shows up for a brief goodbye, the tension between him and my parents palpable. Good luck and a handshake. That's it. We proceed down the long hall, and, with a brief stop at the front desk to pick up a handful of papers, we're free to leave. Exactly six months after being admitted, incarcerated, I walk out that same front door, down the steps, and into the warm sunshine of freedom.

GETTING OUT SUMMER

Cobleskill and home. The house looks familiar: Dark green-black shutters frame tall sash windows, a curtain of glossy ivy covers the chimney, thick slab redwood picnic table and benches on the red-and-gray flagstones of a backyard patio. I feel sure this is our house when Dad draws a brass key from his pocket and unlocks the back door. I follow them in, carrying my small cloth bag of toiletries and a few letters. Dad goes ahead of me, insists on carrying my Samsonite suitcase. Is my room upstairs? Why can't I remember? At the hospital, I heard that shock treatments would affect my memory. I guess it's really true, even though the last one was more than two months ago. Dad knows how to guide me, but I can't let on that I really don't remember any of this.

All summer I live in my head, in my stuffy bedroom, the whirr of the reverse window fan in the hall soothing me. I don't initiate phone calls, but wait to discover who are my best friends. At first, when someone calls, I pretend I am who I used to be, and wonder if they're fooled. Does my voice betray my lack of confidence? I fake it: Names, facts, colleges where friends are going, places I should know, have known since I was five years old and before; birthdays, jokes we've laughed at since junior high. My loyal girlfriends' voices begin to trigger memories. Oddly, I remember words and phrases in Latin — "*quis, quo, quid; tempus fugit*" — and thank God I can still laugh.

My parents seem relieved. We never talk about my "incarceration" — not ever. I don't want to remember either. The summer slips by, hospital memories fade like old Polaroids, filed somewhere I'm sure to find again.

My second senior year begins with surprising ease, though I long for my old friends. Absence from Cobleskill for two years, and the fact of being a year older than the other seniors, set me apart, but in a good way. Linda, Jody, and Ruthie, three sweet girlfriends from years before, seem to still like me, and our easy friendships put no demands on my secrets. We party, hang out, plan for life after high school. I feel included even though I'm different. Lucky. I guess I can live with that.

IV

Interlude

1962–1963

Hometown Senior — The Lie

A miracle! I feel normal. I take six classes, including French II, Drivers Ed, Art, and Chemistry for Masochists, with Ham Acheson. School places few demands on me, aside from keeping the secret of my whereabouts for seven months, and why I'm repeating my senior year. The story goes like this: I needed some extra courses for college after Northfield. Simple. Everyone's own stories consume them, so no one pays attention to mine. And besides, all my old friends are gone, college freshmen now. We see and talk with each other at Christmas and breaks. Even my best friend doesn't know what happened. Only Aunt Mabel, Uncle Ed, and the local Lutheran minister are in on my secret.

Art class captures my interest. For the first time, I'm allowed, even encouraged, to express my creative side. Mr. Jackman works us hard on perspective drawing. Recently he requested a pen and ink drawing: "How you feel about something; go ahead, show your feelings." What I came up with scares me. The girl-figure in a black leotard crouches beneath dark ominous clouds and lightning; behind her sit shadow figures, ephemeral images, disappearing. I can't explain the piece, but Mr. Jackman loves it! I guess he has his own interpretation of teenage darkness and depression. Maybe he understands more than I imagine.

Winter descends, with SATs just around the corner, then the Regents Scholarship Exam and college applications. My ability to remember facts — historical dates, place names, vocabulary — is very challenged. I manage to memorize the periodic table of the elements by staring at the picture-window-sized chart high on the chem-lab wall. Bringing the images to mind, like focusing my inner camera, I see the letters for copper, iron, zinc, potassium, sulfur. My scores on the SATs are decent. I'm surprised and proceed with college visits, interviews, and applications. Dreams of attending Middlebury College in Vermont keep me motivated this year to make up for last year's disaster. I seek a small, coed liberal arts college. I carefully select three with the help of my parents and guidance counselor, emphasizing science, where I achieved my highest test scores. Science isn't my passion, but I can see the sense of it: career potential. My folks don't believe I should count on marriage as the complete answer to my future. Very enlightened. And with me, they don't count on much.

We gather up my high school records and send them off in neat bundles to meet the schools' February deadlines. Applications, fees, recommendations (3), medical records, test scores, grades, activities, even vaccination records. They want it all, and I look pretty good on paper. Interviews and campus visits go well, and all seems hopeful. I love Middlebury. Aiming high, my bow strung tight, I know it's a long shot to the Ivy Leagues. Ithaca College seems like my best bet, pretty much a sure thing. I cautiously begin to picture myself there on the campus, the town with its steep gorges, magical woodlands, and cool coffee houses. Yes, this will work and I can be happy there.

The letters arrive, all three before my April Fool's birthday. Ithaca comes last, and that rejection hits me the hardest. As with the others, no reason is given. It must be a mistake. My parents call and write, and finally we receive the answer. My seven months in New York Hospital has ruined it — my chances to recover a normal life — the one I'm supposed to have. None of the colleges will accept me.

At graduation, I win the school's Art Prize and a Regents Scholarship: Full tuition to any college in New York State. The only problem — I can't get into one. On the list of seniors and where they're going to college, I'm left out again, which is how I feel most of the time.

THE DANCE

In April, a huge surprise: my classmates nominate me, along with Candace and Judy B., for Queen of the "Coronation Capers." I throw myself into decorating and avoid thinking about a date. The large mirrored sphere that spins from the gym's rafters scatters diamond lights across the basketball-court-turned-dance-floor. As I hang midnight-blue drapery on the bleachers and mount silver stars, I try to imagine myself here dancing, but I can't picture it with any of the younger guys from my class.

My close friend, Jody, hatches a plan. Her steady guy, George, now attends Union College in nearby Schenectady. George has a friend, Harry, and apparently he's quite cute. In our fantasy, they could drive out here together and we could double-date. The bottom line for me — without a date, I can't go to the dance. Amazingly, he says yes! One week before the dance, I have no dress and haven't even met Harry. Still I feel excited and go on a shopping trip with Mom. Albany's too far, so an after-school drive to nearby Schoharie and a small dress shop will have to do. Annual Prom shopping ended weeks ago; racks got picked over, the best pastels chosen by others before me. Still, I find a flowing apricot one, soft and curvy with a sweetheart neckline. Too low, Mom says. Then she spots a sheer black organdy dress with a white windowpane design over black taffeta, sleeveless, with a boat neckline. It hangs on the sale rack and she insists on my trying it on — the fit perfect. No alterations needed, so we buy it for $25, ignoring that it looks more appropriate for a cocktail party than a dance. My plain black patent-leather flats will do, especially since I heard that Harry is about my height, five-seven. With a college guy for a date and my strange outfit, I'll probably feel out of place. Not a new feeling. Still I'm happy that I'm going.

Friday night. The doorbell rings twice and I see Harry's outline through the sheer pleated front-door curtain. Dad answers right away. From the upstairs hallway I catch a peek at him. Dark gray suit, neat short-cropped sandy hair, and handsome. I'm hot and flushed, grinning to myself when Dad calls me.

"Judy, Harry's here. Are you ready?" I slowly descend the stairs, and Harry's smiling brown eyes show me that he likes what he sees. What a relief! A small clear plastic box holds a perfect white gardenia and he holds it out, offering me this gift of faith: that we will like each other and have a good time. He talks politely with my parents for a few minutes, and then tries awkwardly to pin on my corsage. He moves closer, fumbling with the long pin. It's like we're already dancing. This unexpected intimacy feels charged with expectation, the fragrance of my White Shoulders and his clean pure smell, not spoiled with too much aftershave. I think he's perfect. He offers me his arm as we step out into the steamy cicada-song night and George's Volvo station wagon.

I've forgotten all about my candidacy for Queen. It's like a popularity contest voted on by the student body. I hate these sorts of things, yet I feel honored to be nominated to the Court. When they call out my name as Queen, I can't believe it! Jody nudges me hard so I'll walk up to the bandstand. The lights flash and everyone claps and cheers. My throat grips so tight I can't speak and tears rush to my eyes, threatening to dissolve my mascara, as I'm presented with a bouquet of long-stemmed red roses. Up front, I stand in the center with Blair, who's King and class president. We are crowned. The lights dim and the band croons our theme song, *Moon River.* We casually approach the middle of the floor. Neither of us is a good dancer and we're both a bit shy. As my hand slides tentatively around the back of his shoulder, he leads me gently in a slow waltz. Soon other couples join us at the perimeter, in the shadows, sprinkled with starlight on ballet-length gowns and glossy hair. When I join Harry for the rest of the evening, he seems proud of me, pulls me close, and between songs holds my hand. At the last break, as we drink pink lemonade punch, Harry invites me to go to Union College with George and Jody the next afternoon and spend an overnight at a guesthouse on campus for their Spring Weekend. Jody had warned me that he might ask, if he liked me. Oh, yes! Of course, I really want to go. When I discuss the plan with my folks on Saturday morning, they're reluctant. But at nineteen, I don't need their permission. I assure them that all is safe.

Harry, George, and Jody pick me up just after eleven the next morning, with my train case and a small overnight bag in tow. They plan for a tour of the campus, picnic on the lawn, and a dorm party in the evening. Even with kegs of beer, it turns out mellow, not like a wild fraternity party. These are the unpledged guys, left behind by the fraternity scene. I enjoy my date with Harry, feel relaxed, comfortable, and part of it all. What a special weekend. When he kisses me goodbye, I know I could get serious about Harry.

SUMMER JOB

Just my luck: After only one more date, Harry leaves for the summer. I'll probably never see him again. I land a summer job nearby at the American Hotel in Sharon Springs, a hot sulfur springs resort. The town sits in a canyon twenty miles away from Cobleskill, populated by Orthodox Jewish rabbis and families from New York City. The job goes from Thursday through Sunday. As a chambermaid, I have very specific duties. When weekend guests arrive, I supervise "the Annex," a large two-story building with cheap rooms and a big dorm-style bathroom at the end of the long hallway.

I monitor the refrigerators also, keeping track of which one's for meat and which for dairy; these must be stored separately. I turn lights on and off between sundown Friday and sundown on Saturday, the Sabbath according to Jewish law. In years past this would have meant a busy job, with all the rooms full, people coming and going to the baths, "taking the waters" for their various ailments: Arthritis, lethargy, rheumatism, anxiety, but now the patrons from New York favor the Catskills to the east. Rustic mountain resorts, with their cool air, comedy shows, and cocktail parties provide a popular social scene. Bridge games and status trump the old-fashioned vacations at the spas. Times are changing. On Saturday afternoons I'm left with little to do. After cleaning up the bathrooms and kitchen I still must stay close to the Annex. I adore the main hotel down the street on the other side. It has three floors and its crisp white paint and late 1800s architecture, with a full-length broad porch lined with large comfortable rockers, make it the shining jewel of town. It sits about halfway down Spring Street, slightly above street level, with generous lawns set up with croquet courts on two or three levels. On the back porch, umbrella tables overlook the grounds, giant maples, and elms. Midday, hardly anyone relaxes outside in the sticky heat, 90 degrees or more. Inside, ceiling fans softly whirr as couples play canasta or cribbage, read newspapers or old romantic novels, and wait for the breeze to come up the canyon and cool things off before they head for the baths. Later, guests will dress up for a late dinner, after sundown, gathering first in the spacious lobby. Screen doors bang as couples step in and out, porch to lobby and back again, like a ritual mating dance. Their voices form a crazy chorus, punctuated by emphatic tenor lines. High-pitched laughter, lilting female alto tones, and a rumbling base ground the whole melody. I love my little side job here. No one notices me as I cruise around to fill pitchers with ice water, pick up empty, sweaty cocktail tumblers and soaked napkins. This pace suits me fine. I circulate in the center of it all, happily occupied, accepted, and totally invisible.

Several weeks pass without incident. Unfortunately, I can't seem to stay out of trouble. A handsome guy, twenty-five or so, with jet-black hair and dark steamy eyes, moves into the Annex down the hall from me. One Saturday night, he invites me to have a drink on the porch, and then talk upstairs. After our drink, I feel extremely turned on, and against my better judgment follow him to his room. We share cigarettes, have another drink, and make out a bit, but I refuse to take off my clothes. Something feels terribly wrong. He becomes pushy, obnoxious. Somehow I escape to my room, lock the door, fall into a dead sleep, fully, but scantily clothed in the summer heat. I awaken to a fire alarm. Smoke fills the hall, pours out of his room. Apparently, he fell asleep with a cigarette, and his bed is in flames. Acrid black smoke sends everyone outside coughing. He escapes with minor burns. Now he acts like he knows me, sidles up to me, wants something. I'm freaked out! That's it. Over. Sunday morning, early, I pack my things, stop at the main hotel with my time card, and quit. Once again, it's time to leave. At least this time I have something to say about it.

The Lie Continues

For the rest of the summer, I commute to a filing job an hour away at the state capitol in Albany. I learn to drink coffee with sugar and Coffee Mate on breaks in our air-conditioned cubicle-filled office. On Saturdays, I double-date with my girlfriend, Jody, and two brothers from the next town. Jody already goes steady with George, and when we park, I get nervous. All I want is to. talk, hold hands, and maybe kiss a little. My early curfew usually keeps things safe; at the same time, the screwdrivers we drink at the Colonial lounge help to loosen me up. I'm a virgin, not in love with this guy, and very uptight about petting.

"They just want one thing," Mom says. "Boys won't respect you if you let them do what they want," referring to petting and going all the way.

So why does he keep asking me out? Maybe it's just that we like each other, are friends, can talk and have a good time. Maybe that's enough. It feels safe. Jody talks about Keuka College where she's going, an all-girls college in the Finger Lakes region. I see Keuka as a good possibility. I need to go somewhere, can't remain at home. Our family doctor agrees to leave out the "black marks" on my medical records, which he'll submit with my application. Bless him. Otherwise, I have little hope of getting in. Within two weeks, I receive my acceptance letter. Apparently, there are no problems. I feel elated, like I've won the Kellogg's Sweepstakes. My prize: a permanent ticket out of town, leaving home forever.

August is full of intricate plans, endless lists of toiletries, clothes, summer booklists — and hours of reading. Hot sultry nights, windows open, single thin sheet draped half off the bed. The fan sucks out hot air, pulling in the thick, cooler night air. I lie awake, worrying. What if someone finds out? Will they kick me out? My hair has grown long again, and I refuse any more permanents — I'll wear it straight. And I won't sleep on large coiled rollers with bristled cores, aggravating my insomnia. My waking hours fill with thoughts of the future: A college campus and my roommate Linda. My new life shimmers before me like an orange-and-gold tropical sunrise. When I fall asleep, I'm not afraid. My future seems secure.

FIRST LOVE

Arrival and orientation — I made it! Mom and Dad are thrilled with Keuka College, and help me get settled. They've already arranged for me to ride home to Cobleskill with Jody at Thanksgiving. Dad unloads the car outside my dorm. We scurry back and forth carrying boxes of books, duffel bags of linens, and two suitcases to my new room. I adore my gray tweed Samsonite train case, stuffed to the gills with Golden Breck shampoo, Secret deodorant, Excedrin; enough supplies to last the whole semester.

The two larger suitcases mostly contain winter clothes, as there will be frost later this month: Wool crew sweaters and straight skirts; tweed slacks and thick black tights; mittens, gloves, and pull-on hats. But for now, it's Indian Summer, still gloriously warm during the day, and I can get away with culottes and my new sweater set of brushed angora, a delicious buttery yellow. With my shoulder-length straight blonde hair, I imagine that I look good and fit in.

Linda, my roommate, stands petite; dark curls frame her lightly freckled face and winning smile. When we meet up in our room, she seems happy, warm, and we like each other on sight. What a good sign, I think, that my life is turning around. Linda's dad is a psychiatrist, and when I spend a weekend with her family, I feel comfortable opening up a bit to talk about Mom and her nervous breakdowns. I even allude to my own troubles, but no words about my hospital experience. Decades might pass — unimaginable, actually — before I can speak of it.

Prior to Homecoming, our brother college, Hobart, hosts a fall mixer at their campus. A new friend from my dorm, Susan, and I sign up and take the bus over for pizza and the dance. A mixer can't be that bad, not like the ones in high school, so tense and embarrassing. Susan and I will stick together. We dress in our pencil-straight skirts, sweater sets, flats, and a little make-up, then climb giggling onto the bus. Susan has already met someone she likes — Bob. She'll meet up with him there, and promises to introduce me to his roommate David. Maybe we four can hang out.

Once there, Susan disappears, leaving me to munch pizza and stick to my favorite role as observer on the sidelines. Cute boys attach themselves to attractive girls with perfect figures. As I stand there, invisible, it hits me that I've never had a real boyfriend. I remember J.S., my very first date ever, for the high school freshman dance, my first kiss too. Sophomore year, Matt, the not-my-boyfriend fantasy guy, intrigued me with his black, slicked back D.A., leather jacket, motorcycle, and soft-spoken friendship.

As juniors at Northfield, we had chaperoned parlor dates and Sunday campus walks, which went nowhere. Following my senior year, I flirted with a brief but intense, impossible, summer romance, spiked with deep kissing. This ended abruptly when he decided to get back together with his girlfriend. I was crushed, but what did I expect? My secret hope — that he loved me, would choose me.

The nice guys I fantasized about didn't seem interested in Plain Jane me, flat chested, shy, and inexperienced. Summer dates with college guys two years my senior concluded with them trying to feel me up in the front seats of parked cars, while I wondered how it would feel to be in love. That about sums it up. Nineteen and still waiting.

"There you are. Are you hiding?" Susan approaches, smiling, two guys in tow. "Here, meet Bob." She grabs his hand and pulls him close. "And this is David, his roommate... I was telling you about him...." Awkward, we smile, say hi, but don't touch. David stands tall; I'm guessing six feet two, with brown hair, soft, dark, intense eyes behind horn-rimmed glasses. Good-looking. And he stares at me like he knows me, sees into me. I feel a bit of a flush and turn away. Bob and Susan take off to get some pizza and Cokes while David and I make small talk. I figure he'll excuse himself soon and disappear, but I figure wrong. He seems attracted to me, my long hair, summer freckles splattered across my nose, shy nervous laugh. By mid-evening he tells me so.

We dance. I stretch my neck up, while he bends down, sniffing my hair. I want to catch every word he says. He pulls me in closer, and in the dimmest light, we shuffle and sway to the Everly Brothers. We turn with tiny steps, lost in the feeling of our bodies pressing together, losing our separate identities. One moment blends into the next, seamlessly, like the tide's rhythmic motion. At the end of the night, amidst couples entwined outside the bus, we promise to meet next weekend.

The next three months fly by like wildfire. Autumn blazes crimson and bright gold, awakening in me a deep passion for life, for connection. I feel it beating in my chest, hot in my limbs. I see beauty everywhere, in the ever-shorter snappy cold days, hoarfrost on dying grass, endings and beginnings. I have never been in love before, not like this, not the real thing. Gradually I slip into David's embrace as easily as day becomes night with its soft blanket of comfort.

All semester, the four of us double-date, delighting ourselves with long weekend drives to our favorite rural bar, the Crossroads, for burgers and drinks and endless hilarious games of pool. In the back seat of Bob's car, we steam up the windows with hot kisses and needy embraces. David presses me for more, always a bit beyond my comfort zone, with hands all over the place, on top and under my sweater, pants, desire flaring. We feel weak with wanting, dazed, but I can't go further. I'm not ready, always the one holding the line. He wants to go "all the way," would probably do so right in the back seat, yet he clearly respects me and steadfastly promises to honor my wishes. We made an agreement to wait. Finally I can relax and enjoy our time together.

We feel that we've known each other forever. In a past life, Egyptian royalty, we are lovers bound by some ancient tie. Images of gold and lapis flit through my dreams, guardians surrounding a sacred love. Knowing that we are meant to be together, we face down the heat, play at the edge. We will choose our time for consummation with care. It would be easy, in a way, to give in, follow the flames that lick their way to the center of us. I find tremendous security in our stance together and the deep trust we nurture. Mom was right, and I love that I have my special gift to offer. Almost twenty and still a virgin! Hopefully we will share this moment on our wedding night, I dream. I'm sure we can hold out.

Whenever the dorm phone rings, I know it's David. Actually, I know before the ring, the moment he breaks into my mental concentration: calculus and anatomy go to hell. I feel him reach for me, and, smiling, I dash down the hall to grab the receiver, breathing hard. We share air space all the time, indulge our E.S.P. world, compare notes. I don't even try to shield my mind but leave it available, open, like a delicate rose ready to be plucked. I trust him and know he would never hurt me. Love poems appear in my mailbox, in my sweater pocket. He stares at me, his dark moody eyes filled with such love, pure devotion. Destiny has certainly brought us together. In the deep of winter, David further shows himself to me. Dark moods, frustration, acute perception, and sharp intelligence: He reveals his inner life gradually, carefully, wants me to truly know him. He struggles, broods. His hoped-for career as a jazz pianist was dashed one Fourth of July, when someone tossed a cherry bomb at a party, blowing off part of his left thumb and forefinger.

He pounds the keyboard. Angry syncopated notes create a magic tension, compelling melodies. Music pulses in his veins. Rhythm pours from his hands, white-hot, even the stub, left hand angling to make the rough, hard contact. He makes love to the piano. I am touched and even a little jealous. I adore David's passion for jazz, his courage, and persistence. I have never known anyone like him.

I feel sure he is the One.

V

Lost

1964–1965

Lost

I wake up groggy and squinting. At that moment, a nurse pulls back a thick white curtain; prism-like light floods the room and fans out like a kaleidoscope. My mind struggles to make sense of what I see. The nurse, a student in her crisp striped uniform, comes right to my bedside and speaks softly.

"Well, I see you're coming around. You had quite a time of it; you've been asleep half the day." I look hard at her. Who are you? Why am I here? What happened? I slog around inside my head for something familiar. I notice that my arm is bound to a splint-like device, with IV tubes taped to the inside of my right elbow. "Don't worry," she says, noticing my alarm. "The medicine will help you recover, return to normal. The doctors had to pump your stomach. Nasty combination, pills and alcohol. Lucky you're still with us." Pills and alcohol? What does she mean? Now it's coming back, bits and pieces, a mosaic, like shards of colored glass. That cool fraternity party, David being rushed by Phi Sig. We made a good impression, I think, toasting sparkly glasses of champagne to celebrate. Everyone seemed so nice, the party a bit rowdy for my taste. He was proud of me, and I think I looked good in my black wool cocktail dress skimming my knees, and new suede pumps. Then, the motel... what happened?

I remember when we got there we checked out the room that Susan and I were supposed to share. A nice room, heavy floor-to-ceiling drapes that shut out the lights from the parking lot, one big bed, and a couple of bucket chairs. Then Susan and Bob excused themselves and went to the room next door. I felt a little uncomfortable, as David and I had never actually been alone. "What's up?" I ask.

"Oh, they just need a little privacy," he answers. "Come here, baby." He steps close, gently puts both arms around my shoulders.

I feel his familiar large hands slide across my back, surrounding me; he kisses my hair. He wants to lie on the bed. I want to, but don't want to — dangerous territory. We have a solid agreement, so I know I can trust him. Then, everything shifts. Suddenly I feel scared. We're wrestling, and I'm shouting, "No! Stop!" I push him away, struggling... it's all fading.... A nightmare. And then I wake up again.

I'm screaming, ripping the tubes out of my arm. I've got to get out of here! But instead, I swoon into the arms of the nurse, who also screams and holds me tight. A couple of nurses and an orderly push me back onto the bed. A shot, and I'm out. This feels so weirdly familiar.

When I come to, it's dark outside. Through a wide slit in the curtains, I can see eerie streetlights shrouded in swirling winter fog. The metal side rails of the hospital bed confine me, tubes reinserted, my arms securely tied down to the rails. Only the signal light, at the end of its cord, is within my reach. I feel totally alone and frightened. Old pictures of Albany Hospital and that orderly keep cropping up. Then, memories of the previous night begin to crowd in and I can't stop them. I alternately cry and then stare out the window; a familiar panic rises in my chest, my heart races like a rabbit caught in the teeth of a steel trap. I hate to lie on my back. So vulnerable. I squirm and struggle, pull up my knees to change position. I can almost feel his weight on me — heavy thick thighs, strong muscled arms pushing, pushing me down. His face too close, dark and menacing. His voice, his musky smell... uninvited, and I wonder how it has come to this. I just want to curl up in a ball and pull a blanket over me. The agonizing scene in my head slows down but won't turn off.

"Baby, baby, you know you want to, you know you want it as much as I do," I hear David say, but I hardly recognize him. His big hand covers my face, trying to muffle my sobs. This has gone way too far! *You have to stop!* I'm hysterical, thrash, push on his chest, heave under his weight and try to escape. It all happens so fast! I don't want this, not now, and not this way.

Searing white-hot pain rips into me, through me, like a dagger, like nothing I've ever felt before. Then, it's over.

He rolls off at last. I grab my dress and pull it around me like a beach towel. Full of shame, I head for the bathroom. I can't talk, and I can't stop crying. Once locked safely in the tiny bathroom, I begin immediately to clean up. That's when I discover the blood; inside I hurt a lot, but not like my period, which is due next week. Soap and the hottest water sting, and I welcome the pain. I have the worst headache of my life, like a migraine. My eyes hurt; they're puffy and swollen, and the light seems too bright. I can't imagine ever opening the door. Luckily, my overnight case stayed with me, containing my pills. One Fiorinal usually does it, annihilates a headache, two if it's really bad. Tonight I take two, and a few minutes later, two more for good measure. I just want to drown out the hurt. I can't believe our beautiful, sacred love has come to this.

Outside the door, David begs me to come out and talk. "Are you all right, baby? Come on, open the door. I'm sorry. I feel so bad." Silence. "Please, please stop crying. I didn't mean to hurt you. You know I love you."

Now I cry even harder. I know things will never be the same with us, that it's spoiled, it's over. And me? Damaged, forever lost. What he took from me I can never get back. He hears my sobs, and I have no words. What is there to say? That my life is ruined? My chance for love?

Susan waits outside the bathroom, and convinces me to unlock the door. We sit on the edge of the bathtub, and through bouts of sobbing I attempt to tell her what happened. When we stand up, I get dizzy. As we emerge from the bathroom, the room spins, undulates, and I stumble to a chair. Susan asks if I took something. I should have recovered from the champagne by now, and I wasn't drunk last night anyway. They say I'm acting strangely, and we should go out for coffee to clear my head. By now it's early morning, 5:00 or 6:00 a.m., still dark. We head to a nearby diner. Coffee, Wonder Bread toast, and cigarette smells hit me, along with bright fluorescent lights. I want to throw up. Bob and Susan help me walk — I won't let David touch me. They make me drink the first cup plain. I black out on the way to the bathroom. Back in the car, they tell me how scared they feel, that they're taking me to the hospital to have me checked out. Something's wrong.

"Come on, stay awake. Don't do this," Susan cries softly, shaking my arm. "You'll be okay. Just keep your eyes open." I doze off again. The ride is like a Bergman movie, clips of snowy streets whiz past the fogged-up window in the back seat of Bob's car. My headache slips away, along with the details of last night — misty, swirling, they disappear into the white. Some time later, a doctor asks me about what happened. I won't talk about the sex. I tell him no, I was not trying to kill myself. He explains how the pills, a barbiturate, combined with the alcohol in my system. That even a small amount could kill me. He gives me a medication to calm my anxiety: sodium amytal. After the shot, I feel dizzy, really nauseous and agitated, like being at the dentist's, only much worse. I'm jumping out of my skin!

Then, in a flash, with a heaving thrust, all my strength focuses in one move, like karate. I pitch forward over the end of the bed, tearing the straps and tubes loose from my wrists. I'm shocked when I find myself down on the cold floor, chin bleeding, fractured, wondering what the hell just happened. Later, after several stitches, the doctor calls it an allergic reaction to the drug.

The worst comes later. They inform me that I've been kicked out of school and must go home. David has been expelled too. When my parents pick me up, I know I have failed them in the worst way. Thank God they don't know the whole story, about the sex, my lost virginity — only that I illegally signed out of my dorm, took some pills and alcohol, and that somehow my boyfriend and I wrecked my chance to go to college. And the only good part? No one seriously considers sending me back to the loony bin.

Home Again

Going home this time, pure hell. No delicate state of mind or fragile memory, just the intense shame of being kicked out of college. Inside, I'm going crazy with the feeling of violation ... and the irrational desire to hear from David. Someone claimed he came with Bob and Susan to see me at the hospital. I'm sure the staff wouldn't let him in. And my parents? His existence banned, like prohibition, and we can't even speak his name. Like before, my friends aren't aware I'm home, most of them off enjoying college. When the phone rings, Mom picks it up. And I know David's been calling.

"Don't call again," I hear her hiss. "She won't be talking to you."

I feel David reach out, hear his voice in my mind. "Baby, baby, I'm so sorry. Please, please be all right. Say you'll talk to me again, that it's not over, somehow we'll be okay...."

Alone with my parents, I'm totally cut off. The iron-gray sky, deep snowdrifts, and dirty icicles freeze all hope for me this winter. I can only dream that somehow I'll find a way to get out of here, even see him again. Could that even happen? And what would that mean? My heart aches whenever I think of him. Next week I'll start looking for a job.

One Saturday morning, the mailbox door bangs, not quite closing around a fat bundle of mail and magazines. The folded *Life* sticks out, and I step onto the porch to retrieve it. From out of nowhere, Mom appears and rudely snatches the letters right out of my hands.

"But there might be something for me," I complain. Ignoring me, she sorts with intense focus. I see a small plain envelope, plump with folded paper. "Is it for me?" She holds it back, not answering, so I quickly grab it. The return address, "Susan Ames." The letter's from David.

"Give me that," she demands, but I'm already on my way upstairs. Skipping steps and breathless, I tear into the bathroom and lock both doors. In a minute, she's there, demanding that I open the door. But I'm safe — safe at least, until I read his letter.

Dear Judy... This will be the hardest letter I've ever written... I am so very sorry... if I could only take it back... never meant to hurt you... only love you so much... lost control... Please forgive me... I see your face in my mind every day, crying, sad... I need desperately to see you, talk to you... beg you to forgive me. When they wouldn't let me see you, I nearly lost my mind....

I keep reading quickly, feeling the pressure of Mom outside. David's words, so full and poignant, then his beautiful sad poem, like a classical Greek tragedy of love lost. I fall apart, cry uncontrollably. My heart is shattered. It's overwhelming, and I can hardly contain all that I feel. I read the letter three times; the words wash over me and sink in. I memorize as best I can. Seated on the edge of the bathtub, still crying, I tear the letter into tiny pieces, ingest a few, feel the bits roll around on my tongue. I drop the rest into the toilet, watch them float there — the dark blue ink dissolves, colors the water a pale lavender — then flush the pieces away. Now Mom can't know my secret life. Shoved in my bra, a small torn scrap — Susan's address. She will be my contact, as I have no idea where David is.

It takes forever to compose myself. I finally tell Mom I'm fine, I'll be down for lunch. I won't talk about any of it. I wish I could have kept the letter, but she might find it somehow, digging around in my stuff.

The letter assures me that I am not alone in my pain. I can't imagine how, or when, we'll meet again, only that there's some destiny about David and me, and it's not finished. Injured to my core, I also feel tightly bound to this man that I deeply loved. Tonight, I will try to answer his letter.

DISCOVERY

One month at home and I know what stir-crazy means. I'll do anything — wait tables at Hoagland's Drug Store, clerk at the A&P, maybe be a bank teller. Needs to be respectable. I need to earn back my parents' approval. Just turning twenty, I feel pretty much at zero.

Ever since high school, the local hospital calls Dad and me to donate blood. They love us there, us and our A-negative blood. Sitting in the lab, pumping it out ever so slowly, we hear about a temporary job opening in the medical records department. Heck, I can do that. I always loved libraries and filing. Hospitals intrigue me, regular ones, that is. And two hours a week as a candy striper doesn't get me out of the house nearly enough.

I land the job easily: Thirty hours a week and quite boring, actually; nine to twelve, one to four — filing charts, Xeroxing records, delivering charts to the upstairs nurses' station or ER "stat." I like most of the staff, love being recognized by doctors, nurses, and aides, most of whom I've known all my life. They seldom ask questions, like why am I home and not away at college. Small-town folks want to know everything, are hungry for details, yet often won't pry or ask direct personal questions. Perfect.

After a couple of weeks, putting away charts like Fiore and Firman, a name jumps out at me: "Fisher, Judith A." Curious. I've never been in this hospital, so why would there be a chart? My back to the doorway, I open the chart to be certain. A strange coincidence? Someone with the same name?

But I'm wrong. Same address, same birth date, it's mine after all. What the heck is going on? My heart races when a clerk walks in, and I nervously stuff the file into its spot on the shelf. Going through the motions at lunch, I can hardly eat my peanut butter sandwich. Even with ice-cold milk to wash it down, the dry bread sticks in my throat. The cafeteria's fluorescent lights seem harsh, too bright, and I feel exposed. I'm afraid to see what's in my chart, but even so, I leave lunch early because I can't wait to look.

I stand in the far corner of the records room, completely hidden, and quickly read through the pages. Now I'm in an absolute panic, as the implications of what I see sink in, confuse and clog my brain.

Vital signs mostly absent on arrival... apparent overdose of sleeping pills, probably pentobarbital... mother's prescription... suicide note... pumped her stomach... five days in hospital... no other known history or incidents.

I slam the file shut and cram it back where it came from. My pulse pounds, face hot and flushed. I want to run outside, up the hill into the woods, with its fresh young leaves and innocence, but my feet stick to the floor. I can't move, can hardly breathe. I simply don't remember. How is that? Can shock treatments obliterate everything? It feels like this never happened, and I want it not to have happened, to disappear. How can I make peace with this — a fifteen-year-old girl, me, who tried to kill herself?

What else might I discover that I have forgotten?

MED-TECH JOB

April 1. My birthday comes and goes, unremarkable. At twenty, I still live at home. Medical records proves a dead end, and though grateful for a job, I begin again to dream of a future away from Cobleskill and my parents. Filing, so tedious. Mostly, I love visiting the lab. Jeannie, the head lab tech, buzzes around like the queen bee, curly honey-colored hair pulled back in a bouncy ponytail, petite frame covered by her short white lab coat. She always takes a few minutes to chat with me when I come by to pick up reports.

"You seem really interested in the lab," Jeannie says to me one day.

"Yes, I am. Always loved chemistry and biology, kind of fascinated by blood."

"The reason I'm asking, I need another tech assistant. I could teach you everything, and if it works out, you'll have a better job and more money."

I immediately accept. This seems like my big break. The following week, I begin training. Much looks familiar to me, and the work feels so natural. First thing, I learn to make slides: carefully place one drop of blood at the end of a sterile glass slide; then with a second slide, slowly drag it across, spread out the cells to view and count through the microscope. Labeled tubes of freshly drawn blood, with rubber tops, are placed in the centrifuge to separate out the components: plasma, red and white cells. Some samples are stained, cultured, and analyzed in search of disease-causing organisms; secrets are discovered, hidden in the viscous ruby fluids. The work mesmerizes me.

Urinalysis, another big part of the lab: Specimens show up, amber and clear gold; light brown and pink; cloudy, clear, or containing suspended particles. So much can be learned from the first viewing. We measure the urine into narrow beakers, hold it up to the natural light from the north windows, and make notes on our observations. Then we proceed to a closer look under the microscope, searching for crystals, cells of all kinds that might indicate bladder or kidney issues, inflammation, stones, infection. Lab analysis feels like magic, the key that can turn the tide. It's all about making a difference, discovering the specific cause of an illness, being part of the team pulling for a treatment or a cure. This is what I'm excited about. Perhaps I've found my calling.

As the hot sticky summer progresses, I'm called upon to perform various overtime tasks. I like to be busy and don't mind staying after five or coming in on the weekend. Jeannie takes me along on blood draws, and soon has me doing them: Tourniquet, palpate for a nice fat vein, wipe down with alcohol; steady my hand, stick, allow the tube to fill; withdraw, apply gauze, press. Easy! She observes for several weeks before she sends me upstairs alone to draw blood when she's too busy.

One day she invites me to watch a spinal tap. Sweat trickles down under my lab coat collar, more from nerves than the 95% humidity. Jeannie takes her tools from the shiny sterile silver tray, and makes a precise puncture into the spine of a very sick young man. He groans and I cringe; almost feeling his pain, I grit my teeth and feel nauseous. I manage not to faint or let on that this bothers me. Afterward, I rejoice that the analysis of this precious fluid saves his life: Spinal meningitis. Surely I am in the right place.

Jeannie brings it up first: "How about you go to school, get the real training to become a Med Tech, a degree. You're headed in that direction anyway. Soon you'll be required to have a license to work in a lab. Med tech is your ticket out of Cobleskill."

And so, the research begins. By July, I apply to Rochester Institute of Technology, which has two- and four-year courses in medical technology. The department's reputation is excellent, and includes many premed students as well as "techies." With my hospital's recommendation and good SAT scores, especially in science, R.I.T. accepts me for the fall. Even my Regents' Scholarship is still valid. I'll live in a dorm I've never seen, in a city I've never visited. In two months' time, I leave home on my great adventure — and this time I won't screw up.

BACK TO COLLEGE, 1964

I'm two years older than most freshmen at R.I.T. Secretly, I feel the difference, am enthusiastic to fit in, become a normal college girl again. Dorm assignment lands me in a rambling corner suite with three other girls. Sally and Betty both major in retailing—very hip. Perfectly coiffed and attired, they make college life look so easy. Besides, they are fun loving, good students, and best of all they like me. One day, a junior from our dorm invites us to a sorority rush party. I know nothing about this world, yet I'm pulled along by the excitement, the feeling of being included.

The members of Alpha Xi seem mature, dress with a flair, and fit in so well with each other: the "cream of the crop." They court us. I find myself drawn in, like the embrace of a long-lost family. One evening, at a final get-together before pledging begins, the sisters of Alpha Xi stand close to us and sing in harmony one of their melodies of loyalty and connection. Sally squeezes my hand. This gesture moves me to tears. Sally's blue eyes lock with mine; overcome in the moment, we hope we'll be chosen. I feel sure that she and Betty will make it.

Monday through Friday, our alarms go off, painfully, around 6:00 a.m. Outside our windows, the predawn glow shimmers through the expansive maples and elms that still grace the streets of our neighborhood. We take sequential showers in our tiny bathroom. Some of the old tiles are cracked; little white hexagons cover the floor, just like at Grandma's house. We luck out, having a tub; it's often full, hung with drying bras, panties, and stockings. We dress by 7:00, concentrate on make-up, hairdos, toast and coffee, then start to collect our notebooks for the day. I feel blessed with just one eight o'clock class this semester, Western Civilization 101, the most boring prerequisite class of every college freshman.

Our dorm, Bates Hall, with three floors of studio apartments, a small entrance lobby, and an elevator, once served as a residence boarding house. Our corner apartment is packed full, with two beds by the windows and two Murphys that flip down from French doors. They never go up. Mine is one of the pull-downs, and though I have a desk, chemistry formulas and biology illustrations are strewn across my madras bedspread.

We take turns making dinner in our miniature kitchen. Each of us cooks easy family recipes. My favorites are meatloaf (from the Quaker Oats box), tuna noodle casserole (from the Campbell's mushroom soup can) and Mom's tasty Betty Crocker apple crisp. Everybody does baked potatoes, Rice-a-Roni, and iceberg-lettuce salads. We all sort of know how to cook, except for our other roommate, Penny, who flatly refuses to participate. She isn't interested. Sometimes she eats with us anyway. Mostly she hops in her Porsche and disappears into the foggy night, goes who knows where, and slips back in before curfew.

On Friday nights we head out for pizza and beer, one block away at the Past-Time bar. The place fills up by 6:00, dark, smoky, and loud. At first it's hard to pick out familiar voices and faces. Then a hand pops up. "Over here, Judy!" and I recognize my roommates and a couple of Alpha Xis. "We scored a table," they croon excitedly.

Somehow, they've claimed one, just big enough for an extra-large pizza with everything, a tall ribbed-glass pitcher of draft beer, glasses, and an ashtray. Nothing else fits. Five or six of us squeeze around to eat, drink, and share the week's happenings. We sink into the amazing comfort of belonging, and flirt with the cute guys. Our Past-Time Friday evenings become a ritual: No dates required, just hitch up with a girlfriend or two, after a long week of classes, labs and homework, and walk down two blocks to the campus "watering hole." I pretend that the hodgepodge collection of old buildings taken over by R.I.T. on the edge of a "bad neighborhood" translates into a real college campus. Some of the structures are century-old homes, transformed into apartments, fraternity houses, and the School for American Craftsmen. Still, it's not the same as rolling lawns and ivy-covered colonial buildings of the country campuses of my dreams — like Middlebury. Or even last year at Keuka, the little jewel of a girls' college snuggled between two Finger Lakes. Still, I feel settled and lucky. One evening, three small ivory envelopes that look like thank-you notes, appear at our door. Mine has my full name written out in a beautiful loopy script. Sally, Betty, and I are all goose bumps, hoping it means what we think it means. It's true! The three of us are invited to pledge Alpha Xi Delta. Now we scream, cry, and hug each other. At 9:00 p.m., we shall meet in the dorm lobby if we want to pledge.

As we gather, we sense the muffled crying, quick hugs, and nods as we look around to see who's been chosen. The older sisters shush us and lead us to a dimly lit meeting room. One by one our names are called, and they question us about our intentions, loyalty, and commitment to become, through pledging, sisters of Alpha Xi Delta. Cathy hugs me; she will be my Big Sister. Tears of joy stream down my cheeks. After the ceremony, they explain that Barb, a senior, will be our Pledge Mistress. Her words rule us. Loyalty to our pledge group becomes a top priority, and we will be tested on this over and over. Our very happiness depends on surviving the next several weeks. Serious business. We leave the room elated and scared. In whispers, we agree to meet the following night, before our weekly trek to the P.T. We have a lot to figure out.

The next quarter is chock-full of challenges. I experience a new feeling of closeness and bonding with my pledge sisters. By spring we have made it — Initiation! The beautiful ritual: older sisters circle us, magical candlelight, everyone in white dresses, holding the symbolic pink roses. When I repeat my vows, I feel them in my heart. I am surrounded by the love and support of a sisterhood with high ideals and values, as well as some guidelines to keep me from getting lost. Whenever I dress up, I proudly wear the beautiful gold quill pin with tiny seed pearls over my heart. I feel truly happy. My parents aren't thrilled with my decision to join a sorority. Where will I get the money, they ask, for dues and clothes? I start a part-time job at the alumni office, doing keypunch entry. My Regent's Scholarship pays the tuition, and Dad cosigns a student loan for the rest: room, board, and books. He sends small checks whenever he can. At least there's no car payment or parking expense. I walk or take buses everywhere.

Biology and chemistry labs take place several blocks away, off campus. Following the afternoon labs of three hours plus cleanup, the streets are dark. Sidewalks shimmer with frozen slush, making it treacherous to walk in my knee-high Frye leather boots. Some days I try to pick my way through it, often give up and catch the bus at the corner. When I get off near the dorm, I pass a small Catholic church. It seems so inviting: faint organ music plays, and its simple arched windows are aglow. Kids too young to be out at night play chase. I walk quickly past a chain-link fence on the corner where an old building was demolished last year. Only piles of rubble remain. This area of the city is "mixed"; houses overflow with large black families sharing space for low rents. Right next door, students occupy a once lavish home. With these charming turn-of-the-century buildings in bad repair, the entire neighborhood teeters on the verge of being torn down, disappearing, forever lost to its residents. Luckily, it's still considered safe; I don't feel threatened here. Secure at last.

Meet the Guys

In the wild flurry of pledging and initiation, we party with our brother fraternity, Theta Pi. Those guys are so lucky to have a frat house, and we meet there for keg parties in their basement. It's hard to know what they expect of us; pressure and guidance comes from the sisters to act ladylike under all circumstances. This means not getting drunk (or hiding it well) and not being "loose." Our brothers, however, have different ideas. At parties, some guy always hovers at my shoulder with another drink, pulls me close to his hard body, tries to make out on the dance floor or in a dark corner. Attendance at these events is required, but I dread them. The nicest guys, the ones who are respectful, smart, funny, and cute, like Eddie, are quickly spoken for.

One Friday night I meet Frank, who pursues me with his friendly manners and sassy mouth. He makes me laugh, we have fun together, yet I sense I'll never fall for him. I see him moving in the direction of "serious," and I feel squeamish, can't lie to him. He looks sad when I tell him it's not happening. His chubby dimpled face shifts from open and smiling to distant and guarded. He is hurt, and I feel bad. I'd welcome his friendship, but I know how rejection feels.

I need something more real. We made it through pledging and now enjoy our new status: sisters. As for relationships, most guys seem so immature it's hard to be interested. I simply don't fit into this dating scene. I meet a couple of nice guys, but nothing clicks. Roger claims to be in love with me; his tall, blonde good looks and sweet manners make him seem perfect, but I just feel numb. No juice. And I still can't forget what happened with David. What's wrong with me? I try to kiss back, be clever and interesting, even affectionate, but Roger feels my distance. I'm not in love and can't make it so.

At a Theta Pi party, I meet Johnny, adorably cute, slightly shorter than I am, shock of blonde hair, and sparkly blue eyes. We hit it off. I learn that he's an "art photography" student. In his room, he shows me a portfolio of his current work, and I'm impressed and fascinated. Black-and-white and sepia images, slices of life: shoppers caught on street corners with bags of groceries, kids on playgrounds, icicles frozen in motion as they slide off roofs. He wants to show me his darkroom, which he shares with two other guys. The very next day I walk over there, down a dirt driveway, to the small converted garage they use as a studio. It's like entering a chapel, or secret cave with ancient pictographs emerging from the dark. Johnny flips on a single light. All the windows are sealed with black cloth stapled tightly to the frames. Flat vinyl trays line up, filled with clear fluids an inch or two deep.

The whole place is surprisingly neat. Amber glass one-gallon jugs sit on shelves, mysterious developing chemicals in them. Overhead, strung across the room, are two clotheslines from which photographs hang, once dripping, by clips; ghostly faces peer out, give me chills. Dreamlike, incredible. I can easily pick out distinct artistic styles. One shows undulating landscapes, like naked women covered in soft new grass, shrubs tucked into low crevices, like lively thatches of hair. Another features haunting faces, portraits of known and unknown people, some black, some old and wrinkled, kids with runny noses and coal-black eyes. I feel overcome with desire to know more, to enter this world in some way.

Johnny likes that I'm intrigued, and casually invites me back in a few days to meet the guys. During the week, I usually study. As I wade through my formulas, the species and genus, from algae to trilobites, all I see in my mind are those photographs: faces, crisp edges, shades of gray, glossy skin, another world already imprinting. I can hardly wait.

On Wednesday when I arrive, the door sits ajar, and even outside I can smell the sharp, pungent chemicals. They tickle my nose. Johnny drains out old developing fluid and carefully refills the first tray. He wears rolled-up jeans and a light blue chambray work shirt. "Come on in. I want to show you what goes on here — if you're still interested, that is. Bob and Blake will be over after a while. Once a week we all meet here. Mostly, each of us works here alone, between classes, on projects."

"Yes, show me everything."

When we close the door, the room goes completely black for a minute, until Johnny turns on a soft light. He shows me where a roll of film has been stretched out in a coiled canister, sloshed in developer. Then the strips are hung up to dry in a special dryer, weighted with "negative clips." He takes down a dry one, and we look together at the tiny images over a light box. The desired negatives are selected, and film is put into an enlarger, photo paper below, with a strong light timed to expose the print. Next, the paper enters each of several baths in succession — developer, fixative, and two rinses — gently sloshed through each one. As we peer into the bath, a woman's face slowly emerges looking up at us. After a thorough rinse, Johnny hangs the photograph by its clips, to drip dry to its permanent glossy state. Haunting. Complex. Pure magic.

When Johnny realizes my excitement, he asks me to help in the darkroom on weekends. I really like him. Maybe things could go further, but for now he feels like a friend, a brother. Safe.

"Hi, guys, this is my friend Judy. I think I've found us a convert, a fan, maybe an assistant. She fits right in and wants to help out. Cool, eh?"

Bob grins wide and his warmth feels genuine. He's the serious type, and when he talks about photography, his devotion to both the art and the science becomes obvious. Blake proves more of a mystery, hard to read. His sandy hair, casual loose clothes, and sloe-eyed good looks catch me a little off guard. Who is this guy? From the art crowd? He subtly flirts with me, but at the same time acts aloof. All three guys attend R.I.T.'s art photography program and are students of well-known photographer Minor White. This universe attracts me. I start to feel comfortable, "simpatico," as Blake says.

A couple of weeks, and I know I've found a niche, a place to be useful. Blake starts to show me about point of view and cameras, large ones; how to "see," frame the image in my mind, then compose it through the lens. He takes special interest in me, though not romantic, and I learn more about this special art every week.

Blake has decided I should learn to shoot a gun, though I can't imagine why. He insists we go to his apartment, pick up a couple of revolvers, and drive to a remote country location for my training, to face my fears — both scary and thrilling. When I hold the gun, it feels evil: cold, hard, heavy. I'm determined to go through with the challenge, however, and manage to get off a few shots, which hurts my arm. The vibration goes straight through my whole body, shaking me to the core. I tremble, want to run away, curl up and become invisible. No explanation. I just hate it and can't wait to get out of here. Why did I ever agree to come?

Bob and Johnny, both so easygoing, instantly become my buddies. For frat parties, Johnny is my perfect date. We dance and laugh, and I feel safe from the preying attention of lonely single guys looking to get laid. No sex, no passion, just our affectionate friendship. And we both love to dance. Elvis still remains hot this year, and a new group from London — The Beatles — gets more popular every day. We twist and jitterbug. Of course, there's the ever-popular slow dance, not really a waltz or a foxtrot, more like an excuse.

My guys are just right. And I have my sisters too. When the year ends, I score decent grades, enough to keep my scholarship and continue in the Med Tech program. I've fulfilled my basic requirements, counting the semester of credits from Keuka and now a year completed here. It feels so good to establish a place of belonging, to be settled and doing well — at last.

APARTMENT

Betty, Sally, and I find an apartment for the summer, close to downtown. We're thrilled, out on our own and off campus. Alicia, an upperclassman, helps me get a job in the urinalysis lab at St. Mary's Hospital. The position pays well enough for me to afford the shared rent, and I can stay in the groove of Med Tech. Sal and Betty both land summer retail jobs at Magnin's department store. Adults now — it's the real deal. The minute spring quarter ends, we scurry about in Betty's station wagon, looking to find items for our scantily furnished apartment. It's basically a small '30s-style house, close to the street, with three steps leading up to a porch just big enough for a single chair. Only shadows show through the frosted-glass front door. We acquire a comfortable couch and overstuffed chair, and with the coffee table, there's just room enough to squeeze through. Someone gives us an old TV, which we add to the living room. My dark green folding butterfly chair splays out in a corner of the dining room, along with the giant extendable table that nearly fills that room.

Each of us brings dishes, pots and pans, whatever we have from the dorm, and we cobble together a functional kitchen. Everything I need to furnish my upstairs bedroom, including a twin bed, dresser, and floor lamp, costs under $50 at the Salvation Army store. We haul and arrange with much exuberance: art posters on the walls, second-hand curtains, and after a long weekend's work, we begin our jobs and our summer together — two great roommates, our own place, home-cooked meals, and freedom. No curfews! Who could ask for more? Home sweet home.

VI

Seven Weeks

1965

KNIFE DREAM

Fragments of a story replay in my head, like strips of film edited from a movie, discarded, but not destroyed. I can't be sure it actually happened. Part of me says no, it must have been a dream. Then again, the "dream" seems insignificant in light of what happens the following week.

The story consists of specific images that my mind attempts to string together to make sense of it all. I'm alone in the apartment that I share with Betty and Sal. A man stands in the living room. He waits as I go to the kitchen to get him a drink of water. He is a black man, and a stranger. How did he get in here? Why would I let him in?

The kitchen has no windows. Dark. I feel trapped. He's coming after me now — intense, threatening. We circle round and round the kitchen table, the only obstacle that prevents him from grabbing me. One of us snatches a long knife from the drawer — I think it's me. We struggle. I scream, but there is no sound.

Then nothing. He's gone. The memory/dream ends there. Only frozen fear remains — my heart pounds in my ears, heaves in my chest.

How could I be so stupid?

THE CHOICE

Sitting on the couch in Blake's apartment one Friday night, I feel comfortable, easy. We've become friends via his studio, and hang out sometimes. Thelonius Monk plays on the stereo. Hot night, tall windows, sashes thrown open. Blake emerges from the bedroom. His eyes catch mine. He's harboring a little surprise nested in his hands like a fragile butterfly.

"See here, I have some really good grass. I thought we could get high."

Warm memories of another time with someone else, let me quickly answer, "Oh sure, but just a little; I haven't done this much before, just a couple of times."

A knowing smile, almost protective, spreads across his gaunt cheekbones. Sitting down beside me, he lights the joint, inhales deeply, and hands it to me. I take a toke, not too much, promptly exhale, coughing, and hand it back.

"No, you have to hold it in, like this," Blake demonstrates.

"Okay, I'll try again." This time I'm careful, take it in slowly. As the fragrant smoke meanders down my throat and into my chest, I begin to feel lightheaded. It must be the heat, I think, so muggy.

I watch smoke curl from his mouth in columns, disappearing up into his flared nostrils. "A French inhale," he tells me. Next thing I know, a smoke-like mist swirls into the large landscape over the mantle and I begin to drift, leaning backwards into the recesses of the deep sofa. Then I'm melting into the painting: I travel down a road toward the hills, clouds race overhead, water churns in a ditch beside the path. Then… slow motion. Dreamtime takes over as I slip into another reality.

A voice startles me. "Here, eat some of this orange — and you'll need water, too. Drink this."

Vodka. Yuck! The taste rocks me back into my body like an ice-cold shower.

"Hey, what's happening? I don't feel so good…."

"Here, come lie down — you're just having a little reaction. Don't worry, it's really good smoke."

Blake takes my hand. Trusting, I follow him to the bedroom where I sit down on the bed, exhausted.

Sipping the water, I feel confused, fuzzy, and hot. I really wish I were back in the dorm, sitting around with some girlfriends eating popcorn, sipping Cokes, and fantasizing about exciting dates we could have with guys we haven't met yet. Too late for that.

Propped up by a pile of pillows, I feel the smoothness of his hands stroke my face, play with my long hair, his soft touch on my arms. I'm cradled in a summer night's dream. Wait…wake up! A voice goes off in my head, my eyes fly open. Blake has half rolled on top of me, gropes with my pants zipper and pulls at my tee shirt, all at once.

"No—stop!" I protest.

"Shush." He covers my mouth but doesn't let go of my zipper.

"What are you doing? Stop it!"

Then I'm sobbing and pushing against his chest. I shove with my feet and legs until he's mostly off of me; all the while, I'm pulling my shirt down and my pants up, zipping, crying, grabbing for my sandals.

"Where are you going? You can't just leave now," he argues. "It's after midnight."

I head for the door, trying to escape. Damn! I forgot my purse. I feel disoriented, unsteady, and still I have to sidle over to the end of the couch to grab it and again make for the door.

"Come on, Judy, stay." Blake tries to block me, gets in front of the door.

I punch him, hit him hard. I'm in a really bad movie, sobbing more now because I know I've been in this movie before.

As I run down the block, elm trees swaying above in the warm night breeze, I feel light, like I could run all the way to New York. My heart keeps pounding. I race over the uneven squares of cement lifted up last winter by repeated hard freezes. I've become a frightened animal dashing for cover. I duck behind the hedgerow of a once-opulent house awaiting demolition, and crouch there while my heart slows its panicked pumping. I walk, slower, headed for somewhere, and I sense it must be a couple of hours past midnight by now.

I cross the main thruway underpass in the middle of the night. Big lights expose me, though only to the occasional teenager in his convertible, or an all-night truck driver. One of them stops to offer a ride, but I just start to cry again. I've decided to head for Dan's apartment—he's my sorority sister's boyfriend—on the other side of the city. I'll just pick my way over there.

It seems to take forever. A familiar cross street comes into view, and I turn left down a less-traveled street to avoid being followed or seen at all. If I hear a car or see headlights, I slip behind a big tree or trimmed hedge and become invisible. The humidity wraps me in its embrace like a puff pastry, delicate layers about to fall apart if touched. Overnight dew has condensed from the air; the lawns are wet, sparkle bathed in streetlight. I'm so tired, want to lie down on soft green summer grass, curl up and sleep. But I must get to Dan's.

A dark van pulls up beside me; it's Blake, and he's telling me he is sorry. How did he find me? "Get in," he says. "Where are you going? You can't just walk around like this. I've been looking for you for hours. I'll take you wherever you want to go."

I try to ignore him, walk on, feeling like I'll collapse soon. Finally, I give in and climb into the high passenger seat of the van. "I'm going to Dan's. You know, Diana's friend. Two blocks, over on Center Street."

Silence. He drives the short way, and then pulls up to the curb. "You okay?"

"Sure," I say, not turning to look at him. I get out, slam the door, and start crying.

Climbing up three flights of creaky wooden stairs, I feel a bit weak and out of breath. My sandals are soaked from the wet grass. Sweat runs off my back and makes my thin cotton blouse cling to me. My hair hangs limp and sticky on my shoulders. Nothing is right.

It's the middle of the night and I feel a bit sheepish knocking on Dan's door, disheveled, crying, still slightly stoned. I do it anyway. I stand in the hallway of the house-turned-apartment building. After a long silence, Dan opens the door, sleepy, in skivvies and a thin white tee shirt. He's very surprised to see me, especially looking like I've been to hell and back. He pulls me in the door, pats me on the back, and we go in to his living room to talk.

"What happened? You look terrible. Did someone beat you up?"

More tears. Then the story of my night spills out in bits. I finally slow down like a percolator squeezing out its last muddy drops.

Exhaustion spreads over me like thick fog, penetrating all the cells down to my fingers and toes, up into my heart and belly. I want so badly to curl up on his funky old sofa and sleep awhile.

Dan has other ideas and keeps probing me with questions: "Did you take something? Was it just the joint or was there something more? Did he rape you?"

I'm confused, not sure of all the answers. I stare out the double windows into the tips of maples and elms, silhouettes of leaves just starting to fade. It's already early morning, in June. Dan hands me a cold bottle of Coke, says he'll be on the phone for a while and I should go into the other room. Now I'm crying again and beg him not to call the police. That will be bad, and I don't think I can deal with it, so he decides instead to talk it over with Diana and figure out what to do. As he picks up the phone and turns his back to me, I step into the long hallway holding my icy Coke to my chest to calm myself.

The night fades, exchanging dark for light, every second imperceptibly different from the last. It's so astonishingly beautiful that I decide to sit on the windowsill and watch the sunrise, follow every change. That's all I can do at this moment. Dan's still talking, pacing about, tethered to his phone in a heavy conversation with Diana. They obviously disagree about what to do with me, and I fear that my future is drifting out of my hands, has been ever since I showed up.

Deep lilac, edged in peachy cream, becoming the bluest blue — a backdrop to the maple leaves closest to me, like hands reaching out their delicate fingers to the sky. I feel heavy sitting here, feet dangling, mind swimming with details, like frames from that bad movie. The soft warm air and approaching dawn soothe me. They hold hope.

In the other room, the talk goes on. Dan is worried; his voice gets louder. I catch bits like "he can be arrested," and "it's not her fault," between other muffled lines. I can't imagine how this will turn out.

The sun creeps up through a high fork in the tree in front of me, and fans out its rays into the muggy morning. I am stunned that anything can be so beautiful right now. My heart breaks to feel the sun's pure light cover my bare arms and swollen face with warmth. I feel grateful, want to be part of it all.

"Can I go there, to the sun? Can I fly?"

Surprised, I hear an answer in my head. "Yes, you can fly. Go ahead, it's okay, just let go."

Already, I imagine the air rushing past me as I lean out, ever so slightly, from my cool perch. Freedom, wind, leaves caress my face, torso, and arms. When I open my eyes, I find I am actually falling! My heavy legs pull me down, down, my arms flail out reflexively, grab at ancient ivy embedded in the brick wall. And in a moment, it's over. I hear one long wailing scream penetrate the early morning silence, as all breath, all consciousness, exits my body.

Then, she lies there, crumpled on her right side, like a broken doll, arms and legs at odd angles. People crowd around, and no one dares touch her. Some are crying as the high-pitched scream of the ambulance turns into the driveway, and people move back to make a path. Several men in medic uniforms bend over the body to assess. Carefully they support and lift the body onto a board, strap and bind the lifeless form, load her through the rear double doors of the van.

* * *

A voice. "Do you want to go back?"

"I don't know. What's involved? What would that be like? And why would I want to?"

The scene below me is fading. I am being held in a soft place. Light from somewhere ahead increases, very slowly, like the sunrise. It draws me, and I feel the Light come closer and bathe me in its comfort. Time has vanished. There is only now.

"It's all the same, just a choice. If you choose to go back it will be very painful. Your body is severely broken."

"So why would I choose to go back?"

"There is something important you can do in your life, if you choose it. You've forgotten, but you will remember."

"What is it?"

"It's about showing your pain to others... about healing, and witnessing."

"Oh, a reason. Yes, I would need that. I have forgotten. When did I know? And it's true, I do know about pain." Silence. Calm. "Yes... okay. I will go back."

* * *

Voices begin to filter through the dense fog that surrounds my brain.

"Why did she do it? Will she make it?"

Pain slams into me like an armored truck. I hear screams — mine! And underneath it all, the question: What have I done?

MORPHINE DREAMS

They wheel me from the ambulance into the ER. Every little bump screams agony. I hear them tell me they can't give me anything for the pain until they know more about the concussion. Blessedly, I pass out. When I wake up, I beg: "Please, please, give me something! Help me." I can hardly take a breath without feeling like shards of glass are raking my side. I can't stand this.

"Be quiet! You're disturbing the other patients," someone hisses. Doctors and nurses come and go through my own personal hell. I scream and cry, and can't help it. Finally, a nurse gives me a shot, some morphine, and I start to slip away....

As I dream, I hear them talk in hushed voices, feel their hands working on my head, my body, cut off my clothes, probe, wrap. "Better call her parents, get them here right away. I'm not sure she'll make it." And later, "Bad concussion." And "She definitely won't walk again."

Shit! How can that be? What the hell happened? The side of my head feels huge and swollen, not mine, as if I had been slugged. And now my body's waking up from this bad dream. I'm aware of my own voice, loud, shrill, and raging in a cruel nightmare of pain. It's unclear what hurts the most, so I shift around to feel where the pain resides. White-hot swords shoot up my leg, hip, torso, neck, and head. On fire! From my mouth, more anguished screams.

"You'd better settle down, honey. Two more hours before your next shot."

"No, please," I sob, barely able to tolerate this extra movement of my chest — heaving, crying. "I can't make it." The nurse looks at me sadly, offers to sit with me and hold my hand for a few minutes. Sometimes I leave my body, look down on the jumble of ropes and pulleys that suspend my right side in a delicate balance like I'm some weird marionette tossed aside between performances. Then a tornado slams me back into my broken body, where voices come and go, play tricks with my perception.

Every movement hurts. I'm trapped in my hospital bed by a framework of pulleys and weights, attached to and pulling my right leg and hip. Traction. Whenever a visitor, doctor, or some orderly, carelessly mopping the floor, bumps into the weights, searing pain shoots up my leg through every bone in my right side. I beg each hour for morphine, grit my teeth, try desperately to be quiet, to be good. My moaning disturbs me as well as everyone else. Soon... it must be time! The four long hours between the shots drag on, especially that last hour, like a gruesome punishment. Then it comes, relief, and I can slip into heavenly sleep, float dreamily away from my tortured body.

DAYS AND WEEKS

One day runs into the next; all the same, like the slimy custard they try to feed me between shots. The next injection is all I care about. After two hours of numb relief, I can't wait for my nurse to say, "Okay, honey, it's time," as she pokes around my good left hip and leg to look for a new spot to stick me. Too bad that won't happen for another two hours. After a couple of weeks, they let me see myself in a hand mirror. Shocking! I've never even had a "shiner" before. The whole right side of my face has turned mottled shades of purple, swollen, hard, and puffy around my eyes and nose. I guess I'm lucky that my foot, and then hip, hit first, jamming the right femur two inches up into my pelvis.

Thirteen fractures, I heard them say, plus a few broken ribs and concussions. But no surgery. I'm not in good enough shape for that. Thus the traction. Dr. Winslow hopes to pull my leg down to its normal length over a couple of months' time. This is quite an experimental approach, but hey, what's the alternative? And my face — they say someday it will look normal.

Mom and Dad visit. The first time, I'm hardly aware of their presence, yet I can see the worry and disappointment on Mom's face. Dad is so sweet and caring, tries to hide the concern he carries for both of them. They hope to move me home, to Cobleskill Hospital, so I'm not 200 miles away. I feel bad when I see how hard this is on them. Obviously, I screwed up. Again.

One morning, after a couple of weeks, Mom presses her hand to my forehead, says I'm really hot, and goes off to find a nurse. I guess they missed something at morning vitals, or the fever came up really fast. I can't tell what I'm feeling any more; storm clouds of pain mask everything in my world. Then, the nurse summons the doctor on call, and he checks my catheter bag. Bloody, not good. Next, they drag me off to X-ray, wheel me, all propped up, on a heavy steel gurney after unhooking all the weights. The X-ray room must be several blocks away. Halls, elevators, thick double doors with warning signs pass by in a blur. I have spiked a high fever and they're trying to determine what's wrong.

It turns out that a bone splinter from my pelvis punctured my bladder. I have peritonitis. Suddenly life becomes a fevered nightmare as they pump my body full of antibiotics for several days. It's all the same to me. Weeks go by, dreams start to return, and I rarely scream any more. The big surprise, I made it. One day my doctor says, "It looks like you may walk again after all. Your bones are beginning to knit nicely. But don't expect too much. Most likely, you'll always limp, and having children will be out of the question."

You're wrong! Dead wrong. I didn't go through all this for nothing. You'll see. Now that the worst has passed, they allow the police to interview me. Two plainclothes officers show up one afternoon. They want to know what I remember, and obviously they've gotten some of the story from Dan.

"This Blake guy gave you dope — marijuana, right? A joint."

"Yes," I mumble. I am careful and a little confused.

"It couldn't have been just pot. Must have been laced with some other drug, DMT or DET, probably. So you were hallucinating. And Blake gave it to you, right?"

What's that — DMT, DET? I just remember being so stoned I couldn't think. "I don't know. Just had a couple of drags, I think. That's all I remember." Tears. Silence. Please go away.

"Giving you drugs is a crime. All we need from you is to confirm his name. And sign a statement that he gave you the illegal drugs. We'll take care of the rest."

I shake my head, can't meet their eyes. The floor nurse, the young one who's so nice to me, has been observing the whole thing. She sees me crying. They press again: "Here, sign this now, get it over with."

No. I can't do it. The nurse tells them they have to leave now; she'll call them if I change my mind. Just go now. The psychiatrist comes in the next day with his questions; wants the whole story, but mainly, why did I do it — jump out the window... or fall. And what about sex — was I raped?

An accident, I tell him. Sure, I was upset, but I wasn't trying to kill myself. I feel sure of that, even though I can't quite put it all together. I remember sitting on the windowsill; hot night, dangling my feet, watching the world quietly light up. So beautiful. Wondered if I could fly. Then I was falling. What happened? It must have been the drugs. So stoned. Thought I could fly into the sun. And that voice, the one that said it was okay to go out the window. That must have been it then... the drugs. The doctor says there's a psychedelic substance called DMT (dimethyltryptamine), or DET (diethyltryptamine) that can cause hallucinations for hours, with delusions. "That could have been in the joint you smoked," he says.

Maybe that's what happened. We both accept this version of the story, and move on. After five weeks, I begin to work with a physical therapist. He comes to fetch me, wheels me to a room with lots of exercise and rehab equipment. My work is mostly with the parallel bars. I'm so weak at first I can barely hold myself upright, much less imagine walking. Soon, though, even with my heavy leg cast, I start to feel my strength and stand upright. No weight bearing. Lots of pain. They've switched me to Demerol this week, and I sure miss the morphine.

The following week, my cast comes off, and I'm horrified by what I see. My thigh has shrunk to almost half its normal size, every bit of muscle tone gone. The skin appears puckered, hairless, and so ugly. But since they promise me crutches by Friday, I hardly care about this development. Most of the swelling in my face is gone, along with shades of purple and yellow.

Miraculously, after seven long weeks, my doctors decide that I'm ready to be discharged. Mom and Dad arrive to pick me up, sign all the papers, and take the thick chart and large envelope of X-rays for my new doctor. When they wheel me down to the exit doors, I make them stop.

"I can walk by myself," I insist. "Give me the crutches." With everyone watching, I push myself up, awkwardly tuck the crutches into my armpits. The door opens and I hobble out to the car, triumphant. My favorite nurse is clapping, her face wet with tears.

I briefly glimpse the journey ahead, and thank my Guardian Angels. Now I know they are with me.

VII

Second Chance

1965–1967

RETURN

Shielded by a vague sense of purpose, I return to my parents' home with determination. Seven days a week I will go to the town swimming pool, behind the bowling alley, and rigorously do my exercises. It's already mid-August, and I hope, somehow, to return to college in late September. There's a lot to accomplish and not much time. The great part about my parents' refusal to talk about what happened, they leave me alone.

I get Mom to drop me off early at the pool, right when they open, so I can avoid encountering old friends or acquaintances, but of course this is folly; I live in a small town. Mostly I see parents of young children, five to ten, there for summer swim lessons. I arrive already dressed in my bathing suit with a light sundress over it. At the edge of the concrete I set up my spot, awkwardly pull the sundress over my head, and wrap the turquoise fish towel around my waist to cover up. Before I slip into the chilly water, I slather on some Coppertone to cover up the strange whiteness of my leg. I hobble to the edge of the pool. As quickly as possible, I grab the ladder, abandon the towel and crutches, and lower myself into the cool water. I stay near the deeper end, cling to the side, work my skinny right leg in circles, the "bicycle," then the dog paddle, easy movements to rebuild muscle and strengthen the knitting bones.

A few people already notice me when I limp through the gate on crutches, beach bag on my back. I feel sure they wonder what happened, why one leg is shrunken, looks like a pale sapling stripped of its bark. When the doctors took off the cast, after nearly seven weeks, my thigh didn't look like it belonged to me. It's such a relief to be here. I'll have an hour and a half before Mom picks me up.

Each week I progress, and when I measure my leg, it's getting bigger. In a month, after my checkup with the orthopedist, I'm allowed partial weight-bearing. Using crutches, I gingerly walk on two legs.

All month, letters fly back and forth from my parents to R.I.T.'s president. When I left in June, my grades and status were fine. Of course, he and everyone at school know about the accident. They mainly want assurance that I am physically and mentally fit to return for my second year. Several doctors send reports that describe my remarkable recovery, given the severity of the injuries, with glowing recommendations for my return. Finally, word arrives: they're letting me go back!

The drive to Rochester is somber. We load up in the morning, and stop near Cooperstown for lunch. Even on the thruway, the trip takes almost four hours. In the balmy Indian summer, with colder nights, the nip of fall teases the pointy tips of leaves to lose their summer green. Windows are partway down, catching the aromatic breeze, relieving the tension as we play one of our traditional car games: Apples (at the fruit stand); Barn (so easy!); Cow; Dairy, East Springfield. So much is left unspoken, falls between the simple words of the alphabet game.

Upon arrival, we check in with the dorm mother, Miss Molinari. She seems happy to see me, gives me a warm hug. I know she was supportive of my return, and I sense openness with her; she's someone I can confide in. We unload boxes and move them all one more time. Then the moment comes, out by the car, to say goodbye. Mom is tearful, not saying much.

Dad gives me a quick hug, gently holds my shoulders, very direct, and says, "You'll be fine, Judy. Don't worry."

He sounds like he knows this. Even I feel confident.

"Call us when you're all settled."

Volumes hover beneath this simple exchange. And even though I don't know what comes next, I sense a new feeling of being alive, committed, and moving forward. I am back.

COOKING FOR LIFE

"Notice: Withdrawal of Regents' Scholarship Funds. Reason: Fall Quarter Average (GPA) fails to meet required minimum." Shit! I am so screwed. When I got my grades last week, I was shocked to see it on paper. I knew I had failed "New Physics," some bastard child of the basic physics I barely understood in high school. The teacher's a dreamboat: Gorgeous and nice, happy to tutor me on the side, a recent Cambridge Scholar with a fellowship — too smart to be teaching a novice class. I faked my way through fall quarter with his help.

The final exam, one-third of our grade, consisted of three questions. We had three hours to complete it. I sat and contemplated, even attempted one answer, but the truth is I couldn't begin to understand how to answer any of it. I didn't even comprehend the questions. After an hour, I turned in my papers, blank. Speechless, I exited in tears. That did it. With other grades floating around B– and C, the F puts me on "academic probation." It's over.

When I returned in September, after the accident, I wasn't all that keen on Med Tech. In my heart of hearts I still long to be an artist. Now, with no scholarship and very little money, staying in school looks hopeless. This feels like a turning point. Even if my parents had the money, they'd never support my going to art school. Screw it all. I'll apply and see what happens. I just can't go back to Med Tech. Before the long Christmas break, I throw together some pieces from high school senior art class, a portfolio of sorts, and submit my application to the Art School. My drawings and illustrations show dark, brooding shapes, scenes, landscapes of my last three years. Lots of black and grays — nothing pretty. My main interest lies in printmaking and design, and photography, especially considering the amazing program Kodak sponsors at R.I.T. Hanging out with Bob and Johnny in the photo lab has been a real turn-on. Sometimes they even pay me to help. I realize that most of my friends are arts and crafts people. I adore the weekend art openings, and find myself longing for complete immersion in the artist's life. I feel a subtle movement away from sorority and frat parties toward the attractive post-Bohemian scene I'm discovering. These are my people.

How will I get by? I think I must be totally losing it. Very little money comes in from my school job at the activities center. Three nights a week, I take a second job at a private men's club uptown as a "coat check girl." In the middle of the evening, when it's slow, I pore over my books. Besides the sometimes-generous tips, the Italian food is top-notch. If I get there by 5:00, ahead of the members, I enjoy a plateful of fancy stew or pasta, bread, and a scoop of salad. I look forward to these meals all week.

At the club, I meet a gorgeous businessman from Argentina. He develops quite a crush on me, has his own plane, and wants to fly me to the Caribbean on an extended business trip. I can't believe there isn't some catch to his offer. Like a dope, I don't go. Too suspicious, I guess. The only things I can accept from him are his warm hopeful smile and the fifty-dollar bills he presses into my hand. And how do I think I'll pay for art school if I get accepted? We'll see. By winter, I'm laid off.

Bob, my existential friend in photography, comes up with a brilliant idea to solve both our problems. He's a guy with a strange "health-food" diet, and spends so much time in the photo lab he has no time to cook. He wants to teach me macrobiotics so I can cook for him. "You're joking," I say. "You mean that vegetarian diet with seaweed and brown rice?"

"Don't worry. I'll teach you everything, all the techniques. You'll learn to like it. And besides making money, you'll get to eat healthy food, free." During my training, the first few meals Bob and I share taste both strange and savory. He directs me to chew each mouthful one hundred times, especially the rice, so I commit to doing it right and getting healthy while I'm at it. Gomasio makes everything yummy. It's the very first thing he teaches me to prepare. We slow roast the brown sesame seeds in his well-seasoned cast-iron pan, stirring carefully as if they're precious gems. When they look and smell just so, I measure them into a suribachi — a ceramic mortar and pestle. Toasted sea salt is then added, and the mixture ground into the world's most versatile and delicious condiment.

As if I don't have enough on my plate, so to speak, I meet one of the school's painting professors, Osmond Guy, at an art opening at the Janis Gallery. We immediately like each other. His story is that his wife lives in a mental hospital and he takes care of their daughter, Misha, who's five, while he teaches art and tries to keep his life in order. The wife will not come home anytime soon. We visit a few times, but not like dating, and Oz asks if I can cook. Sure, of course. It turns out he's having a few people over on Friday night and needs some help to make a special dinner. He promises to do all the shopping and pay me extremely well. If it works out, he'd love some help with dinners a couple times a week. Since I lost my job as a coat-check girl, I guess I'm destined for cooking. Who knew?

Friday afternoon I arrive early, thank God, to study the menu. A dozen people will be arriving at 4:00 p.m.! No problem. Oz will mix the drinks, which turn out to be mostly tequila in salted shot glasses. I will cook "Duck à l'orange," he tells me, with accompanying side dishes... and then, how about flan for dessert? Oh, Shit! How am I going to pull this off? I start to explain that I've never made this — or anything remotely like it — but he's already relaxed, pouring drinks and preparing to greet the guests. "Don't worry, babe, you'll be fine. Here's *Joy of Cooking* and *Julia Child* if you need to check it out."

I can't believe the mess I'm in. I must have been drunk or something to sign up for this job. Okay, I can read, right? And I'm good at following instructions, have read cookbooks before and maybe picked up a knack for cooking from Grandma (certainly not from Mom). The recipe in Julia's looks complex but straightforward. By going one step at a time and ducking out the back door for deep breaths, I manage to get the plump birds in the oven. Next, I pretend that I can produce a flan — similar to custard we made at home. I picture how it looked, in individual cups. I locate a decorative shallow baking dish; it will have to do. Grandma's trick: drizzle a tiny pool of maple syrup on top with a sprinkle of nutmeg, and bake with a pan of water in the bottom of the oven. Now, on to the orange sauce.

I can picture the duck in my mind, deep brown and crusty, my favorite dish when we went out for Sunday dinner. I remember sitting in the Parrot House dining room in Schoharie, a thick white cloth napkin on my lap. The waitress sets the plate before me: Steaming glazed duck, crispy skin, succulent tangy-sweet sauce. Dad always said to order anything I liked, and it was always the duck.

When the aroma of the hot caramelized sauce begins to ooze its way through the house, I know it's almost ready. Salad alert! And asparagus for twelve, with hollandaise. I run around, crazed, set the table, stir sauce, tear lettuce, but nobody cares. An hour late, no big deal. Everyone's into tequila. The dinner goes off well and Oz seems none the wiser, pleased, in fact.

"Thanks, babe, that was great! You're amazing. Are we on for next Wednesday? And by the way, Misha really likes you." After that, Oz always calls me "babe." I'm in. Thank you, tequila.

WEAVER

Art school turns down my late application. However, R.I.T.'s School for American Craftsmen (S.A.C.) accepts me, and I'll get to take most of the art classes I want. When they ask me to choose one of the crafts for a major, it's like rolling the dice, a random pick. "Weaving and Fabric Design," I say, choosing over pottery, silver and jewelry design, and woodworking. I've always loved the feel of silks, velvets, textured brocades, fat handspun wool yarns and linen.

In the basic two-dimensional design class, we play with illustration, color, and printmaking techniques. Art History at 8:00

a.m. proves tough, grueling, especially pairing the more obscure painters' names with their masterpieces. Memorization again. I pull through with a C–, relieved when it's over and I can move on.

The Weaving School, which occupies the entire second floor of the S.A.C. building, has nearly floor-to-ceiling double-hung windows, hardwood floors, and looms everywhere. Some have overhead jacks and multiple treadles for weaving intricate patterns such as jacquard and double-weave fabric. Colorful yarns in rows stretch tightly across the looms, awaiting the weavers' artistry.

In the dye room, large hanks of handspun yarns hang dripping, on clotheslines, over long sinks and drain boards. Deep indigo, reds, and purples stain the walls, and floor. It's as if someone took the wet colorful hanks of yarn and flung them about, whirling like a dervish, spattering color everywhere. Sometimes we see students with hands that match the bright skeins. I prefer to wear long rubber gloves, almost to the elbow, to protect my skin from the harsh Ciba dyes.

Here, setting up looms, I first meet Charlotte. We click right away, see each other often, and become fast friends. She is what I call a natural artist — color and design come so easy to her. We take breaks together, share inspiration on weaving, and bounce ideas around. The head of our department, Mr. B, is a tough cookie: Very demanding, particular, and strongly prefers his own taste. It's clear he just barely tolerates me. The friction between us becomes more obvious when I submit my proposal for the second-year journeyman's piece. I've been working on the idea for several months and feel passionate about it; I hope to pursue the concept in the future, with endless variations.

The proposal: The tapestry loom itself is a sculptural element of the finished hanging. Five pieces of curved maple, with many holes drilled in each piece, make up its structure. Linen warp threads pass through these holes, connecting all five pieces, creating a hanging loom. Each section — the weft — is woven separately, top area first. I then adjust the tension for the next part below. The yarns I've chosen are a mix of Norwegian wool and handspun, hand-dyed (by me) thick-and-thin New Zealand wool. This 3' × 7' "loom" hangs in my dorm room and I work on it all second semester. My "journeyman's piece" counts for the entire grade in my major.

Mr. B reluctantly approves the project. He doesn't like it. I think he'd prefer something more modern, similar to his own work. I don't really care what he thinks; I just work hard and continue to feel excited about my work.

One week prior to graduation, I receive my grade — D. I'm devastated, and furious. What a jerk! When I confront him, he becomes critical and defensive. We have a big argument, but he won't budge, stands his ground. He feels justified since he didn't see the piece in process. D it is. Due to my other good grades, I will still graduate, receive my A.A.S. degree, and can continue the program next year.

But I'm done. Two more years of Mr. B sounds like hell. I decide not to return. At the School for American Craftsmen's annual show of journeyman's pieces, I receive many compliments on my work. A faculty member invites me to bring my tapestry to his home on the lake.

"It's perfect for our dining room," he says. "And the wood matches the furniture. I want my wife to see it in place. If she likes it, we'll pay you whatever you want."

The week following graduation, I drive out to the lake and hang my year's work in their home. And they pay me $600. A great beginning to life after college.

CHARLOTTE AND THE COOP

After three years in Rochester, I feel ready for a change. Charlotte knows some folks out in the country, Fayetteville, near Syracuse, who have a large room to rent, cheap — free in fact. We'd become part of a communal household, share chores and cooking. The group includes a single guy, Ted, his ten-year-old son, Jeep, their friend, Conrad, and the farm's owner, Mrs. Brown, known as Brownie. Sounds fun. Charlotte and I drive over there, anxious to check it out, get out of the city. We hit it off with "the boys," and decide on the spot to move there, start our new life as artists.

When I decided to leave the School for American Craftsmen in June, I felt both elated by my freedom and disappointed for not completing my B.A. degree. Leaving now feels right, however. It's time.

Moving day: We haul our countless wine boxes filled with art supplies, beads, books and portfolios; yarns, looms, and clothes, including my rediscovered navy-surplus bellbottoms. Standing in the doorway of our new room, at the lowest level of a three-tiered refurbished chicken coop, I can see all the way up through the long house to the top bedroom. The spacious "great room" in the middle is lined on the south side by a bank of reclaimed windows and French doors. The small funky kitchen, with an apartment-sized propane stove, functions, barely. We all eat together at a long table with picnic benches. A wooden ladder leads to a sleeping loft, Jeep's room. The whole place is cobbled together with imagination, recycled parts, home carpentry, and love. Ted and his son have converted the large building out of the need for a place to call home. The Coop feels like home to me.

Our room begins to take shape. As the Beatles serenade us with *Lucy in the Sky With Diamonds,* we drag in the rest of our belongings: woven rugs, two foam mattresses, madras bedspreads, beaded window hangings, and clothes in baskets on block-and-board shelves. Soon the room feels like ours, with a table for beading and art projects. Jeep amazes us with his daily psychedelic nature poems and excellent black-ink drawings. He is the family's budding artist.

Indian summer prevails long into November. Amazed, we're creating exactly the life we dreamed of. There's little money — fortunately we don't need much. Our rent's free, we share utilities, Ted care-takes the property. Brownie provides cash for building materials, and Ted fixes up the Coop. She likes Charlotte's and my presence; thinks the boys need some feminine energy, hopes that one of us will hook up with Ted. Connie, the renegade auto mechanic/hermit, joins us sometimes for dinner; he fixes our cars, and provides us working vehicles, smiles, and his crooked humor. Within a couple of months, both Charlotte and I own Morris Minor coupes.

Meals improve with our cooking. Ted is a good dad, but has little imagination with food. We go for the basics: casseroles, rice pilaf, stir-fried veggies, fruit, and mixed salads from the garden. We like to bake cornbread and cookies, and pick juicy berries for cobblers and crisps. Our skills upgrade the Coop's cuisine.

For money and entertainment, we produce artwork for friends who put on light shows, often in combination with rock bands. The shows consist of projected images accompanied by loud music, blinking Christmas tree lights, strobe lights, black lights, and carousels of changing colored slides (made by us).

After breakfast, we share the ritual passing of the pipe; doors stand open, sun streams in, and breezes ruffle our hair. We spread out the paints, brushes, jars of water, and begin to apply droplets of color directly onto blank slide transparencies. The paint pools and partially dries; then, a tiny drop of water is added, perhaps more color or a corner of fine lace overlay. Some slides look like snowflakes, lightning, or leaves with light coming through. The miniature window paintings reveal glassy views into fantasy forests and meadows; they sparkle as if drenched in sunlight. We love our art! Charlotte and I incorporate our individual styles and color sense. We talk constantly while we work, and sing along with Country Joe, John Lennon, Joan Baez, and Mimi and Richard Fariña.

Weeks pass, and we happily linger through the warm fall into a productive harvest. First we pick the garden herbs: sage, dill, oregano, and basil, and carefully hang them in the kitchen to dry for winter soups and stews. Next, we harvest berries, apples, and other fruits, make them into jams. Finally, uprooted just before a dangerous frost would ruin their precious buds, we pull the eight-foot-tall cannabis plants and hang them upside down from the rafters of the barn's tall hayloft. Heat collects there on sunny days, and breezes dry the strong, yet delicate, plants.

In a month or so they'll be completely dry and cured. Some days if I go in the barn and get near the second story, I swear I get stoned just breathing. If Brownie needs something from the barn, we always offer to run up and fetch it, and thereby save her poor old legs, her eighty-two-year-old aching back, and her inquiring mind the trip. Does she ever suspect what Ted's been doing in the loft? I wonder. Guess we'll never know the answer.

VIII

Moving West

1969–1974

East/West, 1969

East Coast winters in Syracuse — not my favorite. Freezing, subzero temperatures, and slick, icy roads. Summer and fall at the Coop were fun and carefree, but the winter was a killer. Lots of huddling by the central wood stove, sleeping under piles of blankets. When I met Bill, his sweet demeanor and exotic good looks — long black hair, dark brooding eyes — drew me in. Then he invited me to live with him; the pieces all fell together and I moved into the city. Bill was clearly in love with me, and I cared deeply for him, hoped that in time I could fall in love too. We tried for a year, but it was not to be. The breakup was agonizing, as by this time Bill, Charlotte, and I were in business together. I rented a room nearby, and soon, too soon, I met Howie.

That winter and three solid weeks of the Asian flu nearly did me in. I've never been so sick, delirious with fever, aching deep in my bones, unable to eat. Thank God for Howie taking care of me — it certainly has brought us closer. His romantic attentions surprised me from the beginning. He would hold me in his bear hug; his broad shoulders and chest felt solid and protective, while my fingers fondled the mass of his curly chest hair. Then there was our brief engagement, the family heirloom ring, Howie taking control. That's where it came apart — something about how he was in charge of our lives. The control reminded me of Mom, and that ended it. I broke off the engagement.

Now, a place I can call my own, once again shared with my best friend Charlotte. My failed attempts at relationship over the past years have left me wondering if I'm meant to be alone: a year with my now ex-boyfriend, Bill, and just a few intense weeks with Howie. In March, Charlotte rents our darling little apartment, the upstairs of Mrs. Mahan's house on Bristol Place. Like Brownie, Mrs. Mahan is quite old, maybe seventy-five, and thinks we're adorable. The feeling is mutual; she reminds me of Grandma. Luckily she doesn't know everything that goes on upstairs, and prefers it that way. So do we.

I love our two-bedroom flat; especially enjoy long baths in the claw-foot tub, opening the sash window where the old-fashioned roses below toss up their fragrance. We set up an arts-and-crafts studio in the front living room alongside our stereo and record collections. Before long, a little group, about six of us, start to hang out together several evenings a week. Our love for music plays a big part. John, Charlotte's boyfriend, shows up with his guitar, and I sing and play along on my Autoharp. I'm learning the chords and words to our favorite tunes: Bob Dylan's *Lay Lady, Lay, Buckets of Rain,* and *Jack of Hearts.* And of course we adore every one of the Beatles' songs. Life feels very full; it spills over like warm bread dough rising, almost too much for its container.

Both Charlotte and I have our Morris Minors: Hers, a coupe, and I've now acquired a cobalt-blue "woody wagon" — my dream car. For music festivals and camping, I can flip down the back seat and sleep diagonally, and when I attend the Newport Folk Festival, I do just that.

My roommate spends a lot of time with John. I'm sure she'll move in with him soon. When we hang out at the apartment, we smoke a little "homegrown," cook dinners on our blue-and-white Wedgwood gas stove, and make jewelry and clothing for our co-op crafts business. Three of us have rented a cool old corner store for our shop, The Dragon's Emporium, where we each have set up workstations for our craft, like a large shared studio. The shop showcases Bill's leather sandals and handbags, Charlotte's textiles and clothing, and my beaded jewelry.

Beading proves so perfect for me. I learned the craft last year when a friend decided to give up beadwork, along with all his worldly possessions, teach me his craft, and travel to India. I inherited three suitcases full of antique Czechoslovakian glass beads, brass and silver wire, intricate filigree, even his finest pair of needle-nose pliers. As I sit at my beading table in our groovy store, I assemble necklaces, earrings, and small window hangings, and I feel almost happy. Some days are a bit tense since Bill and I split up. I know he'd like me to move back in with him, but it's just not happening. I begin to realize that once I leave a relationship, it's over. There's no going back.

Three part-time gigs seem to fit my lifestyle. Jewelry sales and cleaning one large house a week provide just enough to cover rent, food, and gas. A small stipend from the alternative newspaper I help lay out is more for fun than money. I write a popular column for the *Nickel Review,* become "Madame Judith," choose one card from the Rider-Waite tarot deck for discussion, plus the I Ching. Our newspaper leans mostly left: Post-civil rights issues, Eldridge Cleaver, the Vietnam War. Sometimes the paper publishes my artwork — visual comments on the evils of war, racism, and hard drugs.

One particular warm night in April, our group gathers at John's — another music and potluck sort of evening. John's friend, Terry, a dealer in art posters, visits from California, travels back and forth between Syracuse and Berkeley. We are instantly attracted to each other. After only a couple of weeks, we decide to be together and begin to plan a cross-country drive in June. Our blooming relationship thrills me, and I welcome the opportunity to move to California, to leave the East Coast and put some distance between my parents and me. I'm sad to leave Charlotte and John, the store, my sweet apartment. Nonetheless, we box up all our belongings and store them in Terry's folks' garage for later retrieval. The most difficult part is selling my woody wagon. Terry's fancy and comfortable Citroën sedan will take us on the trip, and I must leave my beloved car behind.

June 1969

In the intense heat of North Dakota, we stop at a motel to cool off, shower, and rest. So far we've found nice campgrounds, but we need a break. On TV, we see what's happening in Berkeley: People's Park, men and women corralled, tear-gassed, and arrested. It's unbelievable! Is this where we're going? Terry answers that his apartment should be safe; a few blocks away from all the action, we won't have to deal with any of that mess.

After many days of driving the Northern Route, stopping to camp in Glacier National Park, we wind down Highway One through Mendocino, Point Arena, Stinson Beach. Late evening of the summer solstice, we arrive in Berkeley. The intoxicating scent of night-blooming jasmine surrounds and soothes me, along with the gorgeous rambling passion vine, lush ferns, and cobbled walkways of Fox Court. The small courtyard and about twelve apartments are crafted of brick, tile, and timbers, built in the late twenties, Maybeck style, by Carl Fox. I've walked into a fairy tale and am enchanted at every turn.

Terry's small studio apartment is sparsely furnished; obviously he doesn't spend much time here. The main room features a vaulted beamed ceiling, brick-red tile floor, Hobbit-like fireplace, and a flip-down Murphy bed. In one month, my things will be trucked out here: Grandma's rocking chair, my beads, special dishes, and the deep-blue antique velvet couch. Meanwhile, we go backpacking — my first time. When I load up my new Sierra Designs backpack and hoist it onto my shoulders, I can't imagine carrying its near-forty pounds up mountain trails to Royal Arch Lake — our remote destination in the Yosemite high country. In Berkeley, we meet up with Terry's friends, hang out in their apartments, stay up late listening to Cat Stevens, the Beatles, and the Dead; sip lattés at Café Med on Telegraph Avenue.

In the tiniest closet-alcove, I create beaded jewelry to sell at a hip store on University Avenue. I love the lack of pressure to come up with rent money, and I especially love not being alone. I have an "old man."

I feel little reason to dig around in my past. With the move, 3,000 miles away from my parents and the East, I have left my traumas behind. California and the "love generation" speak to my spirit. The open-minded attitudes, feelings of freedom, and the "summer of love" are so seductive, an antidote to my old, stuck feelings. Berkeley becomes a balm for my soul.

Now I understand how the pioneers felt discovering the treasures of the West: The magical Sierras, golden hills, majestic redwoods, and dramatic Pacific Coast. I'm on the greatest adventure of my life. Everything is changing and growing, each day more beautiful than the last. And inside I feel different. Even my name, Judy, no longer fits or suits me. I am becoming the person I was meant to be, the woman I've been waiting for, and I've grown up. I am Judith.

ADVENTURES

Life with Terry means moving; we never stay in the same place for more than six months. This seems like my pattern already, with four moves since college. I love Berkeley, and frankly, I could stay here in our cozy apartment forever, but stability doesn't seem to be. At twenty-four, we're full of ideals, projects, and unbounded energy. We fantasize about buying land, growing gardens, travel, and refining our vision of the dream life. I'm game for adventure.

October 1969, we return to the East Coast — Syracuse, New York — to visit friends. We have a brilliant idea, and open a health food store. We name it the Good Food Store. The one-room operation, maybe 200 square feet, is chock-full of the basics: short-grain brown rice, wheat berries, sesame and sunflower seeds, all sitting in fifty-pound brown burlap bags. In large tins and five-gallon jars we store Tamari, safflower and sesame oils, and local honey, ready to dispense into quart glass containers. An upright commercial refrigerator with double glass doors displays shelves of perishables: local eggs, butter, yogurt and raw milk from a nearby dairy. Fresh produce, some of which we pick up at farms, spreads out on the bottom shelves of the cooler. Special orders support about half of our business. As the first store of its kind in the city, we are an instant success, through word of mouth and small ads. Quart and gallon jars of dried herbs, from a supplier in San Francisco, fill a short wall of shelves. Customers weigh out precise amounts into glassine bags. All the essential paraphernalia is available too: Corona flour grinders, juicers, baby-food grinders, suribachi bowls for crushing sesame seeds, even small scales.

Late fall, the maple sap flows freely following the hard freezes, and the hills are covered in patches of brilliant gold, burnt orange, true red, and deep burgundy. We rent a house on Otisco Lake, fifteen miles outside of Syracuse, with a college friend of Terry's. It's sweetly romantic to sit at our picture window, watch flocks of geese fly in V-formation as they leave for winter; sun sinking into the lake and darkening hills. The lake freezes solid in a couple weeks' time, while swirling patterns form in its glassy surface. A few brave fishermen drill holes in the ice, then sit for hours by tiny heaters. We spend much of our time keeping warm, hunkered near the crackling fire in the brick fireplace of our poorly insulated summer cottage.

I feel happy with Terry and our nearly one-year-old relationship. We are good together; still feel some of that original attraction, settled into a comfortable rhythm of domestic harmony.

In April, a late-season blizzard threatens to extend our already-too-long winter into May. We say, "to hell with this" and quickly sell our store to some friends; the sale provides the money and freedom for a trip. On a lark, we head to the Caribbean. The trip is cobbled together with three friends — Frank, Ben, and Sara — and no exact plans save flying to Florida, then on to St. Thomas. I contact my old pal, Laura, who's lived on St. Thomas for a couple of years. She plans to meet us and show us the island. As it turns out, Laura is injecting heroin, dealing drugs on the street, completely adrift. She sees us as her saviors, and we accept the role. With her vow to quit "cold turkey" and our resolve to take her off the island and care for her, we decide, on our second day there, to leave the fast-paced scene of St. Thomas with its tourist crowds and duty-free stores. Not our style anyway. A travel agent suggests we visit the more remote island of St. Catherine's, about 200 miles away in the British West Indies. We're off to "St. Kitts."

Stuffed into a six-seat private plane with our suitcases and a twenty-five-pound bag of brown rice (must have our basics), we cross the magical Caribbean. Volcanic islands stretch out like strings of beads, edged by silken ribbons of white sand, trimmed in layer upon layer of pale aquamarine and cobalt-blue surf. We fly over the fairy-tale Dutch island of Saba. Alabaster white houses with neat red tile roofs crown its crazy rocks, which plunge into the rough surf on all sides. Curvy narrow streets spiral up steep inclines. The scene below resembles one out of Tolkien.

When we spot St. Kitts, Mt. Misery's profile against the sky and sea looks like a goddess: large breasts and belly undulating, she floats in her turquoise bed of ocean, last rays of wavy light making her come alive. We put down at the short, dusty landing strip they call the airport, collect and carry our baggage to the only building in sight. There we meet Mr. Hillary Joseph, who readily rents us a perfect house in a small village not ten miles from Basseterre, the largest town on the island, and the capital. We arrange for a Land Rover, and decide we'll rent the house, sight unseen. By now, Laura is nauseated and sweating profusely; we wonder what we've taken on. And Frank — he can't wait to drop off his luggage and take off on his own for some adventure. He's unpredictable. As for the rest of us, simple comforts will do. Dinner and bed sound so inviting.

The house comes with a maid-housekeeper who cooks, cleans, and washes our clothes in the backyard; she scrubs any stains on rough brain coral, and spreads the garments out on lava rocks in the hot sun to dry. The humble stucco building, our vacation home, is the largest, most elaborate house in the village, complete with one bathroom and shower, three bedrooms (Terry and I get the only double bed), kitchen, large dining table with six mismatched chairs; very firm beds, and a couch, coffee table, and two chairs in the living room. The doors are solid, but no actual windows — just gaping holes with shutters against strong winds and hurricanes. Our maid brings bananas, coconuts, and fresh fish from the locals, which she insists on frying up for our dinners. Eggs every day. While she boils our day's drinking water, she mops the floors, makes our beds, and snatches our barely dirty clothes to launder before we miss them. We have trouble understanding her "Biwi" (British West Indies) accent, and try to say everything politely so as not to hurt her feelings.

Just next door, to the north, lives an old man in his one-room shack with its rickety porch. At the porch rail, he brushes his teeth at dusk each day, spitting into tufts of grass that thrive off his watering. He waves and smiles at us, his missing-tooth grin sly and mischievous. I know he's keeping an eye on us and I wonder why.

Easter week. The church resembles a miniature beehive, abuzz with preparations. Palm fronds spread out on the front steps, and bunches of flowers explode from Mason jars. Women and kids come in and out all week. Saturday afternoon before Easter, we pack up blankets and a picnic and head for the town's favorite beach, a ten-minute walk through high grass. Troupes of village children, who always appear just as we begin, accompany us. They skip and laugh, run ahead, intent on being our companions and guides. I wonder about their parents, where they are and if they know their children follow us to the beach. The older ones look out for the youngsters. After a few hours of playing and watching us, they tire and leave in a pack. We, however, have plans to stay up all night on the beach and experience the Easter sunrise.

The slim moon hangs like a crescent ornament, and the

Southern Cross is lit up for Easter. I am stunned. Fine crystalline sand sparkles like diamond dust, illuminated, once the moon has set, only by brilliant stars. We walk back and forth the length of the beach, at the very edge where the frilly white lacey surf laps warm between our toes. We swim, dip, and bathe, held up by the buoyant waters, our spirits caressed by starlight. Magic has taken us over.

After Easter sunrise, we make our way back, single file, on the narrow path to town. A quick rinse in the cement shower cleans off the sticky salt and fine sand, and we fall dead asleep for hours. Only the singing could have awakened me. Silently I pull on my clothes and sneak out, leave the others to dream and sleep off the all-night party. A few doors down, the bleached white church shimmers in the tropical sun. Through half-open doors, voices harmonize in a swingy rhythm: "Christ the Lord is ris'n today... Hallelujah."

I feel so out of place in my white Bermudas, thin tee shirt, and leather sandals. I wish I could be inside, fit in, blend with their dark-chocolate skin and honey-smooth hymns, merge with this feeling of immense joy in my heart. Tears run down my face. An Easter I'll never forget.

Terry and I spend lazy days exploring Basseterre. The city is a jumble of historic buildings, a busy fishing port, and bustling waterfront market. Roasting fish and chicken legs, scented with peppers and lemony herbs, smoke away in clay cook pots over charcoal fires. Handmade goods spread out on tables and sidewalks: Brooms, mats, coconut and palm-frond baskets, of all sizes and shapes. Wide bowls of huge salt crystals glint like gems in the morning sun. Sounds and images collide in my mind. Heads are topped with turquoise, orange, and white cotton bandanas or woven straw hats. Pastel shirts, blousy-sleeved dresses, and pinafores serve the island women as market-day outfits. They swarm and mingle, trade, bargain, taste salt and fruit from neighboring vendors. Their musical voices, punctuated by the screams and laughter of children, are accompanied by steel drums down the beach. The unique Biwi accent charms me — a blend of Colonial English, French, and Spanish, which sounds almost Cajun.

We take our midday meal on the romantic upstairs veranda of The Palms hotel. The ambiance is pure Old World West Indies tradition: ice water poured into thick, faceted glasses; starched white cloth napkins in silver rings; heavy silverware. And the ever-present sounds of steel drums in slightly off-key harmony. Tall palm trees offer a little shade to our table, their trunks fat as elephant legs and straight as the masts of sailing ships.

It's just the two of us in town today — nice to get away from the house and Laura's recovery, like a date; quite unusual for us. Even back home, roommates or friends often linger, leave us little privacy. Alone, we hardly know what to talk about. Everyday living together works so well: cooking, housekeeping, and making plans. Terry and I rarely argue, but are a bit shaky on the communication and intimacy parts, which I think must take some time.

In the shadow of the hotel veranda lies the main dining room, both airy and mysterious, draped in deep maroon velvet and fine lace voile. It feels like *Casablanca,* as rotating fans gently move the fragrant air. Our Earl Grey tea arrives, steeped in a proper English teapot, served with porcelain cups and saucers, cream, and sugar cubes. This is the stuff of tropical vacation dreams.

On a day of island touring, we drive around St. Kitts on the left side of narrow, rutted dirt roads in an ancient Land Rover, most suited for jungle trails. Jostled and carsick, I still manage to appreciate the spirit of the day. A heavy mist shrouds Mt. Misery, and the typical afternoon rainstorm approaches, brings with it a most welcome cool-down and opportunity for siesta. By four o'clock, after tea and snack, we trudge off to the beach for a swim.

After two weeks, Laura has completely detoxed and become more like her old self. Quite cheery, in fact — relaxed and clear, comfortable, as opposed to miserable, shaking, and throwing up. Even her skin, a pallid gray when we picked her up, is a lively pink. This other side of heroin addiction looks good. Frank, our Mr. Adventure, comes in and out; he leaves at dawn, hitches a ride presumably into Basseterre, or thrashes through the rain forest to conquer Mt. Misery. Forget about what he's really up to. At the end of the day, we hear fantastic stories and see a smirk that says parts of the story were left out.

"You don't want to know," he laughs, eyes twinkling like St. Nicholas himself.

The next week shifts from tropical heaven to foreboding nightmare. I lie doubled over with some jungle fever that forces me to visit Basseterre's hospital emergency room. I'm diagnosed with dysentery, so we stop by the island pharmacy for medicine: a bitter black tincture of opium. Several drops each day from the eight-sided blue bottle keep me in a sick but dreamy haze for at least a week. Finally, I'm cured, and a bit thinner. Brown rice with roasted sesame tastes like a gourmet treat. I'm so glad we hauled it with us.

I feel good, just in time for a visit from the police. We — all six of us — are given notice to leave the island within twenty-four hours. What's going on? Frank's not here — he's out on a rampage, but I keenly suspect that this is his doing. He storms in at sundown. "Those bastards went through my suitcase, stole my acid. Probably those damn kids set me up."

I am livid. "LSD? Are you crazy? How could you bring drugs down here? Plus, you promised to be clean if we let you come with us."

"The acid was only drops on paper — you know, the little stamped "frogs." How would they know anyway? Just a couple hundred hits, two sheets, with a few torn off. Always a good trade commodity. How do you think I got that good weed we've been smoking? Traded it for my good looks?"

Oh, my God! We are truly in deep shit now. And Laura. It turns out she feels so good due to a stash of heroin and paraphernalia. I don't get it. Why bother with all the trouble and mess of detox just to screw it up? And why, really, are Terry and I being expelled?

Frank and Laura — they have to go! Out of here. Back to where they came from. Ben and Sara, our sweet friends, have run low on cash and are headed home anyway. Terry and I want to stay, and we decide to fight the eviction. After everyone leaves on the morning plane back to St. Thomas, we go on a fool's errand: to visit the Government House and demand to know why we've been evicted. We hope to reverse their decision. Amazingly, the chief minister agrees to see us, and we're escorted through the halls of the Victorian mansion to a private office.

The Minister is handsome, with smooth dark-roast coffee skin. His intelligent poise hints at royal blood. His black eyes greet us, revealing a keen interest. After a few rounds of polite conversation, he becomes serious. "You know that your friend was selling illegal drugs on the island, right?"

I suck in my breath, angry, trying to be cool. "Yes, we know that now, but of course had no idea when we came here. We found out last night. He's just a casual friend, tagged along at the last minute. We should have realized he'd be trouble."

"There's more to it. Your government watches him, and we received a phone call to keep an eye on him. He's your problem — that's all I can tell you. And since you all came here together, you all have to leave."

Frank the troublemaker. Should have listened to that little voice inside — Warning: Don't bring Frank. All his wild stories. Claims his father's CIA, and after all, somebody has to play the intractable rebel. How much is true? We should have been paying attention.

This is dream-like, to be here talking to "the man" — like a great movie with expensive sets, a famous actor whose name I forget. Still, we must go by tomorrow, he says. Guilty by association, but we have a twenty-four-hour reprieve.

The Dutch island St. Eustatius, across the channel, calls to us — deserted beaches, few tourists, and no nightlife, an island to ourselves. We stay for two weeks before we must go home; pack up our things and move out of our little cottage at Otisco Lake.

Our next destination is a 500-acre pastoral farm in South Londonderry, Vermont. A group of friends, seven of us, will live there communally, grow organic vegetables to sell, harvest hay, care-take the resident chickens and horses, make and sell ceramics and tie-dyed hangings at craft fairs. May, and it's still so cold back there, the ice on the lake barely turned to slush; dirty snowdrifts still line the driveways of our summer-camp neighborhood. Just a few more days of tropical bliss. Then we'll move again, ready for our next adventure, the real country life.

RAY OF HOPE, 1971

The beginning: Love's early bloom, holding the promise, the seed of new life destined to come through us. We want to fulfill that dream, and at some point we talk about being parents, the challenges, fears, and rewards. After two years we're still not sure, even about staying together. "The timing's not right," I say. "We're not married, no commitment. And I don't know if I'd be a good mother." With Mom's voice still echoing crazily in my head, I feel scared. I religiously use the cumbersome diaphragm and gel, though this proves annoying and sometimes painful.

And then it fails. Spermicide allows a gap, just enough for one tiny sperm to slip through and make its squiggly journey to the egg. Its longing is satisfied, despite inappropriate circumstances, aware only of the child, the child.

Another move. Since summer, we've been care-taking a ranch in the Cascade Mountains of northern Oregon. Maintaining a half-acre organic veggie garden and caring for three horses plus two dogs keeps us very busy — a practice run for homesteading. Someday, perhaps, a place of our own.

Late fall air takes my breath away, nearly freezes my fingertips as I squat alone in my herb garden and harvest the last sage, oregano, thyme, and marjoram to hang up to dry. This is the end, before the first hard frost. Once the herbs are ready, I pack them into sets of square jars for Christmas gifts. For each two-ounce jar, I make a botanical label with a tiny hand-painted watercolor sunset.

Waves of nausea and sharp belly pain nearly knock me over. As I gaze at the apple barn nearby, rows of weather-polished shakes reflecting its ageless beauty, I somehow doubt that we will ever live here. Our plans for the barn remodel are completed — drawings with double French doors, dormer bedroom, windows opening out — our dream cottage. But today I know something is coming undone. Searing pain again. I stagger back to the house where we call a doctor and head into town.

It's official: I'm pregnant and have PID, pelvic inflammatory disease. The infection is fairly severe, but a heavy dose of antibiotics takes care of it. Will this harm the baby? I can hardly wrap my mind around what's going on inside of my body. Pregnancy doesn't fit with my life right now, but I want desperately to make it work.

Toast. Dry and light brown, just right. Brewer's yeast in a smoothie with apple juice, not orange, not too sweet. And not too early! Terry brings me hot herb tea, chamomile or lemon verbena. Blueberries work for me, fat and succulent, picked in the foothills of Mt. Hood in midsummer, then stored in the freezer. For two months, nausea arises as my belly swells and my tiny breasts begin to plump up and hurt. I'm adrift — lost and seasick — unsure of my destination. I only know that I'm meant to be here and this tiny beam of light is with me.

Then Terry goes away on a ski trip. I'm alone, sick, and it's all too much. I need to leave the ranch, go back to Berkeley. But before I can go, the animals must have feed enough for a few days. I push bales of hay and shovel grain into the horse pasture. The new colt, Thunder, seems agitated, senses my departure. His wet nose and hot breath press into my face. I feel so sad to leave them, know I may never see this place again. I finish the chores by nightfall, dark by 4:30. Following a fretful night's sleep, punctuated by wild dreams, I'm ready to leave after first light and a cold breakfast.

Overnight, eight inches of snow blankets the landscape, softens the lumpy frozen ground. I try over and over to start the Jeep, but it won't catch — like me, it's low on energy. With my backpack filled, I kiss the two dogs goodbye and tearfully begin the three-mile walk out to the main road. With luck, I easily hitch a ride into Portland. I have just enough cash, $60 to buy a Greyhound ticket to San Francisco. Sometime later, I'll meet up with Terry to figure out what's next. For now, I'm alone.

An acquaintance in Berkeley lends me some money, so I stay in a motel for a few days. A cold snap hits, and temperatures hover in the teens; frozen slush on concrete freezes my feet through boots not made for winter. I feel the weight of everything in my life that has fallen apart, all the dark nights. Eclipses. I feel abandoned by the Light. Alone in my room, I'm calmed little by the drone of the electric heater, and my tears begin to flow. As I lie on the hard bed, I feel cramping, like the start of my period. I roll onto my side, pull up my knees, and clutch my belly.

"No, no, please don't leave me," I whisper to my child.

Emotions tumble out of me like thawing waterfalls, uncontained.

"I want you to stay. Please stay."

There it is. She needs to know I really want her. Unconditionally. Now I know. But how can I convince her? I begin to hum a tiny broken melody that she might hear, to carry my wanting to her. It calms me, too, just the thing — a soothing song for my wounded spirit. Maybe we can both heal, continue on together toward the Light of this world. My humming becomes smoother, the rocking more even, rhythmic. A lullaby emerges from some ancient memory.

Hush little baby, don't you cry.
Mama's gonna sing you a lullaby.

I drift off, and by morning the cramping becomes mild, infrequent. I know she has heard me and will stay. Even breakfast stays down mercifully; blueberries, bananas, and yogurt actually taste good. Now what? I'm not sure, only that I promise, with all my heart, to take good care of us.

BIRTH

In late December, Terry and I marry in a small ceremony with four witnesses. On the way to the tiny church in Oakland, we lose our bearings and arrive an hour late. Afterward, we share a celebratory dinner at Fisherman's Wharf with friends. As a wedding gift, Terry's parents give us a down payment for property; we hope to find something in Mendocino County. Perhaps things will come together after all.

In January we rent a sweet two-bedroom house in Albany, just north of Berkeley. Every day I walk a mile up Solano Avenue for a double scoop of ice cream — good calcium and protein. When my best friend, Charlotte, and her son, Zachary, move west to live with us, we need a bigger place. A generous Tudor-style house shows up for rent on Poppy Lane in North Berkeley, and we relocate. There's a tiny backyard for a garden and clothesline, and a view of the Bay with its bridges.

Pregnancy agrees with my body. I've never felt better. As a bonus, I'm warm all the time, even my toes. My walks take me through the hills near Tilden Park. We settle in, paint the dining room and its crown moldings in sunset colors of apricot and gold, as if we would stay here for years of sunsets. Terry and I attend weekly Lamaze classes, practice breathing and the drive across town to Alta Bates Hospital where we'll go for the birth.

According to a new theory on pregnancy, my obstetricians, two German doctors, twins, try to limit my weight gain to fifteen pounds. Dr. H. is very serious; the other, Dr F., talks like a stand-up comedian. They agree that I should drink one dark beer every day for the B vitamins. Honestly, I can only get down a few ounces. I'm hungry, on my own track with food: three solid meals, three large snacks, my daily ice cream on Solano Avenue, and one small glass of beer.

As for the weight restriction, my body swells and I'm popping out of my new B-cup bras. Despite their rules, I put on thirty pounds. I'm fat and happy. Baby's little elbows bump out, tiny hips tipping this way and that. I walk around with my hands on my belly so I won't miss a beat.

Mid-May, and I'm two weeks late. After a sleepless night of timed contractions, two to three minutes apart, my water breaks, and we streak across town on our well-worn route to check in at Alta Bates. After nine and a half hours of hard labor, I progress only one centimeter. The Pitocin drip speeds things up, brings on a rapid thirty-minute transition, like a freight train bearing down. Feelings come in waves, crashing, coursing through my helpless body. Terry stays the whole time to coach and support; he counts for me as I breathe, pant, and contract in and out of my altered states of being. The doctor insists on episiotomy; next minute, it's time to push — now! In the midst of the chaos, I glimpse her crowning head in a mirror, and then she's here with us. It's the most extraordinary twenty-four hours of my life. By choice, I have experienced intense pain, pleasure, joy, and release, simultaneously.

She is born at 7:37 p.m. The brightest star I ever recall, Venus, as it turns out, shines high up through a small delivery-room window. Her sweet, tiny body is laid upon my chest. She looks from me to Terry and back with glazed, intense eyes, so surprised and awed by the light after her long, dark, and difficult journey to join us in this outside world. Within a day she nurses and we are ready to take her home.

"You must fill out these forms, print her name so we can file her paperwork."

"But why?" we ask.

"She needs a Social Security number. You can't leave till it's done, till you give her a name."

Several hours later we fill in their blank, "Baby Girl Hust." And then we take her home.

Feedings and sleep and diaper changes establish a rhythm. All focus is upon our daughter. After a few weeks, we realize we don't want to live in the city. Our dream of country life starts again. For now, we pack up and take a camping trip with our baby, drive north of the Sierras to Lassen National Park. One evening, the campfire pulls us into its magic under the Sugar Pines. As I stare into the embers of a dying campfire, I sense her name whispered in the wind — Heidi, girl of the mountains. And when I say it out loud, she looks at me. She knows her name.

Camping

I know, in the way one always knows these things, something's not right. Doubt persists deep in my heart, hidden beneath thick layers of protective tissue, and the shield of my daily life — the hopes and pictures of how it's supposed to be. On one screen, *Better Homes and Gardens* shows the wedding, ivory lace dress with sweetheart neckline, bridesmaids in pastels, happy family, all smiles. The other movie clips along like an underground film: hippies, communes, back-to-the-landers, artists — all experimenting with alternative lifestyles. At twenty-eight, Terry and I are searching for our place on the planet, in community, and most important to me, with each other.

"Temporary" describes and defines our lifestyle. As soon as we land someplace, circumstances change, we move, and then move again. Adjustment, new friends, new work. I soon feel so weary of it all, the packing, hauling, settling, unsettling. Amidst the chaos, Heidi holds us together, our common focus and love for her is the glue.

Following our Lassen campout, Terry receives an offer of a carpentry job — the remodel of a summer cabin in Monte Rio, perched on a steep hillside above the Russian River. The job provides our ticket out of Berkeley and away from city life. We camp out in the torn-apart structure, but with the baby, every day proves a challenge: we schlep backpacks of clothes, laundry, coolers; cook brown rice and veggies on our Coleman two-burner. I need a real house, can't do this much longer. Like a delicate spider web, our gypsy skills are stretched thin, as are our patience and comfort level. I love that I can successfully nurse my child, so grateful for our long hours together, Heidi nestled in the crook of my arm. We give each other nourishment and peace. She is my anchor.

Terry's a great dad, as I knew he would be. His attention, when not on the building project, goes straight to Heidi. Diaper changes? No problem. She spends hours pressed against his chest in the corduroy Snugli baby carrier. Evenings, after our simple dinner, nursing, and baby bedtime, we hash out plans to buy some land, maybe remodel an old house, grow our own food — some version of our experiences in Vermont and Oregon. Currently, we have very little money. There remains the $5,000 wedding gift offer from Terry's parents for a down payment. That's it. Regardless, our vision lives on like a fairy-tale pipe dream, a hope for a home.

We yearn for something better than our ramshackle existence. One morning, a FOR SALE sign in the window of a shiny silver Airstream trailer grabs our attention on the way to the Laundromat. Yes! An adorable tiny cabin on wheels with a real kitchen, bathroom, even a shower, and the bed converts to a dining area. We buy it even before we know where to put it.

"Let's go check out the Duncan's Mills Campground, farther out River Road toward the ocean. Maybe we can get a deal for a couple of months while we figure things out. And it's close to your job." I feel hopeful. Ideas start to gel, and puzzle pieces come together and make sense.

The campground caretaker points down a narrow dirt road that fades in tall yellow grass. "Sure, go ahead, look around. Nobody here much during the week anyhow. There are bigger sites for trailers all the way to the back, near the school bus. Just keep going, you'll find it."

The rutted one-lane roadway has a few campsites that veer off and disappear into the grass. Then, as we round the last curve, a small meadow opens up before us. On the south side, it's flat and sandy; tufts of grass struggle where the river floods each year, then recedes, leaving rich silt, broken branches, and mud. On our left sit three or four spacious sites, with picnic tables and fire rings, neatly tucked under large sheltering oaks. Willows huddle together in groups along the river's edge, roots sunk deep; their leaves vibrate and shimmer silvery pale green. Farther, at the very end, sits a sunflower-yellow school bus surrounded by folding chairs, adult and child bicycles, and brightly colored kids' toys.

A woman in shorts with pixie-cut blond hair sets out lunch on the red-and-white-checkered tablecloth, while a tow-headed toddler yells from his nearby highchair. The woman waves to us, flashes a welcoming smile. We can't help ourselves — we have to get out of the Citroën and walk around, stretch. Besides, Heidi needs a snack and a diaper change. Two more kids with their dad tumble out of the school bus doors. Soon we're hanging out with them, talking like old friends.

"How long have you been here? Where are you from? Do you live in the bus now, full time?" We're anxious to learn more about them.

"Nashville, Tennessee," answers Sally. "We were just worn out with our old life, sales jobs and obligations. Always wanted to travel, see more of the world than our hometown where we were born and raised. California seemed so attractive, and now we're here, lookin' for land, a new way of life."

Ron grins wide, pulls gently at his red-brown beard like he's not used to having one. They converted their school bus into a tidy and charming mobile home: bunks for the three kids, a large bed and storage closet in the back, and a comfortable living/dining room with full kitchen tucked behind the driver's seat.

By the weekend, we move into a shady site under a spreading oak and across the meadow from the bus. We tow our silver bubble of a new home down the bumpy road, set up the Aladdin lamp, propane stove, and cooler as the outdoor kitchen; string up a clothesline for rinsed-out baby clothes. We stake out our territory, and, for now at least, we have a home. Sally and Ron invite us over for glasses of red wine; we share stories of wanderlust and homesteading. Simpatico. We enjoy each other's company. We could be friends.

Once we settle in, Terry's job keeps him occupied and I stay alone at the trailer — alone with Heidi, that is. I don't mind, actually enjoy the peace, living outside, walk with her snuggled between my breasts, asleep or bright-eyed, looking at gulls, blue river herons, sparkling water, fast-moving fog clouds, silvery leaves. She listens acutely to my footsteps on river-beach pebbles, the rush of wind, the swish of a heron's wings. Every sound and change of light catches her attention. I feel reverence for this gift of "seeing" each precious moment. Days pass in this simple way. "Chop wood, carry water" becomes my daily mantra. Heidi, the trees, and river are my teachers and companions.

Sunny days ease my tension around being alone. When the fog rolls upriver and shrouds the meadow, I feel more challenged, mostly to keep warm, huddled by a smoky campfire, drinking hot cups of peppermint tea. Heidi and I take extra-long naps in the trailer under a pile of blankets. Daily we go on long walks the length of the campground. When the thick, wet fog condenses on the table and benches, I require a raincoat. Finally, I give up and hide out in the trailer with propane heat and wait for the end of the day when Terry comes home. He's tired, ready for a camp shower behind the trailer by the big tree. We talk about Heidi and our day, and try to keep our hopes alive.

Sally and Ron share the dream of buying land and a house in the country. In August they find property just five miles away up Austin Creek, near Cazadero. Several acres of sheltered property — second- and third-growth redwood and mixed forest — with a spacious, lofted house are perfect for their family. They invite us to move our Airstream to the land and remodel an old redwood cabin as our master bedroom. Our collective vision expands once more: dream house in the country.

Finding Home

Things come undone for unexpected reasons, and that feels like my life story. When Ron and Terry have a serious falling out, we're asked to leave the land. I remember only the pounding on our cabin door and Ron screaming at Terry, "Get out — now!"

We're on the move again. It's hard to count the number of places I've lived, from dorm rooms to stuffy basement apartments, chicken coops to estate farms; the hundreds, maybe thousands of boxes packed, labeled, and stacked. Time for a place of our own, to settle and spread out, flex our skills along with muscles, dig in our own dirt.

In December, we begin to search for land. From the Russian River, we head north to check out Mendocino County, where the redwoods grow thick as weeds and the prices might still be affordable. Camped out at a cheap motel in Fort Bragg, we comb through real estate ads, finding little we would consider. The village of Mendocino perches on a Pacific bluff; its whitewashed New England houses make me homesick for my East Coast roots. The prices in 1972 suggest we're in the wrong place. But, we have specific desires. After two years of research and exploration, we don't want to live anywhere but northern California. Our dream homestead: a charming two-bedroom house, acres of beautiful, forested land with a creek and good spring water year round. Nearby, a flat space for a large garden and plenty of sun. Complete privacy. In other words, Paradise.

We look at Boonville's broad valley, green velvet hills, and vineyards. Not a match: Too open, exposed, not a culture we relate to, and very pricey. Next, we try Willits and Ukiah — too "cowboy," like rodeos and dude ranches. Laytonville seems like a little nothing town: a bar called Boomers, Geysers General Store, and a real estate outpost of Century 21, a one-man operation. As temperatures dip below 20 degrees at night, we continue the search, our hopes dwindling. Dejected, we stop at Laytonville's tiny land office so we can say we didn't give up.

Brad greets us excitedly, like he hasn't seen anyone in days, even a "looky-loo." No, not much in our price range, mostly ranches out here. "But wait... there's this one place out on Wilderness Road, past Branscomb. Just came on the market. A hundred twenty acres with an eighty-year-old house plus a separate workshop. Even has a creek and spring with good drinking water. You might like it — kind of rustic. Lots of original stuff, like a Jeep that runs, wood cook-stove, some outbuildings, even an old wringer-washer. The place needs love and attention. Yes, you folks just might be perfect." He rambles on, quite satisfied, like he's talking to himself. Then, "I'll drive you out there today if you want to see it."

Sure, what the heck. It's a cold, dreary day; the winter sun catches moisture in the air, disperses it like sparklers, glittery and hopeful. Remnants of clouds from the tail of a storm cast drifting shadows on the hills along Branscomb Road. Crammed into Brad's four-wheel-drive Scout, we bump along past Harwood's lumber mill, and just before the turn, Red Bridge Tavern.

Once on Wilderness Road, we enter a different world, a magical kingdom. The valley itself closes in and hugs us in a way that feels comforting and familiar, and at the same time open and wild. An adventure, like I'm five again on a Sunday drive in the country, so thrilled to discover what's around the next corner. Horses graze in lush emerald pastures; expansive lawns surround ranch houses, and low split-rail fences rim summer cottages. Beside crumbling sheds, ancient fruit trees stand dormant, ready to burst forth with their treasures. Here the road narrows into tight curves with a pitted surface. We slow to a cautious 5 miles per hour, and pray hard that we don't meet another vehicle around the bend, the road masked by bushes of redwood sprouts. Approaching the wooden bridge that crosses the Eel River, my focus sharpens to examine the primitive structure poised just a few feet above the thick mocha water rushing below with its cargo of branches and bobbing logs.

Brad stops the Scout smack in the middle of the creaking bridge, like a crazed tour guide who wants to give us a thrill. "Check it out," he crows. "Sometimes it washes right over this bridge and closes the road... briefly," he adds, not wanting to scare us. Soon we're off, north along the river, where the ribbon of road degrades to muddy potholes and gravel. Half a mile in, we come upon the driveway, which crosses two washout spots before turning sharp left, out of sight. The way looks impossibly steep, so we opt to walk the rest of the way up to the house rather than risk getting stuck several miles away from phones or help of any kind.

Terry packs our daughter into the Snugli and straps her onto his chest. I grab the backpack diaper bag just in case, and we set off. The way proves slippery, laced with gnarled tree roots that prevent parts of the road from slipping away, but hauling supplies could present quite a challenge if it became impassable. At the top, we break through the shadows of second-growth Douglas firs into a clearing — into the light. Pure enchantment. Dark-chocolate redwood shingles cover the storybook cabin, its two roofs steeply pitched, the multi-paned windows and doors original. Slanting December sunlight barely catches the tops of the south windows. Within an hour, it dips out of sight into the forest to the west. By 3:00, the house is dark and chilly.

Little House in the Big Woods comes to mind, the back door uncommonly short, not even six feet tall. It makes me want to duck my head. The temperature in the kitchen feels even colder than outside. Dominating the room, like a country queen, stands a blue wood-burning Wedgewood cook-stove. This feels like a Hobbit house with a short refrigerator and apartment-sized gas range. Funky, yet charming. Eighty-year-old redwood paneling makes the living room dark, despite east- and south-facing windows. A mahogany upright piano rekindles my interest in making music. The small bedroom, stuck in the far corner, has no charm at all: chipped linoleum, a couple of high windows, sliders, and a door — but we could fix it up. All it needs is fresh paint, some color to give it a lift. I can imagine Terry's blue-and-white sailboat quilt on one wall, framed Peter Pan print with children and fairies on the other, full-sized crib, Raggedy Ann and Andy dolls. And Heidi, playing, holding on to the crib's rail. This could work.

All in all, we're quite taken with the place, already spinning tales in our heads of how to refurbish the spring, clear some madrone trees for firewood, plant a garden, clean out the attic for our bedroom. Ideas hum like spring bees coming alive, our dream palette manifesting right in front of us, everything possible, within our grasp. With its $25,000 price tag, the property's down payment will be covered by our wedding gift, and the monthly tab is manageable at around $250. We're thrilled, and quickly decide this will be our home.

This time the move feels permanent. By February, the twisty, muddy driveway sports neat drainage channels cut diagonally across the road, holes and ditches packed with river shale. The cleanup takes a few weeks: decades of trash hauled to the dump; cupboards and floors scrubbed with stiff brushes; mice trapped and pitched into the woods; fires built daily to keep us warm and dry out the dampness. Fortunately, the place smells good — no mildew, just dusty.

By next fall we'll have dry firewood of our own. We discover discarded shakes and split them for kindling. Whoever lived here last was, thankfully, a packrat like us. We cut down and buck up the madrone trees near the house. The wet rounds split like butter; we stack them up all around the living-room stove to dry out before adding a couple of pieces to a hot fire. Still they sizzle and spit and slow the fire down. We fill up the stove's firebox before we go to bed, pack it so it smolders all night and wards off the deep chill.

Ukiah Building Supply and Hardware Store becomes our favorite haunt, plus Willits' Happy Belly Juice Bar and health food store. New acquisitions include a chainsaw, ax, and splitting maul. We restore several rusted tools abandoned in the shed, sharpen wedges, and replace handles.

By April 1, my birthday, escrow finally closes, the deal done, and for a year we live our dream. It feels like we can overcome our differences, learn to compromise, let go of that old feeling that we might split up. We focus on the here and now. We have our home at last, and a sweet, growing daughter, the best gift of all. Our hard-won skills for country living suddenly become the underpinnings of daily life. I stand at the baby-bath-sized kitchen sink and happily scrub sticky egg yolk off blue-and-turquoise Fiestaware plates, serenaded by a gurgling baby, and outside, the rhythmic whack of splitting firewood.

Weekly, Terry makes whole-wheat English muffins from scratch: He grinds wheat berries in the Corona mill, kneads the fresh dough, rolls muffins in coarse cornmeal. I swoon with pleasure and anticipation at the smell of them baking atop the wood cook-stove, arranged like a mandala in the black cast-iron pan. Split with a fork, a pat of butter tucked into the craggy muffin halves, the heavenly taste explodes in my mouth. Simple pleasures sustain me, reflect the goodness of our life together; help me override my doubts about the relationship; ease my nagging loneliness, my yearning. Even though trouble brews under the surface, I focus on hope and resolve: I can be a good mother and wife, and keep this family together.

Spring — time to seed the garden, plant ourselves firmly on this land, together. We show our best selves to each other, homesteading and parenting. We thrive. To our friends, and even to ourselves, we are the "perfect couple."

COUNTRY LIFE

The images are perfect: Homesteaders moving back to the land, capturing the lifestyle and solid values of rural America at its best. We resemble my ancestors, Mennonites from Iowa, but with more choices, the freedom and fun of the "Love Generation." Getting our feet wet in the great experiment, we create a way of life that exactly suits us: long days outside working our land; we grow vegetables organically, with love; hang out with neighboring families; share ideas about kids, community, school, ditches, wells, and bridges. We congregate for potlucks and work parties, baby-quilt lunches. How long should those bucked-up tan-oak logs sit out in the woods? How can you keep weasels out of the hen house? Basically farmers with a tie-dye twist.

On hot days we meet up with our friends Tim and Madeleine or Harmony and James while our kids splash in the creek. We exchange not only the week's plans but also a nice joint of fragrant bud, passed around to get the day going. Some days we walk over to their cabin for warm banana bread, aromatic Melita drip French Roast, and conversation. The older children — Heather, Nicole, and Jennifer — run around laughing, bickering, doting on one-year-old Heidi; pick her up, drag her with them, squealing, to weed the garden or play dolls on the miniature lawn. By the time we collect our backpack of snacks and diapers, meander the mile or so back up the hill to home, it's time for Heidi's nap.

Once we're home, there's silence. We talk about Heidi, of course, and about planting our new garden, and fixing fences, yet not a word about the growing gap between us. Days pass like this, turn into months, tapping out a rhythm that both pleases me and makes me unsettled. I feel I have a rightful place with my family on this land. But underneath this feeling sits the nagging question about Terry, about us. I wonder what would have happened two years ago if I had left or not turned up pregnant. Most of the time I smooth it over by remembering what's good in our lives: sun-warmed days with our hands in the earth, the joy of our daughter, all that we create together in our vision of home. Can we make it?

The part I yearn for, and miss, is sharing feelings, those deeper expressions of love, saying out loud what we mean to each other. Will I ever get this with Terry? Some men aren't good at talking about emotions — it's difficult for them. I remember my dad, shy by nature, confronted with so many emotions flung at him by Mom.

I press for communication, try to start conversations, talk about what I feel, what I need. I'm not good at it either, clumsy and awkward like a newborn colt, and it's just not working. In the relationship, I feel stonewalled, frustrated, inadequate. At the same time, I should feel grateful for having such a sweet life and shut the hell up about it. What right do I have to dream on about some soul-mate/best friend/lover all in one? I have no idea what's fantasy or fiction, designed to lure and distract me from giving my all to this marriage. Do the right thing. I think. Something about loving the one you're with. Put away those dreams and questions. Shut it down, or it could be our undoing.

Losing It

I know I love Terry, that's not the question. But is it enough to love him? I adore the way he relates with Heidi, attentive and present, comfortable, a great dad. They are so bonded, in fact, that I feel left out. The tensions between Terry and me simmer, like slow-cooking rice. The lid rattles, must stay on tight or the whole thing will boil over and make a sticky mess. When I try to talk about something that's bothering me (anything, really), there's no eye contact, little or no response from him. I feel invisible.

One morning we're bustling about the kitchen, cleaning up after breakfast, and I confront him about our old issue, my desire to communicate and have a true partnership. He says something, I say something, and suddenly it all explodes. Quick as summer lightning, I flip, and hurl a dish of oatmeal across the room at Terry, low, not aiming to hit him. It shatters, my favorite Fiestaware dish in shards, sticky leftover oatmeal in globs on the floor. Terry's shocked, looks at me like I'm a crazy person, and I am! I yell, cry, run out of the house into the madrone woods, and wander around. It takes me nearly an hour to calm down, stop the heaving sobs and jumbled thoughts about leaving and failing and Heidi.

In the end, I walk back down the hill to approach Terry. Say I'm sorry, and truly mean it. Losing it like that — out of control, freaking out, running away — feels like my mother. And that feels like failure.

DISTRACTIONS

I wasn't sure I'd ever weave again, so meeting Robert and Carol Yelland is a sweet surprise. When I see their amazing woven tapestries, handspun yarns, mohair shawls, and looms, I feel inspired. Over mugs of coffee, we talk about my weaving history and training at college. We form a strong connection, and within a few months they teach me how to spin New Zealand fleeces into thick-and-thin yarns. Common yellow onionskins, magenta plum leaves, and indigo dyes turn the bland yarn into richly colored strands, which they then weave into the borders of shawls. Nubbly yarns form landscapes of textures, their pigments coloring mountains and rivers in rich tapestries. I love this art form. I'm hooked on spinning — the rhythm of the treadle spinner, the lanolin coating my hands, feeding and shaping the fleece's long strands, twisting them into yarn — so soothing, and so distracting.

I begin to weave again. Robert and Carol split up, leaving Robert on his own. Between January and June, a weaving collective forms, four women plus Robert. We gather at his house several days a week. He sets one of us up on his large loom, and then we trade off, weaving pillows for the San Francisco Grant Street Fair and Marin's Renaissance Faire. Our group energy glows, vibrant as the colors we weave: passionate reds, deep sun-gold, cobalt blue, indigo, lavender, and purple. Shawls are Robert's signature pieces, soft loose mohair accented by hand-spun borders, cozy gems to wrap up in. Each of us develops a style in tapestry pillow covers. We take turns weaving; practice setting up warps, threading the loom, spin, dye, stuff pillows, and tie fringe. Julie originally came to Branscomb to apprentice with Robert and Carol. She and I understand textiles, studied the craft in college. Harmony and Joël are eager students. We hum along like honeybees in springtime.

Terry stays home with Heidi on the mornings I work. How odd to call it work, since party time is more like it, totally enter-taining. Still we accomplish a lot, produce a growing stash of pillows, garments and wall hangings for our first craft fair. Each accent pillow is a small, simple tapestry, 18" × 18". We talk astrol-ogy, brew coffee, step outside to share a joint, choose our day's palette, and sing along with Bob Dylan. Robert and Carol, who created this business, have been weaving and selling at craft fairs and doing commissions for several years. And now I'm part of the "Wilderness Weavers," finding my craft and a life of my own.

BREAKUP, 1974

I could just say that Terry and I split up, or I could describe in detail the agonizing months of talks, promises, and attempts to put our troubled marriage back together. Either way, it turns out the same.

Bitter cold winter keeps us huddled next to the wood stove. The rhythm of parenting Heidi anchors our days, allows little time for introspective discussions. Nap time. We put Heidi in her crib after a book and bottle, rock her in Grandma's chair. If we're lucky, we have about two hours to talk — not much time to try, once again, to explore our deep issues, connect with each other and have honest, heart-to-heart conversations.

Our main problem — we're young, inexperienced, naïve, and haven't always made good decisions. We teeter on the edge, unable to fully commit to each other and our marriage. We barely understand what's involved, yet we struggle to maintain and repair our ailing relationship, for Heidi's sake as well as our own. Some of our hopes of family and home are still alive, so we try to focus on them.

When spring arrives we again distract ourselves by planting vegetables in our second-year garden; weed, cook, care for Heidi, and build a tiny play-yard fence from old split rails. We are cautious with each other, aware of the delicate balance, try to preserve whatever remains of "us." But the rift feels like a deep crack in thick porcelain: lost chips, missing pieces. It won't hold together with any glue that we know about.

The crops mature to abundance, carrots fat and long, zucchini out of control, lettuce tender and sweet, then bolting to bitter. Shasta daisies populate the garden, swaying on rangy stems in hot afternoon breezes. The elderly black walnut tree, especially loaded this year, promises a profusion of small hard nuts with an intense, almost bitter taste.

Heidi turns two in May; she walks, talks in miniature sentences, curious as a monkey and into everything. It's so easy to feel wrapped up in her conversations and delightful laughter, her burgeoning use of "no." One day she climbs a ladder to the roof of the woodshed before we notice her missing — an early climber and perfectly confident. Summer comes on with hot, lazy days and long afternoons at the river. Terry and I spend weeks trying to figure out what to do with each other.

Things happen. Accumulated baggage piles up, things we can't forgive. The final unraveling is a long, painful breaking apart that lasts into August. Suffice to say it's over.

In October I move out, into a twenty-four-foot Airstream

parked on a friend's property. Heidi stays with me half the time, while Terry and I agonize over the details of shared custody. I cry every time she leaves. A three-foot-tall pot-bellied stove provides heat, keeps the Airstream cozy, but gives little comfort to my aching heart. I sit on a low cushion and feed the fire with split redwood and short chunks of oak, as if I could make things better with my small offerings. Nothing works. I hang out in my empty shell of a dwelling, wait all winter for a rental house to become available — and in Branscomb, rentals are rare.

The trailer resembles a dollhouse. Luckily I manage to hook up to my neighbor's power by way of thick orange extension cords a couple hundred feet long. A sequence of hoses brings water for washing. The stove and fridge run on propane I buy at the mill store. I haul drinking water in one-gallon glass bottles. Julie and Joël's cabin sits down a narrow path through the woods, and they kindly share their bathroom with me. Most important is their friendship — the nourishing meals, hot tea, and healing talks. They listen to me cry, and their compassionate witness provides the comfort I need to get through.

November, December, an endless descent into darkness; pain dominates each day, a vice around my heart. The short cold days take away my resolve to make it on my own, block my connection to what I want, shadow my spirit like the black clouds with their torrent of angry, icy rain. This winter feels like punishment for my actions, for leaving. I can't get warm or enjoy much of anything. My energy simply seeps away into the night while I sleep, absorbed by the darkness. I hate being alone. It reminds me of "the pit." I'm scared, think I might not be able to pull myself out of this anytime soon.

IX

On My Own

1975–1981

Community — It Takes a Year

"So why did you move to Point Arena," asks my new friend Annie.

"Last summer, I landed an interesting job at a camp. When I first pulled into the parking lot there, I met this guy Allan. We were both hired as counselors at Plantation Farm Camp. Our connection was instant. The two of us were assigned to head up a boys' unit. We spent a lot of time together, really liked each other, and didn't want the summer to end. I was done with Branscomb, needed to move on, what with the pending divorce. Allan had a place on the Gualala Ridge, so I rented a little cabin a few miles away to be with him."

My mind reels with memories of camp. Day hikes to Stumps Beach, swimming and boating at the lake, farm chores that include milking cows; playing my Autoharp at the breakfast sing-alongs, lively square dancing in the hay barn. Bonds with the kids were special, reminded me of my own camp days, but my bond with Allan runs deep. I feel seen and appreciated, and for once I don't question my feelings.

January 1976, I move to the Mendocino Coast, led by instinct and my hopes for an ongoing relationship with this good man. Heidi and I snuggle into the three rooms of our tiny red rental cottage, three miles from Point Arena. This very small town serves as the center for the community: The elementary and high schools, a Montessori preschool, health-food store, movie theater, two churches, Gilmore's old-fashioned general store, and the infamous Disotelle's Restaurant and Bar, host to numerous weekend late-night "boogies." The preschool and health food store are destined to become my town haunts and part-time jobs.

Hired as a Montessori teacher's aide, I hope my job training will eventually lead to full certification. I diligently study an official course-by-mail from London. Also, I join the Natural Food Store

Collective, which functions more like an extended family than a job. Our group, ten to fifteen folks, gets together for Sunday potluck dinner meetings to brainstorm, run the business, deal with store problems, and plan the next food pickup. Whose truck is running this week? Who can make the trip down the coast to meet the supplier, load all the coolers full of produce? As we debate these issues, our kids run around, oldest watching the young ones, a large and rowdy family. Meetings last till we reach consensus or issues are tabled so we can go home and get some sleep.

Our collective venture prospers. We open the "Juice Bar" and continue to extend credit to anyone who needs it. After all, we figure, people need to eat. We're so naïve; with a steep learning curve, we struggle to make money. Our survival, it turns out, depends upon the generosity of a few patrons and a successful marijuana harvest. One man in particular believes that our store serves the core of the community. Late fall, with the store's bank account faltering with overdraft fees, our patron suddenly makes it swell to a sweet five digits. Then we head up Top-O-Hill Road to Stevo's place to celebrate his gift, for a day of swimming, potluck and barbeque, music, and general hanging out in gratitude for gifts that keep us going.

Life is incredibly full. Heidi goes to kindergarten and I work two jobs. On Thursdays at seven, we show up at the Methodist Church for Madrigal and Choir practice. Monday, it's folk dancing. Most weekends we spend at "the Farm" with Allan, share meals and work the gardens like a family, play music with assorted friends. My life feels rich, like thick cream that floats easily to the top. Am I bored with small-town life? Hardly! I barely have time to do laundry.

A few months pass and our little red cottage finally feels cozy. After the split-up, I retained a few special possessions: my large floor loom, which I designed and built last year in shop class; a 1908 upright piano from the house in Branscomb; a 9 × 12 gold Chinese rug; a double bed from a local yard sale; two antique chairs with hand-tooled leather seats; Heidi's maple bed; a white toy box handmade by Dad, "Judy's Toys" painted in primary colors on the lid. My most prized possession is Grandma's comb-back rocking chair, its six coats of paint rubbed and chipped to a soft patina of sage green.

My landlady conveniently left some furnishings: grass-cloth rugs to cover the cold slab floor, a small dining table, lace and velvet curtains. Her enormous plants inhabit the house, including a tiny-leafed begonia in the bathroom that flowers several times a year; it drops hundreds of pale pink blossoms like early snow, and threatens to take over the south window and toilet.

I barely manage the rent of $90 per month. Our well water comes out tinted a light rusty red, fit only for bathing and occasionally, in a pinch, doing dishes; it has a way of staining things like white dishes and underwear. Once a week, we load our glass water bottles in boxes into the back of the red Datsun station wagon and drive out Highway One near the Garcia River to our favorite water supply. At the second pullout, hidden by hanging vines and overgrowth, an iron pipe juts straight out of the hillside; water seeps from this natural spring, ferns and lizards quite at home. Heidi helps me fill and load our one-gallon bottles. A single trip lasts us a week.

By mid-August the well goes dry, with no hope of water until after the rains start, maybe November. The best part of the drought: our agreement to pay no rent during these months. We manage our hygiene taking showers in town, and on weekends, at the Farm. Besides, we love summer days at the river, visits with friends, saunas on a small beach nestled in the crook of the Garcia. There we swim and play and connect to our water source.

The cabin's utility room, with its large water heater, evolves into my weaving studio. Whenever I'm not working elsewhere, I spin thick and thin yarns, dye them, and weave pillow covers and commissioned tapestries. Weaving the bright and muted colors cheers my spirit. Combined income from my three endeavors brings in just enough for us to get by. Over time I learn to trust, to let go of my fear. There is always enough.

STROKE, 1977

I'm asleep in my little cabin when the call pierces my dreams. It's already breakfast time in New York, on a typical muggy-hot August morning. Dad sounds rattled, his voice raspy and thin; it takes a lot to upset his usual calm mood.

"What's happening, Dad? How did the surgery go? How's Mom? Is everything all right?" A sense of something wrong creeps over me like a long shiver.

Silence. Then, "The operation went as planned; they repaired the fracture with a simple pin in her hip. But then, a couple hours later, she started having seizures, "brain spasms," they call them. The doctors don't seem to know exactly what's going on and they can't control the spasms. They just keep happening."

My mind races, reviewing what I've heard over the past few days, about her fall on the way to the bathroom in the middle of the night. She'd walked that path a million times, often half-looped on sleeping pills. Did she black out? The sharp pain in her hip sent her to Dr. Dodd's the next day. The X-ray showed a hairline fracture. "Best to pin it," he said. The surgery was scheduled, quite routine. It was supposed to be easy, no complications, and now this.

"Dad, that's terrible! What does Dr. Dodd say? How could this have happened?"

"He says maybe she's having a stroke. They won't let me in her room right now. Two nurses are with her, and Dr. Dodd is giving her some IV medication to hopefully stop the seizures."

"I'm coming to Cobleskill, Dad, as soon as I can." The tears come fast, my throat so tight I can hardly speak. "It'll take a few days to get it all arranged, with Heidi and work and the plane tickets. I want Heidi with me, at least part of the time." I'm already strategizing how I'll work out vacation time with her dad.

"It will mean a lot to me if you can get away." His words fall softly, relieved that I'll make the trip to be with him. "When you make the reservation, use my credit card. I want to pay for your tickets." And though I feel guilty not having enough money for trips like this, I gratefully accept his offer.

My brain spins with lists of things to prepare, while waves of anxiety and worry wash over me. And I can't get Mom's voice out of my head from the last time I visited: "I'll probably die before you see me again." Haunting.

Several days later, Heidi and I pack the Datsun station wagon and drive down the curvy coast road to San Francisco Airport. I consider staying in Cobleskill for a few weeks to help out. Everything is so unknown at this point, feels surreal, but the prognosis doesn't sound good. Now they're saying "brain stem stroke," completely coincidental with the hip operation. Unrelated. Mom lies in a coma, and yet, Dad says, her eyes stay open. I can't even imagine, but know I must get there as soon as possible.

After the long journey east, we arrive at the hospital, walk into her room, and see her propped up in bed with pillows, side rails up; an IV bottle drips clear liquid into her arm. Sadness overwhelms me. She looks so helpless lying there. I start to cry, feel like I'm falling apart, all my fears confirmed. Through my tears I realize Mom is staring right at me. She knows me! I move in closer, give her a quick hug, and pull back a little to make eye contact, hold her hand gently. Her gaze pins mine for what seems like several minutes. Then, ever so slowly, her eyes drift away.

Behind me I hear Dad choke back his sobs. It takes me a while to really get it. She can't see me. It just doesn't register in her brain.

We stay for a month. Each day Dad and I take turns at the hospital; we sit with Mom, chat, tell her the day's news. The nurses say she might hear everything we say, that any day now she might regain consciousness. Miss Ruth, my favorite RN, talks constantly to her as she plumps pillows, gives Mom her sponge bath, winds her thinning hair into a French twist, feeds her through the tube. How did this happen? Is it a coincidence, the surgery, then right away the stroke? I start asking lots of questions about the previous day, the surgery itself, and how soon afterward the seizures began. All her medications were stopped the day before. Considering the drugs she was taking — tranquilizers, pentobarbital to sleep (two to four per night), painkillers, pep pills — she was in withdrawal, like "cold turkey." Could this have caused the stroke?

Dr. Dodd acts evasive, defensive, and rebuffs my inquiries. And Dad won't even ask those questions, trusts the doctor implicitly and doesn't want to start trouble.

I cry every time I see Mom like this, having spasms every few minutes barely damped down by the anticonvulsant drug Dilantin. It's just not fair and it breaks my heart. There is much feeling between Mom and me, from deep love and connection to anger, criticism, jealousy, and resentment, all of it unspoken for so many years. Now it seems that words will never have their chance to spill out and be heard, lost under a cloak of ether, suffocated, disappearing into the mist.

What's to become of you, Mom? All I can do is whisper the words I want her to hear. "I love you, Mom. Come back. Please be all right."

WHIPLASH

Every day, like a bad dream, Mom still lies there in her "awake coma," seizures every little while, hardly controlled by large doses of Dilantin. She stares straight ahead like a frightened deer in the headlights, frozen in the moment. Eventually I have to leave and go home. After a month, nothing has changed.

Back in California, I live in a trance, just can't get grounded after the trip. I show up at my jobs at the preschool and "the Natch" (Natural Food Store), shop for groceries, and talk to Dad every day. Still no change. I hear the hospital loudspeaker in my head, call buttons beep, Mom moaning. I see her in bed with the pillows, the tubes. Asleep. Awake. Asleep. Not really there.

One day after school, I run errands and need to shop at Anchor

Bay Store. Heidi is playing nearby at Caitlin's for a couple hours. I decide to pick her up later. My mind spins, trying to digest everything that's going on with Mom, as I make the hairpin turn at the campground. Check oncoming traffic. I flip on the left signal and turn toward a parking spot in front of the store. Next thing I know, my ears are assaulted by sounds of skidding, squealing brakes, and for a second I see a black truck hurtle toward me. Before I realize what's happening, it slams into me, spins me around, and hits me again on the other side. Metal crunches, glass shatters, flies like a spray of crystals. Then, silence. Oh, my God! What happened?

I sit perfectly still in my seat till someone looks in the window and forces my door open. Several people run out from the store and the Galley restaurant, ask me if I can move, try to get me out of my twisted, crumpled car. I attempt to turn my head, but that hurts. Otherwise, no pain. Please, just let me sit here. I don't want to move, disturb this fragile moment. "I need to pick up my daughter," and, "Can someone please call Allan?"

The ambulance will be here soon, and the CHP. The guys from the black truck, so I'm told, are four loggers from Boonville who were stuffed into a three-quarter-ton pickup, speeding home at the end of their day. Maybe drunk. They sit inside the café now, down food and hot coffee, talk about how I turned right in front of them. How could that be? I didn't even see them till they were on top of me! I sit and wait almost an hour, thinking only that Heidi is safe; thank God I didn't pick her up early. Someone is watching out for her.

They all show up at once: The ambulance (I refuse), the cops (endless questions), and Allan (to get Heidi and take me home). I'll need to see a doctor later. Without health insurance, I can't afford a ride to the hospital.

It turns out nothing is broken. After three days, the shock wears off. My neck and right shoulder are in spasm. I can hardly turn my head, and everything hurts. No car, no driving, and no work make everything so difficult. For three months, I survive with the loving care of friends, food stamps, and temporary welfare. It feels like I've hit bottom, somehow embarrassed by my dependency on charity to get by.

My ex, Terry, surprises me with a gift of support: $1,000 to replace the totaled Datsun. I feel emotional at this sign of caring from him. Within another month I purchase a lemon-yellow Plymouth Valiant sedan from my friend Nick, only to discover I am petrified to drive. I approach stop signs like a timid animal, looking left and right at least three times, checking the rearview mirror nervously for unseen danger. Instead of swooping down Eureka Hill Road into town, I ride the smoking brakes the whole way.

Right before Halloween, Heidi gets chickenpox. I still stay home some days with whiplash, and try several remedies for the pain: the painkiller Soma makes me stupid and tired, and then there's Excedrin, of course, which hardly touches it. In Gualala, old Dr. Brigham, the osteopath, helps me sometimes, wrestles my groaning limbs into a full-on twist, head to hips, then, practically lying on me, crushes my ribs with his swift hard weight. His treatments bring relief, albeit temporary. I don't know what else to do, so I go back to work and cope, barely, with the pain. Sometimes it lays me up for a few days; slammed into bed with a heating pad, I hide under my comforting electric blanket.

In November, the real pain, that of the divorce, comes to a head with a child custody hearing. I fear I will lose Heidi, that she'll leave the state with her dad, go live in Idaho, and I'll hardly ever see her. She keeps me going, gives me a reason to get up in the morning — I'm determined to become a better person, a good mom. I have acquired a lot of "baggage" to deal with. I wish I wanted all that healing and growth for myself, but for now it's enough to want it just for her.

When, by some miracle, the custody case goes my way, Heidi and I can safely cozy up in our little red house. My breathing comes easier and I let down, let go of so much worry and pain.

Tonight will be mac-and-cheese, Winnie the Pooh, Curious George, and Madeleine — all the favorites. Special-treat ice cream. And tomorrow the school bus will come. Purple flannel-lined jeans, new sneakers, kindergarten. Life can be sweet, and ever so normal.

CLOSET

I imagine Mom entering the dark hall closet, inhaling the scents of her fine wool coats, alligator handbags, and kid gloves. This place always grounds her, connects her to the woman who existed before, who, when she felt well, could dress up for church on Sundays and be seen in her finery. Now she looks for a scarf, needing something to fancy up her simple outfit. *As the World Turns* begins soon, at one o'clock. She floats between lunch and the couch, slips into the closet like a warm wet womb.

Her hands caress the silks and cashmeres, loose summer shawls in pastel sherbet colors to match the sundresses she no longer wears. One particular scarf invites her to wad it up, bury her face in it like she did with Papa's giant handkerchiefs, the remembered smell of his pockets filling her. Then the fabric turns damp, absorbs her tears the way loose gauze holds blood — warm, familiar, one's own essence.

Leaning on her cane as she straightens up, she can pull a long scarf from its hanger, wind its length seductively around her neck. As it brushes past her mouth, her lips taste the faint salt of tears. The softness, meant for comfort, transports her into another time, of blood-soaked bandages wrapped tightly around her wrists, and dreams slipping away. She would give anything to have her life back now — before she fell, before the broken hip, the stroke. Just to be normal again — play bridge, shop for pretty dresses, even read a book. And to talk! It drives her crazy to write everything down on a pad with her shaky right hand.

No one but Dad understands her speech, and hardly anyone visits. Friends find it too painful to see her this way. One thing for certain: her life will never be the same again.

TOM

I should have seen it coming. I might have made excuses to be alone that night.

"You should know better," my mother's voice nags in my head. "You're so gullible. Boys just want one thing from you. Don't you know that by now?"

I hate thinking she was right. I still want a life different from her negative one.

Single again. I feel sad that things didn't work out with Allan. After two and a half years in a serious and loving relationship, we hit a standstill, and no commitment forthcoming. I pushed for a decision, anxious to know if it was going anywhere, like marriage, I guess. At thirty-four, my biological clock was running on, running me. I didn't really want to split up. I told myself I couldn't wait around for him to figure out what he wanted to do, so it all changed. We decided we'd still be friends, good friends, in fact, promised not to lose our connection. But the loss still feels deep, the lost hope of life with this man. I loved not only him but his whole family: His sister, Franci, so open and loving, holds a very special place in my heart; she always treated me as one of them. His parents and brother accepted me unconditionally, and I adopted them as well. I can't stop loving them.

My life feels full, with Heidi — my number-one focus. After that come two part-time jobs, then friends, choir, and weaving. At the Natch, my many companions make up a rich and varied community. Raven Earlygrow started the store several years ago with his partner Luke. Raven carries the torch, a visionary of sorts: Outspoken, passionate, stubborn, and caring. One minute I'm annoyed and frustrated, the next, laughing at his dry wit and keen intelligence. The guy commands respect, holds our business together with clever ideas, creative bookkeeping, and the iron fist/velvet glove technique. Influxes of cash from the local pot harvest mend the gaping holes in the store's charge accounts, and patch the leaks in the store's disintegrating fifty-year-old roof.

One of our collective members, young Tom, works tirelessly, always available to fill in, stay late, and close up the store. His intense blue eyes seem to convey a quiet depth that belies his shy, boyish image. We become friends, and often step outside to talk on breaks or when business slows down. I sense an unspoken attraction from him, but ignore it. Instead, I send a clear message: Forget it. I'm not interested or available. He's engaged to be married this summer, and I'm happy for them.

As the school year draws to a close, Heidi prepares to spend the summer in Branscomb with her dad. During this emotional time for me, I feel her energy draw away like a receding tide pulling on my heart. We pack her summer clothes and all her favorite things, including "Pokey," the cuddly polar bear. At her dad's, her other family includes stepmom Charlotte, two-year-old sister Emily, and stepbrother Zack. Summer for Heidi means days at the river, T-bone steaks, computer lessons, and freedom. I receive the questionable gift of solitude, pared-down responsibility, and a kind of emptiness. I try over and over to fill the space with friends and relationships, but it's never the same as a family.

A couple of weeks before Tom's wedding, I pick up on his nervousness. He asks one day if he can stop by my place after work. It's his birthday and he needs a friend to talk to: "Just a short visit on my way home," he says. I feel uneasy about his request, but I say I'll see him around 6:00, after the store closes. At 6:30 he knocks. When I give him a quick hug, I smell whiskey on his sweaty face.

"Come on in, sit down...so, what's on your mind?"

Clutching a brown paper bag, he sets it down on the table and pulls out a bottle of Korbel Champagne. This throws me off and Tom can see it.

"A little of the bubbly to celebrate my birthday and my last days as a bachelor," he says, already undoing the wire cage, opening the bottle before even asking.

"Well, okay, just a taste. I don't really drink," I say, and fetch two small juice glasses from the cupboard.

We sit across from each other at the small round table and sip champagne. He begins to relax, loosen up, and tell me of his trepidations about his upcoming marriage. Already, he says, he can feel the passion slowly leaking out of their nights, days becoming a regimen of things to do, projects, plans, babies, obligating him to a life that's not his own. He sounds detached and has no plans to change the wedding. For him, there's a release in being able to speak of it, but his confession makes me queasy and uncomfortable. I'm thinking he just needs me to listen, to witness, so that he can let it go.

He goes on talking of passion, the fire of it. Strong attraction, then the cooling... and how he longs for the heat, how he could feel that for me if he let himself.

Whoa! Clearly Tom is out of line, and it's time for him to leave. He seems very nervous about having gone too far, said too much. He wants to make it right with me. "I need a hug," he says.

This should have been a red flag. Why didn't I see it coming? His shy hug quickly swells into a slushy passionate embrace that I reject and push him away. He stumbles, then pins me against the refrigerator. I feel smothered by his weight, acutely aware of the unexpected strength in his thick arms.

By this time, his words and emotions are tumbling out like a storm, uncontrolled, raging. "Always loved you... wanted you... dreamed of us being together... we're meant to be...."

I push, struggling to get out of his drunken stronghold. "Please, Tom, you have to stop. This is no good... you have to go! Now!"

But he pushes me through my bedroom doorway, another five feet and down onto the bed. "Tom. Tom! What are you doing? Stop it!" But he doesn't hear me now, doesn't see me.

"You want this as much as I do, you know you do," he slurs. "Don't fight it."

I shove back, hard, but all the strength I have in my arms is not adequate. His incredibly heavy body is on top of me, holding me down, and somehow I become aware of him pulling on my pants, working them down my thighs, even though I struggle. Tears come fast, my muscles giving way, heart pounding as I try to escape.

"No! No!" I'm sobbing, chest heaving. Can't he see he's hurting me? Can't he hear that I don't want him? Doesn't it make a difference?

I scream when he pushes into me, turn my head from his slobbering kisses, open and close my eyes, seeing only the stained-glass window mandala, and then I'm gone.

I leave in the only way I know how, the way I've always escaped in the past. My body's barely aware of his weight, thrusting, moaning...in crushing waves, like tons of water pushing me under... pushing off of me. Soft, mumbled empty words. Withdrawal.

I am alone.

He tries to reconstruct me, pull up my pants, but I don't respond, still gone. I reach for the silky comforter to cover my body, shield me, though it's too late for that. I turn to the wall, shaking, weeping, as I come back to myself and observe the wreckage.

How could this have happened? And what did I do wrong?

* * *

When I see him in the store, I can't meet his shifting eyes, looking at me like a sad, disobedient puppy seeking my love and approval. I change my store hours and manage to avoid him for months after the wedding.

One day he approaches me. "I need to talk to you. It's really important."

Always wanting to fix things, make them right, I reluctantly agree. We amble up a steep rocky path in back of the store to a small grassy patch overlooking the town.

"I know what I did to you was wrong. I just couldn't help myself. Been thinking about it a lot." The words ooze out of him. I listen. Part of me stays far away.

"I guess I raped you. No, really, I did rape you."

My mind snaps to attention. He raped me? He's admitting this?

"And I'm really sorry. Will you forgive me? I need you to forgive me."

I am shocked. I've carried around a ball of confusion all these months. How did I invite it in? What's wrong with me that things like this happen? Why do I feel powerless to stop it? I feel so violated, helpless, vulnerable. Rape? I hate him.

Yet I consider his need to be forgiven, his admission, see a way to close that door.

"Yes," I say, "you did that. Raped me. Ignored my feelings and our friendship; didn't listen or see me." Silence. "And okay, I will forgive you. But stay away from me. I can't be your friend."

There's nothing more to say. Some imprint of the rape remains, the submerged anger and the loss, again, of myself. But for now it's over.

Healing Begins, 1980

Quarter to seven, middle of the winter, dark outside. My alarm shocks me awake and I roll over to quell its high-pitched ring. Searing white-hot pain jabs me under my right wing bone, into my neck, ear, and temple. I can't move an inch without raw nerves lighting up like summer lightning. Now I'm crying. They've returned: the muscle spasms from the accident over two years ago still haunt me. Agony. I call out, and even my voice, every decibel, every movement, sets it off.

"Heidi... it's time to get up... I can't come get you this morning. It's my neck. So sorry."

She pads in on soft fuzzy slippers; her flower-print flannel nightgown flutters like butterfly wings. Without a word, she surveys the situation and oh-so-carefully crawls under the covers to hug me. Her freshly washed gold hair still emits that baby-fresh smell, reminds me that she is only seven, and yet she takes such good care of me.

"Shall I stoke the fire, Mom? Make breakfast? I'll get dressed and be right back."

Ever since she turned five, after my whiplash, household tasks come easily to her. She knows the whole drill of making our morning tofu scramble — mash, dash of tamari, heat the pan, sprinkle Tabasco — plus toasted English muffins. Standing on her sturdy oak child's chair, she's tall enough to reach the stove, and I can see her from my bed. I feel so helpless, unable to take care of her, be the good mom. Thank goodness she stays so cheerful. When she brings breakfast, I can only manage a few bites of muffin, since I can't sit up.

"Heidi, can you please bring me the phone before you leave for school?" She drags it over to the bed, its long red cord trailing across the grass-mat kitchen floor. A kiss goodbye, and she runs out the door so she won't miss the bus.

What shall I do? Tears leak into my ears and soak my matted hair. I feel so desperate. Can't even get to my Soma pain pills and a glass of water. I thought I was done with all this, nearly two months since my last episode, and two years since the crash. No warning. What did I do wrong this time?

I wait till I can't wait anymore, bladder demanding that I roll over and make my way to the bathroom, crying. Back in bed, I have to lie flat. To make a call, I prop the phone on my pulled-up legs, then dial. Awkward. But I've decided I definitely need help.

Fred answers the phone right away. "What's going on, JuJu?" He hears the angst in my voice immediately, picks up on my desperation, and agrees to come over in an hour, with his table, to work on me.

I'm actually nervous about this massage, never had a massage from a man. I start to shake. Fred and Cheryl are my close friends who started the local massage school, so I feel some trust. He knocks, even though he knows I can't get up. Within ten minutes, he puts logs on the fire, sets up the massage table, and is ready to work — but I can't get up. He tries to help. I resist, groan, and lie back down.

"I'm going to carry you."

Before I can object, he lifts me easily out of bed, carries me to the massage table set up in my kitchen. I feel vulnerable already. At this point I don't even care about the pain. No matter what happens, I'll deal with it.

I lie flat on my back, staring up at the kitchen ceiling, rough boards with layers of white paint and a tiny spider web I've not seen before. Fred begins by holding my hand to his heart, balancing energy, connecting. A part of me begins to let down, just a little. When he tries to turn my neck, check my range of motion, I freeze and start to scream. He applies pressure into my neck, thumb on vertebra. Tears... and then I'm there in my car, in the middle of it; I hear the squeal of brakes, see the large black pickup hurl toward me out of the long afternoon shadows. I feel the impact reverberate through my bones, hear metal crunch, echoes of glass shattering. Then I'm spinning around and the truck hits me again. I scream, out of my mind. Fred pushes, pulls me in all directions, and I lose track; he keeps me present, here, in my body, won't let me escape.

"Right here, Jude. Stay with me, right here, right now."

My whole body heaves, totally alive and present. Explosive pain rocks me. I hear my own voice yell, something about my mother, something about being pissed. It doesn't feel like me on the table, can't be me, bellowing, sobbing out a story of so much anger and sadness. My body continues to shake, and fight, resist. After nearly two hours I begin to give in.

I feel light, and strong currents of energy stream through my body, blood-red-orange, pulsing, flowing, all circuits ON. Then, waves of relief and peace wash over me, and I know I've surrendered to something unknown and much larger than myself.

Soft crying, a salty-sweet release, and suddenly I realize that I can turn my neck without pain.

Fred has one hand on my third eye and top of my head, the other on my heart. It's so peaceful in this moment; I want to stay forever. His compassion and loving care, and our hard work together, have opened a door I didn't know existed. Now I can begin to envision my path spreading out before me, drawing me forward toward the Light. The promised path, the one I was born to follow.

HOTEL, 1981

Last year I lucked out and met Theadora Van Runkle. She and her husband, Bruce, rescued an old hotel on the coast from its boring 1950s conversion to a residence. They lovingly restored it to a magnificence that far outdid its original turn-of-the-century charm. The Old Milano Hotel, a popular B&B destination, now appears on the National Historic Register. I walked into a job as "hostess"; I greet guests, serve breakfast, and arrange flowers grown in the chocolate-cake soil of its coastal gardens.

Thea and I become fast friends, a real soul connection, and I know that I've found a new home here. She asks me to care-take the hotel for the winter while she and Bruce are off to work. Heidi and I move in; spend the winter and spring trying out various rooms. The most glamorous is Thea's own suite. The large bed has a magic energy about it, hand-painted gold, Baroque, covered with garlands of flowers and ribbons of every color. Perhaps the feeling comes from the fact that the bed was featured in *Wuthering Heights*. When I sleep here, gazing out over the hydrangeas to Castle Rock, I feel like I'm in a movie. The room runs to the chilly, so we move upstairs to my sunny favorite, the Castle Rock room with its handsome mirrored armoire, desk, iron bedstead, and a sweet ocean view to the south. Mornings, I feel like a queen lying in bed under the puffy down quilt, basking in the winter sun. In exchange for the room, we keep the place heated and in order while it's closed for the winter; collect and answer mail, make room reservations, manage repairs, and prepare for the spring reopening.

Theadora's career as a Hollywood costume designer has taken off again, so now she's away on location much of the time. She asks me, basically, to run the place. The idea intimidates me. I can't imagine that I know enough, but am also intrigued. Bruce and Thea convince me to try it; they have faith in me, more than I have in myself — and it's working out. Whenever I can't figure out something, like tax issues or bookkeeping, I consult with Daniel, the new accountant, whom Thea allows me to hire. I learn so much it's like getting a college degree in hotel management, but more like a crash course, on location.

My close friend, Aurora, moves to the coast following a divorce, and soon works at the hotel as one of the innkeepers. As if there's not enough to do, what with replacing windows, gardening, maintaining the cliffside hot tub, and keeping up with the new season, Aurora has a brainstorm and launches a cheesecake business, baking out of the hotel kitchen in her off hours. We're having a ball and so are the guests.

For a few months, Aurora and I share a little cabin down the road from the hotel: Charming, funky, right on the bluff. We enjoy the views but feel hammered by the surf and wind. When we hear of a rental in "Enchanted Meadows" with sun and a decent-sized kitchen, loft, and large bedroom, we move there. We like being roommates; we cook fabulous gourmet meals together and deepen our friendship. Through the cold winter, we struggle with an inefficient fireplace and green firewood. We need bone-dry oak and madrone, redwood kindling, and some guy to split it and haul it into the house for us. When Aurora's boyfriend comes over, he helps. Otherwise we'd be stuck, making do with a lukewarm fire and two electric space heaters. How we long for good old-fashioned forced-air heat to warm us with the flick of a switch.

The house has the additional charm of an intriguing story attached to it. Theodora Kroeber, author of *Ishi in Two Worlds,* lived here in her old age. She's the mother of writer Ursula Le Guin, but that's not the best part. The house, so the story goes, was designed and built by Theodora's lover when he was in his late thirties — and she was nearly eighty! I lie in my loft bedroom, gaze through the railing to the distant ocean, and with my 20/40 vision I see whales breach in the blue water. Did the couple make love in the middle of the afternoon on the sun-warmed window seat? Daydreams of Theodora Kroeber and her husband/lover keep me enchanted as I imagine their romantic life in this house: he, padding downstairs in sheepskin slippers to bring her coffee, toast, and blackberry jam in bed, on a tray. Their little love nest. If only it were mine.

I feel settled and confident with my hotel manager's job, best-friend roommate, and comfortable house. Nothing can rattle me. I've got it made.

THE LETTER

One freezing-cold February day, a letter that really shakes me shows up in the mail. The postmark, St. Helena, CA. The green-ink return address displays a name from my distant past: Blake. I can't breathe! How in the world did he find me? I can't even open it; have to wait till I'm at home with Aurora just to read it. I can't face this alone.

The letter explains how he found me: Ran into a mutual friend from college who told him where I live. Page 1 starts out all about him, where he's been and what he's done for the past sixteen years. Currently, he lives at a meditation center just two hours from here. How weird, so close. By page 2, the letter takes a sharp turn, and I'm riveted by its implications.

I know on some level that we are not responsible for what we do—that we are not the doer. That God is the doer, but I find I am still feeling I was responsible for your injuries in Rochester, New York. It was my intention by giving you marijuana to seduce, to loosen your will so that I could have sex with you. I feel very bad about that. I was being abusive and hiding the truth from you. If I wanted to have sex with you, I just should have told you, and if you said no, what I should have done was accept that that was your wish. I truly apologize for trying to take advantage of you.

When I was driving away the night I left you at Dan's apartment, at about six miles away, I felt something horrible. It was as if you asked me, in my mind, if it was all right to go out the window, and I said yes, it was. I didn't know you were talking (thinking) about your body, I thought you meant you in some subtle form, like astral body. I said yes. Then I felt something horrible, that some catastrophe or disaster, something horrible had happened. Then I turned the car around and started to drive back to where I had left you. I heard the ambulance siren, or police, or fire, I didn't know what. When I got back, there were many people, a crowd; I was still sort of stoned. I started to walk through.

I saw police and then I saw you (your body) lying on the ground. I didn't know what had happened. I thought you might be dead. I *thought, if I talked to the police I'd make things worse, so I left. I called a friend. He said I should be still and he'd do what he could. I thought or knew he could pray. I felt that somehow I made that happen (the accident). If not indirectly by giving you the marijuana, then directly by thinking, "It's OK to go out the window."*

If you see the event as something that wasn't caused by me, would you write? And if you did go out the window because of some thought you felt you heard from me, would you write that? I've wanted to talk about this with you for a long time. It's good to make a little contact with you after all this time.

Holy Shit! I sit stunned, reviewing, try to understand what I read. It's so strange, because what he says makes sense to me, perfect sense. I did hear a voice in my head, telling me "Yes, it's okay to go out the window." I never imagined it could actually have been someone else's voice answering a stoned question in my head. And here Blake's telling me things only he could know, like the other side of that conversation.

I read the letter over and over, still in shock. There's no way I can write to him. I wouldn't know what to say. Tell him, "It's fine, don't worry about it. No problem"? I'm not ready for that.

Three months later, I get a phone call. "Did you get my letter?"

Oh, well, my number is listed in the phone book. I've ignored the whole thing, trying to forget Blake's letter. Can I forgive him? Do I even want to talk about it? I reluctantly agree to meet him at the ashram. Maybe I can put all this to rest.

RECONCILIATION

My teeth clench as I maneuver the hilly curves, headed toward Napa Valley. Images of seventeen years ago flash through my mind. I remember sketches of our conversation several days earlier, and phrases from Blake's very disturbing letter. How dare he show up after all this time! At the next curve I panic as a midnight-blue Jaguar screeches toward me, crosses the centerline of the narrow mountain road, and forces my car into a gravelly pullout. Heart racing, limbs trembling, I burst into tears. For the first time, I allow myself to weep, grieve, for the deception, the pain, all of it. What the hell am I doing now? Why did I agree to see him? I must be crazy!

In Calistoga, I turn south onto Highway 29 and finally relax a bit, roll down the window of my '60s yellow Plymouth Valiant and let my body unwind, feel the warm sun across my arm and face. Ah, there it is, Warm Springs Road. Probably named after an old hot spring, long abandoned, replaced by truck farms and orchards. My destination. What to expect? I have to let go, out of my hands now. After all, I decided to meet him.

The road narrows to one-lane dirt, a grass ribbon down the middle. Ahead I see several white buildings, willow trees, and a small parking area with three or four cars. A few residents, dressed in white muslin with ties at the waist, roam the grounds. I sit for a moment to catch my breath, calm my jittery mind, prepare. I spot Blake walking toward me and recognize him right away. His face seems serene, lacking expression. Immediately though, I feel his intensity beneath the shroud of white he wears, his guise of peace. At closer range, I remember his eyes, soft yet penetrating, subtle half-smile and neutral good looks. Innocent, harmless, and I remember how I was drawn in.

"Hi, Judy," he says tentatively. "Did you have trouble finding us? The compound I mean."

"No, it was easy. Good directions. It seems so far out here, but

I went slow so I wouldn't kick up lots of dust."

"Yes, quite a ways. I haven't left the property in a few months. I tend to forget. So good to see you."

I reach out to make some kind of contact, old habit I guess. He quickly holds up his hand and steps back, like a Tai Chi move. "We don't touch here."

Relief floods in. At least there's a boundary, and, we're standing in a public meeting place. "Judy, how are you? Let's walk out past the temple so we can talk."

I feel oddly angry, want to turn time around and go back home, before the letter came. I had made my peace with the whole mess years ago, and even though questions remained, I didn't need Blake to answer them. With my peace broken, I wonder just exactly why I'm here. Can I truly forgive him, acknowledge what happened and move on? That's what I want. Now I'll find out what he wants. For me to relieve his guilt?

The sun is hot on the open part of the road as we move away from the big barn, past the dormitory buildings and large garden, out toward a small hayfield.

"It's the rule," he explains, "about not touching. This means we can let all those physical feelings go and feel safe in our work — you know, the enlightenment."

"I'm here about the letter, what you said about causing the accident. Why now? Why are you telling me this now, after seventeen years?"

Silence. We walk a bit, light breeze blowing in the space between us. "I just want to come clean about what happened, to clear the karma between us. And I am sorry. I need your forgiveness to move on from this."

I stop and look at him, standing there in the dust, pleading eyes dulled by years of practice at detachment. Overcome and confused, I start to cry; want closure, yet feel like punching him at the same time.

"Yes," I manage, "I too want to move on."

"And then there's that time I hit you. I shouldn't have done that...."

His words sting like sand in a windstorm, nearly as startling as the day he hauled off and slapped me in the face so hard I fell off the chair and briefly passed out.

"Somehow I'd managed to forget," I say slowly, trying to control the movie that flashes in my mind. "Now I remember."

"I am sorry about that. It wasn't my place, and I hope you'll forgive me."

We continue slowly down the dirt road, dry grasses wave and shimmer golden on the hillside. His short bursts of explanation punctuate the quiet.

"But why? I mean, why did you hit me? Let's start there."

Silence, as he processes the answer before delivering it.

"You were falling asleep. Gurdjieff says everyone is asleep. I was trying to help you wake up."

I remember our meeting at my apartment after class one muggy spring afternoon. He had brought a new Gurdjieff book and was reading aloud to me, wanting me to understand, be excited about "the Path" to Nirvana. I was exhausted, had been up late to finish my Journeyman's Piece for school and could barely listen or follow the sentences of this longwinded philosopher. I felt both mesmerized and completely bored.

WHAM! Everything went black. In one split second I crashed to the floor. Then, I'm holding my jaw and looking up into his dispassionate face in disbelief. It comes back as clearly as if it happened last week.

"I remember now. It just didn't make any sense."

In the end, I do forgive him. He meant no harm, that's the bottom line. It's hard to imagine Blake being hung up on his guilt for over a decade and a half. I disconnect and say goodbye. How fascinating. Not only is the future unknowable but even the past turns out a surprise.

X

Healing and Building

1981–1991

JUST COOKING

Managing the Old Milano Hotel absorbs most of my time. I've worked out a system whereby four innkeepers alternate shifts, including overnights, and I don't need to live there. This gives me a Monday through Friday day job, and I'm still available as full-time Mom, free most evenings and weekends. Sometimes, Heidi and I take our turn at a hotel shift, sleep together in the alcove's double bed behind the kitchen, get up early, put on the first round of local Thanksgiving coffee for the guests. I enjoy juggling the schedule and working with a collective of women who cook, garden, greet and serve our guests. Work and fun. We like one another and communicate well, makes the job so easy.

One of the innkeepers, my friend Cheryl, is the wife of Fred, who helped me heal after my auto accident. When they first arrived in the community, in 1980, we met at musical theater workshop. Fred and I danced together; he played the street sweeper, and I, Eliza Doolittle, nervously singing *Wouldn't It Be Loverly.* Cheryl and Fred tangoed in a sexy scene from *Hernando's Hideaway.* Through rehearsals, performances, and potluck get-togethers, the three of us began to hang out and became good friends.

That year they pulled a trailer onto their newly acquired acreage on the ridge. Already they had established the Pacific School of Massage and Healing Arts, and transferred their school from Marin to the north coast. They hold the first session of the 110-hour training at the nearby "Re-Newell Center," and twelve local students attend. Cooks are needed to prepare the gourmet vegetarian fare for the weeklong sessions. From my days at the Natural Food Store, I reconnect with Ananda, Shiatsu healer and good cook. I recommend her and jump in to assist, for some extra money and the pure fun of it. The tasty vegetarian meals include dishes like my old favorite, Walnut Cheddar Loaf, from *Diet for a Small Planet;* Rice Italiano, with veggies and cashews; Tofu Supreme for brunch, with its aromas of sautéed onions,

235

garlic, mushrooms, sweet basil, and paprika; Diamond Sutra Carrot Cake, a recipe lifted from the popular '60s restaurant in the Haight. Our meals become a big hit, and we love sharing our creative talents.

I recall the exact day: resting after lunch cleanup, I felt a pang of jealousy, like a child on the playground left out of the game. I wished right then I could join the students, many whom were friends, in the large sunny living room for an intimate afternoon session of deep bodywork and inner growth — Fred's approach to massage. I promised myself I would talk to him about my attraction to this alluring work that had helped me heal.

Summer session draws to a close. One hot breezy afternoon, I stop by Fred's for a chat. We sit in deck chairs with icy-cold mint tea, on their deck outside the trailer. I ruminated for a while about attending massage school and feel compelled to bring it up with him, satisfy my longing and curiosity about the whole thing.

Massage School, Fall 1982

"I worry about my hands, Fred. I mean, I like giving a massage, like a good shoulder rub, but then my hands ache and give out after just ten or fifteen minutes. How would that work? Maybe I'm just not cut out for it."

"Don't concern yourself about that, JuJu. I can teach you to massage for an hour and a half without feeling tired, and besides, you'll have more energy than when you started, ready to do another one." Fred sits back, eyes me, a knowing grin plays at the corners of his mouth.

"Really? Seems impossible, but okay, if you say so. Honestly, I'm attracted to the work from my sessions with you and spending time with your students. They seem so open, and different in some deep way, after just a few days at school. I can't explain; I just wish I were part of it, instead of doing the cooking. I think I feel a little jealous."

"I get that. So... how about signing up for the fall session, starting in October?" Fred throws out this tantalizing offer like he's one step ahead of me.

I hadn't anticipated this development. My questions were intended to explore future possibilities, dabble in dreams, a distant fantasy. The big holdup, no mystery here: money. I see no way to spare either that much income or the time involved to study, practice, and attend the weeks of classes.

"Just don't have the money, Fred," I say, disappointed, embarrassed. "I manage my rent these days thanks to my Old Milano job and Theadora. This part-time job, cooking for massage school, makes up the difference. Besides, Heidi needs me — I can't be gone for days at a time. Single mom, you know."

"If you want to learn massage, or anything else for that matter, JuJu, it's possible. Part of your paycheck for cooking could go into a trade account. Of course, you decide. And then, there's 'slash and burn.'"

That's our code term for the work of clearing portions of their property to make space for Fred and Cheryl's ever-evolving visions: below the house, an expanse of meadow will flow down to a pool, amphitheater, and hot tub. The possibilities are endless, with stately rings of third-growth redwoods, blue-water ocean views, and a magical sunny ridge location.

The drill for clearing the land goes like this: Fred and I meet for coffee around 8:00, just after Heidi catches the school bus. I pull on my Levis, then an old pair of hiking boots, thick and protective, and long-sleeved work shirt, wrap my hair in a blue bandana, and grab a pair of well-worn leather work gloves. We attack the edges of the meadow. By 11:00 we've piled together enough slash for a fire: Piles of manzanita branches, dead oak limbs, whole young trees, blackberries, creosote bush, scotch broom. Mostly, we leave the huckleberries alone, allow them to rim the meadow in a bonsai thicket with exposed rocks and small trees. Fred is the visionary when it comes to sculpting the landscape. Their home site takes shape, dreams become manifest. I love the small part I play, and start to believe that I too can create my dreams.

Fall approaches and my credit account swells like a ripening pumpkin. Fred and Cheryl receive notice that the Re-Newell Center, where they held massage school, is no longer available. With their house and classroom still under construction, they must find a new facility immediately.

"Fred, I have a crazy idea about school, and I think it'll work," I suggest. "This October's session begins just after tourist season ends; school starts on a Sunday and ends Friday after lunch, right? I could close off guest reservations for the two weeks of massage school, and you could take over the hotel! Picture this: Group meetings and classes in the wine parlor; six massage tables set up in the William Morris living room; lunch out back on the loggia at the edge of the garden. Enough rooms for all the students to stay right in the hotel, including me. Ocean-view hot tub. Transformation. All with Theadora's approval, of course. What do you think?"

"I love it, JuJu. Brilliant! Let's do it."

Theadora agrees to our idea, and with a bit of logistics, Fred and I set the plan. We do a hotel walk-through and mock up the week's session: students will arrive on the tails of relaxed hotel guests departing.

Suddenly, it's October, Sunday noon, and it's all happening. Lavender-scented sheets fly onto freshly made beds. In the kitchen, the Innkeeper and crew madly wash the breakfast dishes, while Terry, our cook, chops veggies for a gigantic salad to accompany the garden-fresh herbed tomato soup and warm bread for lunch.

During the hour of final transition from hotel to massage school, Fred and I scurry around; move overstuffed sofas into a cozy, but wider, semicircle around the stone fireplace, to allow for all twelve students, plus Fred and Cheryl, to gather. Six massage tables are set up in the "parlor," fitted with pastel flannel sheets, with just enough room to move around. We finalize the timing for lunch, and Fred double-checks the list to make sure everyone has arrived.

Early that morning, before 8:00, I had hauled my suitcase upstairs to the "Madame Butterfly" room, number six. I felt much too nervous to unpack, flitting about like a mother swallow, keeping track of every detail of the changeover to make it perfect. Front gate locked. Check. Ready to go.

"Relax, Jude, it's time for the class to gather. You can let go now; you're not in charge. You're a student, remember?"

A single tone of the small Tibetan brass cymbal hangs in the air, seems to absorb the excess energy. Stillness. And again. By the third ring, my fellow students and I wander in from the guest rooms and assemble in "circle."

"Great digs!" sings out Andy, the lanky cute one with sandy brown hair, engaging eyes. Jan and Diane, sisters sharing a room and queen-size bed, giggle; the younger claims our B&B is more like a resort than a school. We look around shyly, check each other out like kindergarteners, nervous, wondering, excited.

After Fred gives an inspiring demonstration of foot massage, it's our turn. We partner up; one lies on the table, one prepares for "hands on."

"Don't worry, I'll talk you through it," Fred assures us, confirming our nervousness as total beginners. "First, center yourself, feel that connection to the earth; visualize the muscles and structures in your mind's eye, like the charts we looked at earlier. Picture the Achilles tendon running up the back of the leg from the heel. Now, lightly grasp the foot, right hand on top, left hand cradling the ankle and heel. Listen... and trust yourself. Now, I'll guide you."

Only two hours earlier, we'd met for the first time as a group. Now I'm flat on my back in my Jockey cotton bikinis, which I refuse to remove, covered with a light flannel sheet, a strange man flexing my foot and rubbing my toes. This is weird! Soft background music begins to take the edge off. When I peer around at the other tables, I see that everyone is focused, listening, trying to get the moves right, and by the end of the hour, when it's my turn to work, I feel relaxed, relieved, and my feet feel so good I could dance all night.

By Monday dinner, after a long day of anatomy lessons, discussions, the amazing demonstration by Fred, and back-to-back sessions of neck and shoulder massage, we all find ourselves giddy and pleased, having uncovered some natural abilities and confidence. As a group, we seem compatible, with enough variety and eccentricity to prove interesting. At thirty-eight, I'm third from the oldest, yet have no specific career plans or ambitions; I'm following my instinct, an inner voice that says, "Go for it." Who knows where it will lead? Maybe some extra income, good connections with friends, a trade for eggs or firewood, a better life for my daughter and me. Still, I search for my "passion," that mysterious something, my own special talent, purpose, place in the larger scheme of life. Could this be it?

Each day I can't wait to climb out of my luxurious feather-bed nest, splash cold water on my face, pull on thick sweats and a tee shirt, traipse downstairs to pour a cup of fresh-brewed coffee, and hang out with my new friends before we formally begin our day at 9:00. And each night, at 10:30 or 11:00, so exhausted I can barely brush my teeth and pull on my nightgown before collapsing, I whisper thank you. Thank you to the stars, the rolling sea, and my angels who brought me right here, right now to this place where I am meant to be.

THE RECIPE

Dawn, around 6:30, last day of week one, massage school. Barely discernible light creeps in through antique lace curtains and the slumped glass of the hotel's original double-hung windows. I hear a soft rustle, then a metallic click of the loose brass doorknob of my cozy bedroom. My heart picks up its rhythm, accompanied by a hot rush of adrenalin. With minimal movement, I shift under the down quilt to face the door, my head half-covered and vulnerable. The door now stands ajar, exposing the hall window with its white ruffled curtain puffed out, moving as if blown by a sudden gust of ocean breeze.

Bert! Oh my God, it's Big Bert! The thought flies into my head, like I knew it instantly. Bert Luchinetti, the Milano's builder and resident ghost who can't seem to let go, is visiting me. Calm spreads through my rigid limbs like lavender balm, releasing any fears I harbor of attack. After all, he's proven to be completely harmless, and I'm not afraid of ghosts. For the next half-hour, I lay in bed, propped up by a mountain of soft pillows, and gaze out at the sea as dawn light catches the tips of waves. I mentally review the numerous tales of Bert's cavorting in and out of upstairs windows, startling the hotel's female guests — always, and only, the women. He especially had a thing for redheads, and has approached our feisty innkeeper, Jennifer, "with the hair like fire," several times, according to her. One time, in the downstairs parlor, Aurora and I were talking about him, recounting the tall tales and myths. All of a sudden, our aprons flew up like laundry on a line, whipped up in a gust of south wind. We chuckled over that one, both of us sure that Bert was making his presence known. Though I can't claim to have actually seen him, I know he was at my door that morning.

On the last day, our class faces a challenge: a final practical exam. We quickly breakfast on fruit, granola, and coffee, knowing we won't eat again till lunch. At 8:00 we meet on the front lawn with Cheryl for tai chi, to wake up, ground ourselves, and settle into our bodies. At 8:30, a half-hour of silent meditation, and at 9:00 we gather to focus on our last sessions of the week. The assignment: Give an eighty-minute full-body massage with all the trimmings, as per our "recipe." Performance anxiety settles in, and we channel inner guidance to help with our newfound skill.

Throughout the week, each day had focused on a different area of the body. We assemble our recipe, which lists the moves and strokes and their sequences; we feel ecstatic, as if we made the whole thing up. Such unique terms! No one else would have a clue as to what we're talking about. The recipe goes like this:

Prepare: Cross-crawl; ground, run energy, set intention.

Begin: Tuck in top blanket; head, hand, and foot contact with symmetry; head rock/neck stretch.

Face, neck, arms: Face press; double thumb walk; forearm Fisher stroke; hand-finger teepee; arm cradle bicep-triceps, scapula crawl; lat spread, compression stroke; sternum pivot; Heart to Heart. Repeat left.

Torso: Trapezius thumb press; feather spread, spine drag; shoulder shake; clavicle dive; waist pull, torso rock.

Legs and feet: Jin Shin Safety Energy Lock Number One; foot, ankle, calf, and double Fisher stroke; thumb-cross kneegasm; infinity thigh stroke; gluteus medius and maximus; integration shakeout. Repeat left.

Backside: Backstroke (swimming); trapezius flare; spinal focus; fist push, arm turn, elbow fall; railroad tracks down the spine, finger flare, pull up.

Finish: polarity rock, chakra swirl, body balance, body brush; tai chi aura sweep. Blessings, and Gratitude.

Wow! Can I really remember all that, plus what the terms actually mean? Fred claims it's all in our hands; the knowledge lives in the body, its wisdom. The recipe spoken aloud sounds more like a Beat poem than a plan for massage, takes on a rhythm like a conga drum, and soon we're laughing, sing it out and put it all together.

Thursday evening, Fred demonstrates, gives Cheryl a magnificent session for our viewing, choreographed like a ballet by a tai chi master. His moves are smooth and strong, arm over arm; he caresses, reaches deep into her muscles and tissues, creates pathways for energy to move, flow, and release. Fragrant lavender oil glistens like satin on her light amber, smooth-as-silk skin. Fred and Cheryl create a sacred space that inspires us to be our best, aspire to the highest level of healing.

And then we're the ones massaging, swimming in the river, healing energy pouring out of our hands, bodies imbued with focused life force, giving out what we have taken in and sought to learn. Truly magical.

Friday afternoon, after a gourmet lunch of tabouli, spicy falafel, and mixed green salad, we join hands in a circle on the freshly cut lawn of the Milano. We stand firm, observe the way the grass sweeps down to the cliff's edge, the sea rolling in and out, energized, with each stroke of the tide. We feel heady, infused with clean salty air; our bare feet draw up courage from Mother Earth. We vibrate with the eager anticipation of our upcoming four weeks of practice and study before we meet again. Astonishing. In only one week of intensive study, 9:00 a.m. to 10:00 p.m. each day, we've learned to give a full-body therapeutic massage. Not just a good one but "the best massage I've ever had!" Beyond the basic treatment, we experienced the giving and receiving of nurturing, compassionate touch. Now, we are privileged to go out into our communities and offer our talents as facilitators of healing.

Each morning, toes and heels planted on the wet spongy grass, we've met, practiced tai chi, balancing, centering. We open our hands and hearts to receive, and then give; feel the energies of heaven and earth meet within the temple of our own bodies. We are ready, having collected that energy, to take it on the road.

Tears of gratitude stream down my cheeks. Clear eye contact and warm hugs cement our connection with each other. This group bond feels new, yet ancient, deep and enduring. Surprising, even shocking, in its breadth. I imagine I will know these people, deeply know them, forever.

LEARNING TO BUILD

Home, such a precious concept. My teenage daughter and I still share the cozy two-bedroom rental where we've lived since 1982. As I water its blue hydrangeas and apricot trees, weed-eat the yard, and grow cherry tomatoes, I wonder how one day a place like this could be mine. Though I feel grateful for this sweet house, my heart isn't here. I'm stuck. Do I still wait for the right man to build my dream house with? Is that Warren, my "significant other," who lives two blocks away? We still choose to live separately, spend a few nights a week together. Our arrangement means no strings attached; so comfortable, and yet my dream remains unfulfilled.

Over nearly five years, we've happily designed and built three spec houses. Warren is a master builder and talented craftsman. Under his tutelage, I've learned the ins and outs of construction; together we created two gorgeous houses, and they sold easily. A third is in the works. This process engages two parts of me: the creative artist and the organizer.

I design from the inside out. It's all about the flow, how people move from room to room, relax, prepare and share meals, relate, need privacy — every aspect of daily life. Light, the most important consideration: Sunrise, windows, views. In my vision, when I sit by the fire or at the kitchen table, I want to look out arching windows that frame blue-water views, light dancing on wave tops, or a slip of canyon. Sunset. The upstairs could feel like a tree house, tips of firs and redwoods sway like giant feathers, catch the final rose-gold rays and fly around in the fury of winter storms. All the while, I'd snuggle up, safe and cozy in my second-floor nest, looking out in three directions.

Each time Warren and I design a house, I fantasize. This one's mine, I live here. When I draw floor plans, place doors and windows, I imagine that I stand in the space, look around, feel the proportions as right. Envisioning how the furniture will fit, I make tiny scale cutouts from manila folders and move them around the plan: beds, dining table, chairs, TV, couches, dressers, even the fireplace. I mentally play house.

Warren built homes for many years before we met and developed a refined aesthetic. When I was growing up, Mom remodeled our entire house, and I observed every detail of the process. All those rentals since college — probably over twenty — I loved to pretend they were mine and I could fix and change them into something magical. With Warren's projects, I assist in several aspects of construction: Product research, price comparison, ordering. I learn about building codes, framing, and foundations. So many choices at every turn.

We work well together, a balanced team, and rarely argue. Warren has the final word on everything, with me the eager volunteer. I sketch and draw, then he drafts the final plans, visualizes the building as a whole, considering the outside first. Workers dig trenches, place rebar, and pour cement. Footings, piers, girders, joists, I learn all the terms. Meanwhile, I order materials. With only one or two helpers, Warren frames the house in a month. Just two months before, we had cleared and prepared the land. All so fast! What a complex process.

Midwinter, and interior finish work nears completion. Warren hires my good friend, Victoria, to paint the walls. I show up too, fill every single nail hole in the pine window and door trim. By spring, after eight months, the house is ready for market. We stage the rooms with some of my family's antique furniture, fill the place with bouquets of fragrant roses and wild azaleas, and put on a charming open house. Within a month, a full-price offer comes in. Now we believe that the realtor's "priced to sell" listing amount was set too low. Still, we feel excited and already plan our next project: remodeling an in-town office space into a healing center.

With building, Warren and I can communicate, commit to a goal and manifest that goal. My longtime dream has been to create a center where several practitioners could work together, offering various "alternative" healing modalities. One day I spot a FOR RENT sign upstairs at Whale Point Landing in Gualala, and suddenly the dream comes together. Within a week I sign a lease and start to design two treatment rooms, an office, and waiting room. Ocean views add to the mood; waves breaking on the beach provide a restful backdrop. I draw the plan and Warren builds it. My artist friend, Diane, creates gorgeous sky-blue-with-clouds faux-painted walls. The result, the Healing Arts and Massage Center. In December 1988 we officially open, and my new professional life begins

My love relationship with Warren, however, remains tenuous, our history laced with fears, failures, and the need to protect vulnerable hearts. After five years, with no plans of a future and no commitments, things fall apart. Warren moves on. Eventually I will feel lucky, no longer stuck in a relationship that's going nowhere and lacks the validation of love. Then, maybe I can see our parting as the right thing. But for now, it just hurts.

THE MOVE

Sixty-two East Main Street, Cobleskill, New York, my home for twenty years. My parents have spent forty-five years in the same house, the 1840s fixer-upper they bought in 1945 when I turned one. Its gardens, chicken coop, carriage house, and apple trees reminded Dad of his childhood farm life in Iowa. Amazing, when I think of all the work they put into that house over the years — no hired hands, all Dad's own labor. Mom designed, and together they covered every square inch, from scraping off layers of stained wallpaper, to pasting up and rolling on the new Williamsburg patterns. I was there, handing wet rolls up to Dad on the ladder. Mom ordered the furnishings, and of course designed the kitchen.

Most projects happened on Saturdays, one room at a time, in the good weather, so doors could be propped open, paint venting. When the inside was complete, Dad started on the outside — scrape, sand, climb, paint. Thinking back, it's hard to imagine how one person could do almost everything, plus go to work and take care of Mom and me. A magician and a saint.

It's 1990, and Dad's having a tough time. His prostate surgery left him weak and tired. But mostly, it's about Mom: She requires more and more care, can't stand up alone, get to the bathroom, or take a shower. Dad can barely lift her. And the house isn't set up properly; the bedrooms and the only shower are upstairs. Mom's mostly lived in the converted dining room for twelve years. So in June, when Dad calls to say it's finally happening, they're moving to Greencroft, a senior community in Indiana, I'm not surprised. I feel unexpectedly sad, deflated, like I didn't see it coming.

"Great, Dad, definitely a good plan for you. So now, Mom's finally agreeing? I know you've had your name on the Greencroft list for about three years, right? And you even turned down a place that was available last year."

"Yes — and yes, you're right, she's giving in. It's too much here, with the big house to keep up, the book business, and in the winter..." He falters, overwhelmed just to think of it all. "I can't get enough help for her. Even your mom agrees it's time. At Greencroft we can get all our meals, or just dinner, at a nice dining room right down the hallway from our apartment. We'll have a full kitchen too, and someone available whenever we need help." He sounds wistful, like he's describing a vacation rental, seeing a peaceful environment. "Then, when she needs more care, we'll be close to their full-care nursing unit."

"Sounds good, Dad, the right thing. You've needed this for a long time; you would have moved to Greencroft years ago but for Mom's resistance. Perfect, near your brothers and sisters who live in Goshen."

"Right... but the move seems daunting. So much stuff! Our collections, the books, the shop. Your cousin George and his wife Debbie will take many of the antiques on consignment, to sell for me — "

I interrupt. "Dad, I'm coming to help, you know; a lot of decisions to make. Let's think about this and make a plan."

My dad, the organizer. He'd already figured it out long before this phone conversation, this moment of telling me his decision. He'll arrange an auction and some private sales. Cousin George will hand pick what he wants for his antique business.

"Judith," Dad says, almost apologetically, "you know you have first choice, you can have whatever you want. Make a list and send it."

"Never mind that, Dad, I'll be there soon enough. Then I'll choose some things, and help you sort, pack whatever you need. When will you move? Is your house for sale yet? When will the apartment be ready?"

I imagine a few months, maybe moving in late fall, plenty of time to plan. But he says early August, less than two months away, and right before the '89 Fisher family reunion, which happens every three years. My mind races with jumbled ideas, dates and plans. My partner at Healing Arts can cover for me. I think I'll need two to three weeks off to do it all — sort through forty-five years of their life, and mine; pick and choose for his apartment and my house.

So here's the plan: Before I arrive in Cobleskill, Mom will be moved to Greencroft with a nurse, by train, to the nursing unit until Dad arrives and gets settled. Mayflower movers will pack up everything and meet us in Indiana. Meanwhile, the two of us will stuff his station wagon with precious valuables plus our two suitcases, and drive to Indiana.

When I arrive on August 1, chaos reigns everywhere except for two upstairs bedrooms where we'll sleep. The kitchen is Grand Central. We sit at the round black table, make lists and phone calls, watch the news, eat our meals. We visit each room together, label furniture, paintings, and photographs, antiques to be sent out to California. The pine jelly cupboard and its contents, including the white Wedgwood china from childhood holidays, will now be mine. So many treasures, and not enough room.

A few weeks before I arrive, Dad sends me the floor plan of his new abode. We've talked on the phone about what he'll be able to fit in the smallish apartment and what must be auctioned off and sold, and then, what he must give up — to me, that is. My memory of each piece of furniture helps to clarify a good lay-out, and so I propose a plan that includes many of their favorite antiques. Dad loves it.

During our enormous undertaking — boxing and sorting — he becomes talkative, chatty almost, tells stories I've not heard about growing up on the farm in Iowa. Anticipation of his new life in Indiana slips in. I think this change will provide great relief from his role as primary caregiver, and will offer comforting connections to his new community as well as the family he has missed.

Our drive takes us straight across New York State on the thruway. Then we angle southwest to Cleveland, where we check into a Best Western motel. When we call Aunt Mabel, we learn that Dad's sister-in-law, Aunt Evie, has died rather suddenly. The funeral is Saturday, in Iowa. How can we handle it all? Another day's drive lands us in Indiana. The rest of the week turns into a whirlwind of activity: meet the van at the apartment (the movers conveniently place each piece of furniture); quick visits with relatives for dinner; drive to the family reunion Friday afternoon, then get up early and drive several hours to Iowa for Evie's funeral.

The simple white Mennonite church stands on a corner, surrounded mostly by cornfields; the crops, now tall and tasseled, billow in the hot summer wind. I have visited this church only twice, though Dad was raised here and his father was the preacher. We barely reach Kalona in time for the service, ushered into a pew a couple of rows behind Uncle Wally and their kids, my cousins, and the grandchildren. Family connections feel so strong. I'm already crying as I make eye contact with Aunt Evie's daughter, Gretchen, whom I love and haven't seen for several years. The day is muggy, sweltering hot, and the large side windows of the church tilt open to allow a breeze.

As the service begins, the sun suddenly disappears, displaced by blackening clouds. The breeze becomes a gale, flutters the programs clutched in people's tense hands; relatives nervously look at each other at the close of a hymn. Thunder, lightning. Wind whistles through doors and shutters, and starts to compete with the minister's words of comfort and promise. Then, the rain—sheets of it. We look at one another in disbelief. What's happening? This feels crazy! Gretchen and I lock eyes, connect; both of us know that something else is going on, some other energy is with us. All this is nonverbal, of course. Bright flashes of lightning, followed, one second later, by loud thunderclaps.

Silence. In that still space, the sweet, innocent voice of Aunt Evie's granddaughter rings out: "Grandma's gone up to heaven."

The storm passes, it seems. The service continues, but the energy in that room feels charged. Hushed whispers, inattention; each of us wonders what has just transpired. Soon the family and parishioners file out through double doors into bright sunshine.

The only evidence of the storm rests in the occasional puddle, full from the brief downpour, and leftover gusts ruffling skirts. On the corner opposite the church sits the cemetery, where several cousins wield shovels to finish the task of preparing the grave. Gretchen joins her brothers. I can't remember ever attending a burial, though I probably did when my grandma died thirty years ago. Something about seeing that rectangular hole in the ground, her children digging, makes my heart shudder. I feel so much compassion for Gretchen and her siblings, and Uncle Wally — what they have to go through right now. How does one prepare for losing a mother, a wife, a sister? The heartache, the stark realization that they are gone. We gather around, toss flowers first, then dirt on top of the casket. Suddenly, out of a swirling cornfield, a whirlwind lifts the white tent right off her grave and flings it into the air. The memory of this day feels both sad and rich, blessed with so much love within this family.

The next day, Sunday, most of the family meets back at the reunion camp for a few more hours together before we head off in all directions. Dad and I, Aunt Mabel, and Linda drive the few hours back to Indiana. Whew! So much driving! Tomorrow I'll visit Mom in the nursing unit, see how she's doing. Dad hopes to get unpacked this week, and maybe get set up for Mom to move into the apartment. I'll head back to California. I worry about Dad, and hope it won't be like the last thirteen years, him caring for her every day, never getting any rest, or even a good night's sleep. At least they've come to Greencroft — life's bound to be uphill from here.

LAST VISIT

She lies still, breathing softly. Small teddy bears and other stuffed animals sit on a shelf behind her bed. A green-and-white crocheted afghan partially covers her small bony frame behind the aluminum side rails. Nearly a year has passed since I saw Mom. Her anger can't touch me now, shaken out of her thirteen years before, in weeks of seizures, cleansing her of its poison, releasing the bitter blame.

A hot flush passes through me, seeing the stroke's damage, her silent life without a voice, yet without conflict for over a decade now. Peaceful. I sit with her; reflect on our lives together, the difficulties, and before that, our close connection. After half an hour or so, she stirs and rolls over, opening her sea-blue eyes, immediately engaging mine.

I reach through the bars of the bed, touch her shoulder. She fumbles for the controls. Slowly I help her, raise the bed so she can sit up.

"Hi, Mom, it's me, Judy."

Eyes brighten, staring into mine. Recognition — fading — then returning.

She nods, no longer tries to speak. She knows who I am.

LOSSES

March 1990, a landmark year of celebrations, endings, and beginnings. Mom will turn eighty on March 20, and Heidi flourishes in her senior year at Castilleja High School, loving dorm life. College is secure with acceptance at UC Santa Cruz, a partial scholarship and Pell Grant. We plan for her graduation, two months hence, with a trip to search for the perfect white dress for the ceremony. Planning for the busy graduation weekend takes my mind off the sting of my personal heartache — Warren has left me, moved on to a new relationship. We've been together five years, and now, so quickly, it's over.

In the midst of my crying binges and full-time work, my friend Beth dies from an aggressive leukemia. Aurora, and Beth's daughter, Nancy, are staying here for the weekend memorial. Early Sunday morning, I lie in bed, sad and upset, and wrestle with my feelings about losing Warren. When the phone rings, I get a sinking feeling. No one calls me this early.

"Hello," I manage, agitated, groggy from crying. "Who's calling?"

"Judith... hi. It's your dad." His hoarse voice betrays his anguish. "Your mother — she's gone. This morning. She slipped away, they said, around 5:30 when they went to check her vitals." He chokes up, can't really talk for a minute.

My throat tightens, a sob stuck there. I can hardly breathe, much less talk, but I have to pull it together. We sit, silent, thousands of miles apart. Then, "Oh, Dad, I'm so very sorry. They called you then? What did they say?"

"She died in her sleep, just stopped breathing. I went right over, of course, and sat with her for a while." He stops, can't go on. "Then, about seven, I called Mabel, Ginny, Bob, and Rachel. They all came over right away. Mabel's here now."

"Dad, I'm so glad you're not alone. I'll make arrangements to come to Goshen, as soon as I can get a flight. Hopefully, I can leave tomorrow." My brain launches into planning mode. I must leave Monday. Aurora's here, and I know I'm not fit to drive, so maybe she can give me a ride.

"Rachel says she'll help plan the memorial. She's a minister, remember? But I'll wait for you to meet with the people at the funeral home near the College Mennonite Church. We can decide together, if that's all right with you."

"Yes," I reassure him. "I'll be there soon. Don't worry (we always say that to each other). I'll call and let you know my arrival time." Not much else to say right now. I set the receiver back in its cradle, turn my face into my pillow, and sob like my world has fallen apart.

My feelings... such a surprise! I feel caught off guard, again. After all, we've expected her to die for years. Amazing that she even survived the stroke thirteen years ago. I always wanted to settle things with Mom, talk through the old stuff, let her know I forgive her for signing me into the hospital. That I see how hard her life has been, that I really do love her despite all the difficult times. I am so sad for her years of pain, and always have felt helpless, guilty in some way, that I didn't stay back east to help her. When I tried to talk about things in the past, it never worked. She was angry that I left her and then it was too late. She couldn't even speak, talk about anything. So many years... and now it's really too late. What would I have said anyway?

Eventually, sounds from the waking house creep into my awareness: Nancy and Aurora rustle around, the teakettle whistles, bathroom door opens and closes, hushed whispers seep under my door. I emerge from my hideaway, sniffly, puffy-faced and tell them the news. We are a house full of mourning. Even as I cry for Mom, I feel so sad for Nancy's loss of her mom, Beth, only forty-six years old, with half a life still ahead, cut short.

The day inches along. Phone calls, reservations, packing, work arrangements. Friends always wait in the wings to take over for me. It's complicated. Currently I'm juggling three part-time jobs in addition to the Center. When I return, it will be Heidi's spring break and we're going to Yosemite for a celebratory "senior trip." I'll return home, shift gears, and pack for cold weather in the mountains: boots, parka, heavy sweaters, scarves, and mittens. Sadly, midterm exams prevent Heidi from joining me for Mom's funeral.

Images tumble through my mind with so much letting go — Warren, Beth, and Mom. I remember the last time I saw her, last August: her deep blue-eyed gaze connected with mine; her frail body, a bony silhouette, rested quietly under a thin cotton blanket. So sad, vulnerable, yet finally at peace. Yesterday's gathering, a circle of friends holding hands in Fred and Cheryl's sunny meadow: Beth's memorial. And only last weekend, Heidi and I shopped at Stanford Plaza for her graduation dress and shoes.

Late Tuesday, I land in Indiana. The next few days feel swathed in gauze, foggy. We go to Yoder's to arrange the viewing and funeral. I never imagined how hard it would be when the director takes us downstairs and we're faced with a roomful of caskets. We stand, frozen. Of course we want something nice, and eventually get over our emotions and choose one of polished dark mahogany.

At first I stay with Uncle Bob and Aunt Rachel, then in a guestroom at Dad's retirement community near his apartment. I cry alone at night, grieve for Mom's life of pain. It's difficult to remember happier parts of her life to celebrate. I'll dig through some albums, find photos of her sunny, smiling face from her carefree youth with her best friend, Lillian; the family camp at Summit Lake, life with Dad. "Sonny," she was called as a child. Hardly anyone knows her in Goshen. It's only been seven months since they moved. All of Dad's family who live close will be here. Dad's siblings have known her for forty-eight years. They'll remember when Mom and Dad got married, pregnant, when she was well, when she was happy.

So many people stop by for the viewing and the memorial the next day. I feel overwhelmed at this outpouring of love, as I didn't expect it. When it's over, the receptions, family dinners, and visits, I stay another week, help Dad just by being with him. We visit Aunt Ginny and Uncle Kenny's farm; see Aunt Mabel one more time. When all the details have been dealt with, it's just Dad and me. And I need to go home.

Back to California, with a quick turnaround, I drive to Palo Alto and pick up Heidi. We head to Yosemite, stay at the turn-of-the-century Wawona Hotel. Fresh snow blankets melting drifts outside our tiny second-floor room. I haven't visited Yosemite in ten years, and the late-winter wonderland — Half Dome, El Capitan, the Valley — lightens my heart. We visit dramatic water-falls and the valley floor, a white sparkling sea studded with tall green conifers, naked ash, and maples. The frozen Merced

River threads its way through the center of the meadow. Glinting patches of ice peek out near the edges, where people have earlier tried to shuffle, skate, or cross. We crouch to peer into the river's mystical depths and see crystal-clear water beneath the ice, rushing to some unknown destination, so powerful that its force causes deep cracks in the thick ice.

On our first and last nights, we eat supper in the Wawona's vintage dining room, watch giant snow-dusted fir tops catch the last tinges of pink-gold light through the soaring windows. We're tired at day's end, having trekked up and down the valley, out to Mirror Lake, over boulders to feel the ice-cold spray of crashing waterfalls. Heidi is especially enamored of the well-known "walls" like El Capitan, which climbers scale during good weather and bad. She has always been a great climber, so it wouldn't surprise me if she took up some version of the sport.

Two months later, Heidi graduates. For the very first time, Dad visits California in honor of this milestone. The classic ceremony and outdoor reception are charged with emotion and tears. Afterward we help pack her belongings into our car and hers and drive north to Napa. My cousin Linda and George welcome us to their hilltop home for a visit. George treats Dad to a ride in his two-seater acrobatic airplane, and we feast on the early harvest from their amazing garden. After two days' rest we travel home. Heidi immediately begins her summer job at the Alinder Photography Gallery. After all these years, Dad will finally meet my friends and see where I live.

I still cry at night, struggle with my sadness, anger, denial, and grief. I even remember the list — feelings that arise during the grieving process — from my hospice training last year. Elisabeth Kübler-Ross, Stephen and Ondrea Levine's workshop on death and dying — such poignant spokespeople for a new consciousness and compassion about death. I find myself feeling regret as I wail about my losses. Eventually I go to grief counseling through Hospice. After ten sessions, my first formal therapy, I work through the anguish of Mom's death. Along the way, I come close to acceptance and gratitude that Warren left. I might never have ended it on my own.

HEALING WITH MOM

Spring equinox approaches, as does the one-year anniversary of Mom's death. I never knew this kind of marking time could feel so important, so difficult. When my friend, Valerie, and I talk about my Mom issues and grief, she suggests a way to bring about some closure with hypnotherapy.

I'm game, since unresolved issues continue to haunt me. Counseling helped initially, walking through the five stages of loss. The hardest part, what's so unsettling, is that I never spoke with Mom about some crucial things: her hysterectomy when I was two and how it affected us both, her three nervous breakdowns when I was nine and ten, and her shock treatments (which I barely remember); my own incarceration and shock treatments at seventeen, when they signed me in; Mom's anger at me. Mostly though, I feel left behind trying to figure it all out.

Val meets me at the Healing Arts Center on a Sunday, where we'll be undisturbed for our session. We hear only the rhythmic crash of surf on Gualala Point Beach. Morning light filters into the front room through the cypress trees; it throws mesmerizing patterns on the walls, adding to the atmosphere of relaxation perfect for hypnotherapy. I sink back into the soft upholstered rocker, and Valerie's voice guides me down an imaginary path, counting slowly, each step taking me deeper. I readily find my way. Her voice becomes muffled, slightly distant, though the words are perfectly clear. After a few minutes, she asks me to look around and describe where I am, what I see.

"A grassy meadow, golden-brown mixed with fresh green, spreads out before me. I'm walking toward an ancient sprawling oak tree. The sun warms my back. I feel at ease, but alone," without expectation.

"Look around," she encourages. "Do you see anyone?"

"No, it's just me." Then, as I come around the oak's huge gnarled trunk, I see Mom, looking calm, serene, and like she's waiting for me. "But how can you be here?" She looks young, almost ageless. My logical mind keeps butting in, tries to come to terms with seeing her, tries to break the hypnotic spell.

Val's voice soothes me: "Remember, you're in 'etheric time,' and yes, this is real too. Now take a deep breath, keep your eyes closed, and return to the oak tree and your mom. Ask her if she's real."

I allow myself to drop back into that deeper place. Tentatively I say, "Mom, is this really happening? Why are you here?"

She smiles, open and warm in a way that acknowledges me. "Because you wanted to talk to me, and you invited me here. What would you like to know? I am here for you." Mom extends her hands and we sit down together.

Her soft words touch me like an embrace and encourage me to continue. I feel overwhelmed, but her openness calms me. Why not? Just step in and see what happens. I begin to confide in her, to speak honestly; eventually, I ask painful questions that have plagued me for so long.

We talk for what seems like hours, lost in time and space to all but each other. "I've always loved you. I thought you knew that. Things were hard, and I'm so sorry you didn't know or understand. You were young."

She shares her anguish over how our relationship didn't turn out the way she wanted. We speak of the times when we felt the sweet mother-daughter bond, very close and connected. Then her pain, depression, migraines, and nervous condition got in the way, and her frustration turned to anger and resentment. How much it pained her when I was in the hospital, how scared and crazy she felt.

In the end, it all comes down to three things, which we are able to say to each other. "I'm sorry. Please forgive me. I love you so much."

We both are crying at this point, embracing each other, letting go of a lifetime of pain and misunderstanding. I feel so light, a heavy weight lifted off my heart. How did our connection get so completely off track while she was alive? I wish we'd been able to reach this beautiful place before she died. Now I'm just grateful to be here at all.

Time to say goodbye. We stand and hold each other for what seems an eternity. I imagine this will truly be the last time I see Mom. But in my heart, I know she is with me, has always loved me, as I have loved her. She is smiling as I walk away. Then I turn around and she's gone. For the first time in years, decades, I feel settled. Finally at peace.

FINDING MY PLACE

A year since Mom died — a painful year of loss. The grief hit me hard, so unexpected, given that she was seriously ill for thirteen years, waiting to die at any moment. So much sorrow for her life, especially the one she didn't get to have. So unfair.

With Mom gone, and Dad's responsibility relieved, I feel I can ask him for a loan, a down payment on a house. He says yes and we establish an amount of $40,000. I'll find a fixer-upper, remodel it over time, and swing a mortgage payment about equal to my current rent.

The dismal experience of looking at real estate depresses me. In Gualala, I locate the best option close to my price range. The two-story vacation house consists of two tiny bedrooms upstairs and one miniscule bathroom downstairs; an old dark kitchen with worn-down linoleum and a slit of ocean view through scraggly bull pines. The listing price is $195,000 and doesn't feel like a home, so I move on.

"You should build your own house. Forget buying someone else's dream. Design your own. You can do it, you actually know how; we've seen your vision. And think of the money you'll save."

Friends Alfred and Cynthia support me, and this touches a deep place in me. My mind begins to spin, everything shifts, and my world lights up. Go ahead and build it! Somewhere inside this all makes sense.

That week, I meet with my designer friend, Paul, and ask his advice about building. Can I manage it? He encourages me and offers to help by drafting the plans. He can walk me through the process as "owner-builder." When I leave his office, he casually mentions, "You should check with John Bower. He owns some property up on the ridge, on Stargaze Drive. None of his lots is on the market now, but who knows? Maybe he'll sell you one."

After a couple of days checking out what's currently for sale — small, overpriced, and unattractive lots — I call John Bower and arrange a meeting. We're on for the next afternoon. Before the meeting I stop by his office, where Jana has laid out parcel maps. She points out three lots. I should go and look first, before we meet.

I cruise down Stargaze Drive, off Moonrise, remembering a time several years ago when I explored this very street, right after the division was created in the mid-1970s. Gorgeous. Wild. Camelot views. Then it was rough, and recently logged. John and his son, John Jr., did a nice job carving out the road and laying out eleven lots.

At the end of the road I park my car, jump out, and make my way up through the thick forest of tan oak, madrone and third-growth redwoods. I cross a creek on a fallen madrone log, like a balance beam. I identify the lot when I reach the telephone pole at the upper edge of a steep drop-off. The view takes my breath away.

This is it, my dream. I feel a surge of knowing, like a return to my rightful place in the world. I clear a little spot in the dirt, like a bird or deer settling into its evening nest. With gratitude, I gather a small bouquet — rattlesnake grass, redwood and fir tips, oxalis with its purple flowers, scotch broom — and bundle it with long supple grass, tie it up with my wishes. I make an offering, accompanied by my tears, to Mother Earth, if she'll have me here.

Back at Mr. Bower's office, I feel anxious and excited. He greets me with a friendly handshake and, "Call me John. I know who you are, heard about you and the business you started. So, what do you have in mind?"

I take a deep breath and jump right in — might as well just blurt it out. "I'm interested in buying your lot on Stargaze, lot seven, to be exact, if you'd be interested in selling."

"It's not on the market, you know," he replies. I nod. "But I might sell it to you. What's your plan?"

He doesn't suggest a price yet, I notice, but I continue. "My dad would purchase the lot. I'll design my house with help from Paul. Then he'll draw the official plans to submit to the building department. I'd be the owner-builder, working with a contractor."

"And where will the money come from for the building?"

Here's where I take the big leap, and a fast gulp of air. "Well, John, I've heard that, under certain circumstances, you make construction loans, and I wonder if that's a possibility. I would prefer that to a bank loan. What actually are the conditions?"

"First of all," he says, "you must own the property outright, which you would. Next, it has to be in my water district, which it is. I would make a standard construction loan at ten percent. Everything must be built strictly to code by a licensed contractor. What kind of budget are you thinking about?"

Wow, I haven't thought about that at all! A number pops into my head, totally intuitive. "I think I can do it for one hundred thousand." Is this really happening?

"Sounds good. So, let me know and I'll have Jana draw up the papers, separate escrows for the land and house mortgage, but they can close at the same time. Bring me a rough budget breakdown. A few conditions, but we'll go over that next time we meet — if you want to do it, that is."

"Great. Thank you, John. And yes, I do want to go ahead."

A handshake and a deal. The beginning. The rest is up to me.

Building for Me

The next thirty days, escrow, progress with a flurry of phone calls and drawings, meetings with contractors for estimates and bids. Equinox — the springtime clock change. There's still light when I leave the Massage Center at 6:00, so every day I go to the property. I tie ribbons on trees, bushwhack through scrubby oaks and huckleberries, and site the house on the flat spot facing the sunrise and mountain view. Just clearing the lot turns out to be a major job.

I particularly love to watch the path of the sun, imagine light pouring through the many windows I plan for each room. Walls will line up exactly with the compass; at spring and fall equinoxes, when the sun rises directly in the east, the structure and its shadow will act like a giant sundial.

Each face of the house has a door that aligns with the "Four Directions." I pore over each detail, work on floor plans and window configurations till the arrangements feel right. The final draft has one and a half stories, two high-peaked roofs that join at a "T," and windows everywhere. Master suite is upstairs; a bright, friendly kitchen, spacious viewing deck; a "great room" partially divided by a dramatic turned stairway with a landing halfway up. In my fantasy life, I descend these stairs in a wedding dress, smiling, my dreams fulfilled.

By June, Paul completes the blueprints. I submit them to the county building department, pay the permit fees, and work begins. Cousin Linda, partner George, and nephew Jerry visit on a record-breaking hot weekend, dragging chainsaws, hatchets, and machetes. George attacks the lot, fearless with his chainsaw, as branches and whole trees tumble over the bank and land on a giant burn pile.

"You want to keep this oak? How about the two redwoods next to it? They'll be in the way; they should go. Up to you, though, they're your trees." Good thing I did some thinking ahead, marking out the house perimeter. Now we carefully stake out the corners and save two redwoods to poke through the deck.

Bam! Huge oaks and madrones, once packed close together reaching for the light, fall, crash through branches, land hard, and make my heart jump. The process is both traumatic and exciting. Within two days, the lot is mostly cleared to stumps. Next, cut a driveway, grade the site, dig the foundation. I barely believe this is happening — get little rushes of glee, smile when I'm alone, thrilled with the reality: I am building my own home!

After three unsatisfactory bids, the first, 30 percent over my budget, I run into Terry at the bank. After a casual conversation, he and his partner, Dave, take a look at the blueprints and estimate finishing the job within the budget. I'm going for it now. With a creative arrangement of "time and materials estimate, with a cap," I'll be more involved, in charge of purchases and subcontractors: plumbing, electrical, sheetrock, roof, cabinets, counters, and floors. Dave and Terry will handle the actual construction; nail it all together.

I invent dollar amounts for each category, organize in notebooks and folders, imagine I know what I'm doing. If I spend too much money in one area, like the matte black Vermont Castings wood stove, or solid fir paneled doors, some other allotment must be reduced. Each day I visit the site and confer with the builders. Once the framing, walls, and roof are completed, I begin the tedious task of varnishing the doors and jambs — all ten of them.

When will it ever be finished? One day at a time. Wake up, make coffee, get going; visit the house site and make decisions. Four days a week, I run the Massage Center, and on Fridays, I do framing at North Light Gallery. Every couple of months, I cook at massage school. And after my workday, I sweep up the construction mess, go home to fall into bed. Wake up and do it all over again. For three months. Every week or two, I make a Santa Rosa run, returning with my car full of light fixtures, sinks, faucets, and doorknobs. The first time I drive down the coast to shop, my hot flashes begin. Soon, they go off at the rate of two or three per hour. How will I cope? I learn to count every second of the three-minute flashes as an alternative to going nuts.

By September, Victoria and I paint the interior. She does all the hard stuff, up high with an extension pole to save my ailing neck. It had taken a few weeks to get the sheet rock perfect, skip-troweled and bone dry, so we can paint. Now we rock into the final phase.

Terry and Dave work outside doing trim, decks, and steps. I oversee the installation of carpet and linoleum, bathroom fixtures, and kitchen cabinets. We're almost there when a glitch pops up: They read the stair plans as specifying a half-wall, inexpensive to build, whereas I'd envisioned a Craftsman-like railing with balusters, polished fir posts, and a dark redwood handrail. We just never noticed or saw the discrepancy. The difference in time and materials puts me about $2,000 over budget.

Some kind of miracle occurs: We complete the house in three and a half months, almost unheard of. The house passes final inspection, ready to move into. All that remains is a giant pile of trash and scrap wood that will supply my kindling for several years.

Such an amazing feeling as I put away my dishes: cobalt-blue, turquoise, and yellow Fiestaware plates and juice glasses practically arrange themselves neatly on the shelves of my own kitchen. Next to them sit my favorite, the milk-glass chicken eggcups, red beaks chirping... I can feel my five-year-old self in my childhood kitchen, reaching for them.

Every day, when I walk into each new room, furniture and objects reflect both my history and the new life I've created. A large golden Buddha rests on an antique blanket chest, eyes closed in silent meditation. Grandma's rocker sits next to the bed, Teddy bears nap, snuggled up to my flannel bathrobe. Dad's bookcase, the one he made in Iowa with Grandpa, holds the special-edition *Peter Pan in Kensington Gardens,* just like in the hall outside my childhood bedroom.

Several faux-painted walls are graced with the imaginative

decorative prints and drawings of Heidi Endemann: Iris Gothic, a nest filled with huckleberries, tiger lily in a shell, the lizard watercolor. Even my old piano from Branscomb will stay with me for a while.

I feel steeped in my surroundings, like sweet Chai tea, a rich, deep, and spicy blend of old and new; mellow, familiar, and comforting. Held in my new home, blessed by my Guardian Angels and all that came before, I take back my life and my power. What a gift.

SEARCH FOR LITTLE JUDY, 1991

I look forward to meeting with Valerie today, time for me to look into my past through hypnotherapy. A steaming-hot mug of peppermint tea and Val's warm, easy smile greet me. Next, her reassuring hug relieves my anxiety and reminds me I'm happy to be here with my trusted friend. Her sun-gold hair swings and shimmers as we walk up the rough dirt path leading to her new studio. This is my third session. After the last one — a profound healing with Mom a year after her death — I feel ready to explore my "inner child." Vague memories before age five flash like twinkling Christmas lights — Grandma, my dolls, singing, nursery school. I want to be more in touch with that part of me, hopefully unlock my more playful self.

Before we begin the session, akin to guided imagery, I settle into a comfortable chair. The temperature is just right, warm, cozy, with a window cracked for fresh air. Valerie begins to speak softly. I close my eyes, and soon I hear only her pleasant voice and morning birdsongs. I feel so safe with her. She guides me down a familiar path, step by step, each moment going deeper, deeper, further back in time, to a place where "little Judy" is seven, six, five, four....

Time stops. I feel stuck, paralyzed. I sense my eyelids fluttering; they will neither open nor be still. I squint hard, trying to keep them shut. My body tightens, rigid. My arms close around my ribs, grasping, as I pull myself into a tight ball.

"Where are you, Judy? What's happening? Can you look around and tell me what you see?" Val's voice breaks in, distant, almost like an echo.

No, no, I don't want to be here!

"No — can't see. I'm so cold." I tremble all over. I can see only red inside my closed eyelids. Then I see that it's coming from her, Mom, her arms limp and open. "Blood... Mom...."

Bloody towels. She's on the floor, leaning against the bathtub, her mouth slightly open, eyes closed, unmoving. What's happening? Where's the blood coming from? Is she asleep? Is she dead?

I am shaking, terrified, freezing cold. Valerie brings the small space heater and sets it up right next to me, wraps me in a blanket, then a shawl — layers to warm my frozen body and spirit. I can't make the pictures go away, especially the blood. I can almost taste its salty presence.

Val, arms around me, gently captures my attention and leads me out of the nightmarish scene, back up the familiar path. She directs me and I breathe into my body; then I'm in the room and the present moment.

"What happened, what was that? So real, like I was there, yet I was watching it." My mind is a jumble, wanting both to remember and to shut it out. My body continues to shake as I tell her what I saw: Mom, the blood, Dad there pushing me away, and how scared I felt.

"Was it real?"

Val says yes, probably I experienced a "recovered memory," something so painful I hadn't wanted to remember, had blocked it completely. We talk more, and I feel that this did actually happen. I wonder where that small child went. Val explains how vulnerable "little Judy" was, in that place where her mom had cut herself, and she tried to disappear.

"More details might come up later," Val continues. "Maybe you'll write something." She makes no attempt to ask more questions, rather focuses on comforting me, the small child, still in shock from walking in on the bloody mess in the bathroom.

"How can I deal with this?" I ask.

"It's a very important part of your story, part of how you were formed, the child part of you."

I feel sad and lost and betrayed, finding this fragment hidden in my psyche, holding me back from my magical child-self, the one who skipped down the sidewalk to Grandma's without a care in her world. Finally, the tears spill out, a warm salty bath of sadness for that little girl, her dad, and the mother who tried to leave her forever.

XI

Found

1992–2004

The List, 1992

"He'll have to walk through my front door. I'm serious."

"You're kidding! You really put that on your list?" Suszan looks shocked. "What do you mean by that, exactly?"

"I want to be specific," I say, "so I spelled out all the essential qualities: Good-looking, smart, funny, adores me, has his own source of income... you know. No more going out there searching for the perfect guy, 'the One,' like a treasure hunt, but I never win. So, I'm ending the search, even the waiting. Now that I've built my own home, it seems easier to spend time alone. As for boyfriends, they're mostly not worth the energy, frustration, and disappointment. You know what I mean, right?"

I love our talks. Suszan gets it immediately. She's a strong, self-assured single mom, tall, elegant, her dark curly mane sprinkled with silver threads. She makes her way in the world with grace, often speaking of the Goddess, Vipassana meditation, and divine intervention. We both were plucked from the arms of death and believe we've been saved for another purpose. Suszan works at the center giving massages and spa facials. Whenever she spends overnights with me, every couple of weeks, we inevitably talk about men. Our friendship grows, so valuable and deep. I finally realize that my connection with women sustains me. I can be happy without a man. In fact, what a relief, like finding my own healing path or right livelihood, created and defined only by me. And so I keep the list, bless it, and put it away in a miniature chest of drawers.

The sting of my last breakup left me tender and sore, like the two that preceded it. Somewhere between my bad choices, negative imprinting and the yearning for a soul mate, relationships haven't worked out. And so, I'm letting go.

"He would have to show up at my front door," I repeat.

That was in May.

My new house provides endless joy and creative opportunity.

I plant a giant banana palm in a sunny corner near the entrance; cymbidium orchids bloom on their own under the oaks. On the east/view side I sow crimson clover, and by late spring, a billowing field of red-tipped tassels appears, humming with bees and life and promise. The sun, now high in the sky, means no need for a fire at night. I sit on the stairs inside my new house, just six months old, and realize that I'm happy and full — have all I need and more.

My Healing Arts Center flourishes. We survive a recession. Six therapists happily engage in work that heals us as well as our clients. Our two rooms are occupied with massage or acupuncture, a facial, or Jin Shin treatment. Valerie's magical watercolor paintings of gardens and healing mandalas adorn our walls. We all get along and have fun, and each of us blossoms.

The Center seems busier than ever in July. Then, the phone call. "Hi, Judith. My name is Peter and I'm a friend of Helen's. She suggested I call you...."

His intro went on: "I'm a Physical Therapist in Santa Rosa... love the coast... looking for part-time work, maybe Gualala... have an appointment with RCMS next week to check out a position there. I might be interested in renting space for a part-time practice, and heard you have a nice center there, might have a room."

I think two things simultaneously: There's really no extra space here, and oh, what a lovely voice this man has. I tell him that the office is quite busy, summer season and all, but he should stop by anyway, I'd like to meet him. And so we agree to meet at midday July 28.

I make myself a note so I won't book a massage at noon and miss Peter's visit. When he walks through the door, I step out of my office to greet him, and feel surprised. He's handsome! Deep blue eyes, nice smile, about my age... and that lovely voice. I show him around as we chat. He invites me to lunch, to talk business.

Out on the upper-level deck of my office, I immediately spot a robin's-egg-blue Alpha Romeo convertible, top down, in the parking lot. Wow! My dream car. His car. We hop in and buzz over to the Food Company; my longish hair, pulled back in a ponytail, streams out behind.

Once there, we sit across from each other on the screened-in terrace, eating and talking intensely for nearly two hours. I tell him about my house. He talks about his work, three kids, and life in Santa Rosa. Off-hours he rides a road bike, works out at a gym, and owns a business with others doing Jin Shin, Pilates, and Feldenkrais. He seems genuinely interested in me, my life. Such a lively and engaging conversation — we could be friends. I feel unsure about the business part, so I tell him I'll think further on it and be in touch.

In the parking lot we say goodbye, and just before climbing into his cute Alpha, he says, "If the office situation doesn't work out, maybe we can have dinner sometime."

"Oh, okay... we'll talk. Next week. Call me, okay?" Heat rises, then a little flush. I'm caught off guard. Does this mean he's single? What am I thinking?

Within an hour I'm on the phone with Helen who says, "Yes, in fact he is single. Married for many years, then had a girlfriend for a while after the divorce. Didn't work out. I've known him a couple of years. He's a really nice man."

Helen's words encourage me, yet I have no expectations — just needed to check it out. And who knows, maybe something more will happen.

COURTING

Within a few weeks of starting his part-time physical therapy practice at Healing Arts, Peter begins courting me, and I love it! We sit on the bench after work, talk about the day, our separate lives, our histories. Eventually, we meander down to the Surf market for wine and snacks, and then continue our compelling conversations. We discuss everything, including our "bad track records" with relationships, and debate whose was worse. We both feel vulnerable and cautious, afraid to open old wounds or create new ones. We start to meet for real dates, and I am crystal clear: no spending the night, and no sex. Not without a plan. And not yet, anyway.

Late one evening at my house, our easy chemistry and the buzz of new love nearly overwhelm us. First come hot kisses as we sit close, perched on tall stools; then smooching on the couch, arms and legs wrapping around each other, grasping urgently.

"We need to stop," I finally interrupt, breathless, reluctant. This breaks the mood. We back up a bit, keeping eye and body contact, sizing each other up.

"Of course we do," he replies softly, also making it clear that he'd prefer not to stop. "Boy, that was fun! But I'd better be on my way. It's a long drive to Santa Rosa."

"You could sleep on the couch," I offer lamely.

"I really don't think that would work," he laughs. "Best to go now." He bids me goodnight with a lingering juicy kiss that leaves me tingling for days, anticipating our next time together.

My daughter, Heidi, is my summer roommate and will be a junior at Santa Cruz in September. We enjoy each other's company, cook together, and share meals like best friends. In late August I arrange for Peter to meet my family — Heidi. I feel quite nervous, remembering that in the past her discerning eye had allowed only one man to gain her guarded approval. I plan a simple meal: pasta with homemade pesto and grilled veggies.

Once they meet, Peter seems comfortable, open, talks with Heidi about Santa Cruz and asks about her major, Environmental Studies. He volunteers to light the charcoal briquettes and steps outside to get the grill going. In the kitchen, the space hums between Heidi and me. Finally, I turn to her, perched on the counter, and without a word she breaks into a wide grin and gives me the thumbs-up sign. Wow! This speaks volumes, as I trust her intuition more than my own. When Peter returns, our smiles greet him, surround him like a warm blanket. The three of us click and it's easy.

Peter and I come up with a mantra, an intention, a way to dispel anxiety and fear: "This can be easy, this can be fun." Our relationship progresses, and after two months, we plan a long romantic weekend at my house. By this time, I've visited his house in Santa Rosa and met his son Jed. Because of the AIDS scare, we get tested. This makes us feel serious, very adult, and we celebrate when we receive clean results. We talk a lot about what it will mean to take this next step.

Our first weekend together includes several hours basking in the sun on my deck; a local art gallery opening, with way too many people, all of whom I know; then ducking out early for a simple dinner at home. Evening progresses in slow motion, as the sun tints the far ridges a pink-gold that fades to deep lavender. We stumble up the stairs to my bedroom and sprawl, entwined, across the bed. Each minute, each movement like a heartbeat, full and alive, together in this new life we're creating. Us. Face to face, we make love, hold each other tight, then fall deeply asleep in a tangle of arms and legs — uncovered, vulnerable, unlike the time on the couch two months ago. In the morning, we bring our coffee and toast upstairs, loll in bed. One minute we snuggle with our hot brews like little kids with hot chocolate; the next, sun drenching our naked bodies, we make love again, and talk way past noon.

Over the next few months, as we become closer, more intimate, I feel alive, like all the lights got turned on. This is so right. Still, questions arise. I frequently review my past and wonder if I should trust myself in matters of love. I'm forty-eight, divorced, and essentially single for twenty years. There were a few relationships during that time; two even seemed possible for the long term, but things fell apart. Bad choices? Too much longing? Old wounds holding me back? I hate it when that comes up.

My fears show up at the door uninvited, like Jehovah's Witnesses. This time I look carefully and see them for the protection they've offered and the questions they pose. I must take this risk in order to step forward and claim the life I desire. My dream come true. All I have to do is continue to say yes, knowing that we deserve this chance to be happy together. And this time, I trust myself.

TOGETHER

By January we say the "M" word out loud; it pops out in a casual way, yet still acknowledges the serious intent of our relationship. No pressure, no wedding date, and now we both know where this is going. Our commuting courtship has us heady from the back and forth of it. Long romantic weekends in sunny Santa Rosa, dining at our favorite "China Room," long walks in the hills of Annandale Park. Or at my place, we lounge on the deck, curl up by the woodstove, or whip up new concoctions for dinner. We love to cook together, serenaded by strains of Van Morrison. Peter, as it turns out, is a creative chef, can turn a simple salad into a gourmet meal — like Tuscan tomato bread salad — which later earns him the family title "dresser of salads." Fruit salad transforms into an aromatic aphrodisiac, cardamom wafts up between chunks of mango, pineapple, tangerine, and seasonal berries. Yum!

One delightful warm day in June, sharing midday coffee on the deck, Peter leans forward, ocean blue-gray eyes locking with mine. "I think we should get married... what do you think? Will you marry me?"

"Yes, yes of course I will," I respond, giddy, overwhelmed, realizing... this is it! And that very day we talk through some crucial details about our future.

Peter offers, "Yes, we'll have the wedding of your dreams, a real one," despite the fact that he's had two full-blown weddings before. Such a special gift, that he would do this for me. We then decide two things: wedding date to be in a year, next June or July; and we'll have the wedding at my house, outside, and plant an expansive lawn for the reception.

July 8, 1993, Peter's 50th! We invite his daughters, Micah and Bessie, and my daughter, Heidi, to celebrate. Once we all are gathered around the birthday breakfast table, we share our plans. Peter says, "You may have guessed, we have something to tell you. We're engaged!"

For just a moment there's a pause, like a tiny intake of breath. Then, as if in unison, they chime, "Great! Fantastic," and they all talk at once, and raise juice glasses to toast us. I love seeing them all together, my expanding, extended family. The wedding's still a whole year off, so it feels a bit unreal, but it's such fun to begin planning. I can already see the girls taking part in the ceremony, all dressed up in nontraditional finery.

Peter tops off his birthday with an incredible journey with Jed, a five-week bicycle trip from Gualala to Vancouver, B.C., and back. Tents, saddlebags, sleeping bags, and pads; food, Whisperlite cook stove, espresso pot. Wow! On the trip, somewhere between Seattle and Canada, Peter tells Jed about our plans. Jed approves.

Fall. Time to prepare the land, take down a couple of redwoods and level an area for the reception. Then, in early spring, once the sun has warmed the soil, we scatter grass seed, mulch it with straw, and make our first purchase together: A shiny red Sears lawnmower. Handcrafted gold and silver heart earrings make a romantic engagement present.

Four months to go. We meet with Joayn Milazzo, experienced astrologer and good friend. Using our charts, along with her intuition, we pin down the date — July 16. So much to prepare and arrange: Invitations and catering; flowers, music. The cake! The magnitude of our event, 150 guests, means organization and attention to detail. I am the bride and my own wedding planner, the "queen of lists." Thank goodness I don't have to do it alone. Peter and I discuss everything. I've never planned a wedding, but no matter. I get out my special notebook and calendar, and list each and every item to be handled. Really fun!

On a weekend jaunt to Mendocino we stop by Old Gold and choose rings made in the *mokume-gane* style: rose, yellow, and white gold folded, then sliced, so that both rings come from the same piece of precious metal, the patterns of wavy gold book-matched.

The morning of the wedding we notice what appears to be rain, that July fog-drizzle oh-so familiar to coastal residents. "What will we do if this fog goes on all day? People sitting on wet grass; soggy tablecloths, and no sun," I fret.

Peter heads out to the front lawn, our ceremony site. Between scurrying around the house and remembering to eat something, I catch sight of him through the French doors. He's burning a small bundle of sage, asking the spirits for a little help with the weather. When he comes in we pull on our jeans and go to work: we set up tables, bouquets of flowers in antique teapots; tarp the tables and chairs, and pray for the fog to burn off. By noon, the sun peeks out and begins to dry the grass.

An hour later, I'm surrounded in my upstairs bedroom by a flock of women: Heidi; my new stepdaughters, Bessie and Micah; my oldest best friend, Aurora; and dear friend Ellie. Christina comes in to style my wedding haircut. With Heidi's help, I slip into my pink silk wedding dress and my new life, descend the stairway of my dream house. Bursting with joy, I walk down the pathway, lined with crystal-blue lobelia and strewn with rose petals, to meet Peter, my love, at the altar.

Many words are spoken this day, of support, wisdom, and love from our many close friends and family. Our own vows express the deep love and belief in this commitment we're making. As we slip on the gold rings, they glimmer in the sun, bright like our spirits, filled with the joy of this moment. Today I hold, with pinpoint sharpness, each precious memory of the happiest day of my life.

Two days later, we pack up the car; head off on our camping honeymoon to Crater Lake. From there we need to figure out when we'll move in together. We're a work in progress as, I suspect, are all good marriages. And the big deal — we're together.

GONE, 1997

Mid-November, clear and cold. Silver frost coats blades of grass, like glitter scattered by winter fairies. I get up at 6:30 a.m., still dark. Peter has left for work at his midweek Santa Rosa Physical Therapy gig. Some days I enjoy going to our office early — to tidy up, put things in order, and ground myself before my 10:00 client, Martha, arrives for her massage.

I bring my spiral notebook and manila folder, thin, scant with this semester's attempts at writing monologue pieces. Lynn Abels, our instructor, encourages us, her budding authors, to write personal stories and memorize them to act out onstage: *Local Heroes.* I signed up for the class with one major caveat: I'll write, but no performing, unless by some miracle (as she predicts) I change my mind. The short pieces I've created so far don't inspire me. Peter and I have attended Lynn's classes together for nearly three years, and my writing cannot, as they say, hold a candle to his.

Nine forty-five. Low, intense winter sun streams into the waiting room, interrupted every few minutes by foreboding black clouds. As I brood about my writing, a sharp ringing jars me back into the present.

"Healing Arts Center. Good morning."

"Judith? Is that you?" Pause. "This is Aunt Mabel."

My heart jumps into my throat. Something is wrong, terribly wrong.

"I'm here, at your dad's apartment. Oh, I'm so sorry." She's crying now, and Aunt Mabel doesn't cry much. She can hardly get the words out.

"He's gone."

The words sting, slug me so hard I can't catch a breath, heart aching, constricting in a way that I couldn't have imagined.

"No, no," I moan. "What do you mean? What happened?"

She tells me in choppy bits how she stopped by to visit, maybe go to the Pie Shop across the street with him.

"I knocked, and when he didn't answer I went in. He never locks his door when he's home... and there he was, lying face down on the bathroom floor. I checked his pulse, and then pulled the emergency cord for the medics. But he was gone. I'm so sorry."

I can hear her weeping softly, people talking in the background.

"What's happening now?" I'm sobbing so hard I can barely speak or think.

"People are just arriving from the funeral home. Yoder's. Is that all right? Someone needed to be called right away, so I called them. I tried you at home...."

Already? Funeral home? This is all happening too fast! My mind flashes back to seven years ago, when Mom died, when Dad and I were at Yoder's together picking out her casket, planning the memorial.

"Yes, of course, Aunt Mabel. And I'll be there as soon as I can." My brain feels tired, flooded with details: plane tickets, the office, call Peter, call Heidi.

"So sorry. He was still warm. Seems like he died right away, or he would have pulled the cord. Come and stay with me, of course, Judith. You and Peter, stay as long as you like, and Heidi too."

"Thank you, Aunt Mabel. I'll call when I know what I'm doing, when we're arriving — hopefully tomorrow."

Gone! How can that be? I feel his absence already, like some portion of my essence has been taken from me. I feel cold, empty. Now we'll never have "the conversation" about the hospital. Any conversation. No new carpet for his apartment, like he wanted. And no assisted living for him. Just six weeks ago we were together, regulated his oxygen tank, lunched at Aunt Mabel's, visited cousins, shared pie. Planning for more good years, though his weakened body worried me. I had seen the tiredness in his eyes, his slow pace, as he held my arm lightly for balance. His heart was failing. Why was I not prepared?

I must call Peter.

"Don't worry, sweetheart," he says. "I'll be home this afternoon, as soon as I can leave work. Then we'll figure it out." Comfort. Peter jumps right in, promises to be here with me. I don't think I could do any of this alone.

Martha walks in, smiling, ready for her massage. Her sunny expression shifts suddenly when she sees me, eyes red, sniffling, trying to get it together. I can hardly speak, say the words out loud, "My dad died."

I do what I can; put a call in to Heidi, ask my colleagues to take over the office. Less than an hour has passed as I lock up the Center and go home; collapse in grief on the couch.

The next morning, Peter and I drive to San Francisco, fly to Chicago, fly to Indiana. My cousin picks us up and we drive on icy roads in the first big storm of the season. Wheels crunch over several inches of unplowed snow in Aunt Mabel's driveway. Dark, starless night. I've lost my bearings. Everything feels surreal, like a crazy mixed-up dream.

Peter helps me through each difficult step of the next two days, holds me in his arms each night. We plan the "viewing," funeral, and burial, choose a hand-rubbed cherry casket, like something Dad might have enjoyed refinishing. Aunts, uncles, cousins, and friends provide meals, love, and guidance through the process. We have a nurturing haven with Aunt Mabel — such a blessing. After a couple of days, Heidi arrives, then Cousin Kathy. Heidi puts together an eloquent blend of Dad's story and her memories of him to share at the memorial. Kathy takes me shopping for black suede pumps in downtown Goshen, a good distraction from the reality of planning my father's funeral.

The next few days are like a family reunion. So many relatives show up, including many of my thirty-six cousins, and even their kids with new babies. Since Dad moved to Greencroft seven years ago, several of his nieces and nephews got to know him. Of his nine siblings, seven remain alive; all, with their spouses, are here for the memorial. We gather at Dad's apartment for a traditional meal. I make oyster stew using the old family recipe — simple, with lots of butter, milk, and oysters, which we're lucky to obtain given that Indiana is nowhere near an ocean.

The next day, the service takes place at Goshen's College Mennonite Church. The gentleman from Yoder's, and Nancy, the minister, meet me in the hall near the open casket, where they offer one last chance to see my dad — his body — for I am sure at this point that he's no longer here. I am weeping, and don't want to close the lid. Peter stands close with his arm around me. The funeral director discreetly reminds me to remove the diamond ring on Dad's middle finger, the one he has worn since Uncle Earl gave it to him. Part of me wants to just leave it on his hand, undisturbed, yet I know he wants me to have it. I reach in, arm brushing against the pale gray water-silk lining of the casket, feel the burnished wool of his suit, the coolness of his weathered hand as I slip off the large ring. One last time, I touch his face, whisper my final goodbye. Stepping back, nodding, I let go, quietly sobbing on the shoulders of my husband and daughter.

Time to go into the sanctuary. First, my uncles and cousins carry the casket to the front of the church. Everyone is seated when Peter and I enter, with Heidi and her husband, Stuart, to sit in the front row. Briefly I turn around. My gaze sweeps across the room; I take in the sight of my large family, women in traditional net prayer caps, familiar faces, and a number of Dad's friends gathered in the pews. I feel held and surrounded by their love and presence.

Most of the hymns we've chosen are not traditional Mennonite music, but rather pieces I recall singing with him in our Methodist Church in Cobleskill. *For the Beauty of the Earth* feels like a tribute to his attitude, forever positive in spite of the difficulties life dealt him. Such a saint he was with my mom: husband for forty-eight years, and her caretaker for the last thirteen. Other burdens that he silently carried cannot be mentioned today or any day soon. I wish I could stand up and speak, so many thoughts swirling in my head, but I know it would be a disaster. Fortunately, Heidi speaks for me, has composed a piece about her grandpa, talks about his adventuresome spirit as well as his caring nature.

"In his sixties, he pursued a new career, earning a master's degree in Museum Curation." Heidi bravely stands at the podium, glances up for just a moment before catching a breath and continuing. "His last career seemed truly where his heart was: an antiquarian, a refinisher, a collector of rare books. This is where my memories of him begin: A house full of books, a carriage barn full of antiques, and pure joy whenever he was in either place. Together we would go into the backroom and climb the great ladders to the top shelves to bring down atlases and storybooks. Or we would put on our coats and head to the carriage barn in search of new treasures. Grandpa was my quiet companion in the discovery of each new day I spent with him."

Thank you, dear Heidi.

Aunt Rachael delivers a touching eulogy followed by singing and warm words of appreciation about this gentle man. *Amazing Grace.* A light snow coats the cars, walkways, and hearse as we head out of town in slow procession to Violett Cemetery on the edge of Goshen. I have been here just twice before, once to bury Mom, once to visit her grave. A shoveled path is packed down so people can walk to the burial site. Standing near the edge of the grave, seeing my mom's casket next to the empty place where Dad's soon will lie, something about the brisk cold air and all the family burials — Grandma Sonn, Uncle Earl, Aunt Evie, Mom — everything starts to run together, overlap, become one event/time/place, flashing by like movie shorts. I think I might faint, and clutch Peter's arm and gray wool overcoat. Following the minister's blessing, I toss in my red rose and the requisite shovel of dirt from the pile. I don't want it to be over now, like this, and yet I can't wait to leave.

The rest of the day, like a blur. Members of the congregation serve a lovely meal at the church: Casseroles, coleslaw, hot rolls, a dozen pies, at least. Aunts and uncles and other relatives gather at Aunt Mabel's afterward for tea and stories. Many of their tales ring familiar, some humorous, a few I've never heard, about growing up as children of a Mennonite pastor. I love observing them together, the siblings: Intimate, chatty, laughing, remembering their long snowy walks to the one-room school two miles away. Or sharing farm chores as kids — feeding pigs, collecting eggs, milking cows, and caring for the family's plow horses. The experience of this close-knit family, though not my own, warms my aching heart and draws me in. I feel their ease with each other, their kindness and lack of judgment. I wish I'd lived closer and been more a part of their lives; I cherish every moment with them now.

Peter and I need to remain in Goshen for at least three weeks to move out of Dad's apartment, to sort, sell, and store his belongings. Aunt Mabel graciously offers us refuge in her beautiful home, which borders the iced-over Elkhart River. One evening, about a dozen cousins crowd the long dining table for "pie potluck" — each family brings a whole pie. Laughter and overeating cheer us from our tedious work. Every day, after coffee and oatmeal, we drive to Greencroft for the day's tasks: pack books in labeled boxes; meet with the lawyer, appraiser, antique buyer; set up a family one-day sale.

Sifting through Dad's clothes, I feel so sad, and yet when Peter chooses a gray plaid flannel shirt, and Stuart his Rockport wing-tips, something in me loosens. Then we pack and load furniture and boxes of antiques into a U-haul truck for Heidi and Stuart to furnish their own home. Dad's legacy.

The windows of Aunt Ginny's two-story farmhouse sparkle and glow with candles against a backdrop of gray clouds. Snow, evergreens, and the classic red barn remind me of a Currier and Ives painting. We pull into the farmyard, having chattered all the way from Elkhart about who will be here today for Thanksgiving dinner. I feel elated, as this will be the first Fisher holiday celebration I've ever attended.

Aunt Mabel has made Macintosh apple pie, and we bring a tossed salad with oranges and toasted pecans. It's about noon as cars pull in after us, blocking us in. Great! I could stay all night, basking in the warm company of my too-distant family. Cousin Barb greets us, takes our baskets, points to the back bedroom where we pile our coats and scarves on the bed. The holiday aromas take over my senses: Roasting turkey, of course, and I even smell the stuffing; cinnamon and pumpkin pie spices; yams; some kind of hot baked cheesy thing, popovers, I think, warm and resting in baskets under checkered cotton napkins. The mélange nearly makes me swoon, and I remember a few Thanksgivings back in Cobleskill, at our house and Grandma's. Funny how these memories translate across place and time and culture, always the same, the joy of family together.

When we all sit down, twenty-five of us, Uncle Wally says the blessing, mentioning especially Uncle Kenny and Dad, both recently passed away. I hold back my emotions as much as possible, quietly wipe tears with my green damask napkin. Soon the voices of children demanding to be fed, the clatter of platters and bowls, clink of silverware, laughter and talk blend in harmony that, to me, sounds like a choir of angels. I feel that I am home.

By Monday, with business complete, we turn over the last of Dad's possessions to an auctioneer. Tears flow as I walk down the narrow hallway, revisit each room where he spent his last seven years, and close the apartment door for the last time. Something of him still lingers in the near-empty rooms, close to his marine-blue La-Z-Boy lounger. And with this leaving, I can let him go, just a little bit more, as he would want me to.

WINTER SOLSTICE, 1998

Nine a.m. sharp and already I hear voices outside, a couple of cars parking below and the beep-beep-beep warning of a large lemon-yellow van backing up our steep curving driveway. I suck in my breath, remembering when the concrete truck — on its way to pour the foundation — slipped its wheel in the mud, turned nearly over on its side. The van sidles safely up next to our back door. Suddenly the house is filled with people, bundled up, mittens and gloves, ready to move us down the hill to our new house, Dad's legacy.

Within the hour, a trail of friends, two by two, passes through the old kitchen asking, "Hey, Jude, where does this table go? Where shall we set up your bed? How about the desk?" I had packed the dishes and books two weeks before; transported them in my car. Today it's just the furniture.

My answers seem to confound them; they look at me like I'm daft. "Just put them in the same place you found them," I answer coyly.

"And what does that mean?" they ask. "A little joke? A puzzle?"

"Why is a raven like a writing desk," I quip. "Now that's a puzzle. Don't worry, you'll see."

After they start on their way — this procession of couples clutching furniture, winding down two driveways — I dash past them with an armload of clothes to get there first. Seeing the look on their faces when they walk in the door is priceless.

"Whoa! Where am I?" and "You built the same exact house! Déjà vu. But it's bigger, the same but different, right?"

"That's right. We expanded the living/dining room, plus added Peter's shop."

Slowly the house fills with antique dressers, beds, blanket chests; a jelly cupboard, hutches, armoire, and benches. The couch, chairs of all descriptions, oil and watercolor paintings — all our treasured belongings. Several shifts of people come and go, eat cookies, move plants, say "goodbye and happy holidays." It's December 18 and we'll sleep in our house for the first time tonight.

As we prepare dinner, Peter and I both experience a certain odd feeling, of being home, but not quite the same. I had been madly unpacking boxes into kitchen cupboards for days, and wrestling cartons of books down the not-code stairway for storage. The really crazy part, we have family coming for the holidays — Heidi and Stuart, plus two couples, friends of theirs.

I say sure, of course, but they'll have to sleep on the floor. And they'll be here in two days.

Saturday and Sunday become a blur of crumpled newspaper, hunger attacks (friends rescue us with hot pizza), vacuuming (dragging around the ancient Eureka by its stiff hose, like an aging pet), and cups of hot coffee and chai. Peter, having flipped his bike and broken his collarbone and a few ribs just two weeks ago, does his very best not to lift anything, resigned to lying on the couch. His accident followed an adamant proclamation: "I hate moving... I'd do anything to get out of it...." You get the picture.

All in a flutter, like a storm swooping over the hills, Heidi and her entourage arrive laughing, talking all at once, and dragging sleeping bags, duffle bags, wrapped packages, and half-eaten snacks. After a supper of my hot butternut soup, we're all ready to tuck in for a long winter's nap.

Daybreak, solstice morning. I hear faint footsteps pad about the bedroom. "Jude, look! Come here — you won't believe this — it's snowing!"

My eyes fly open, look out the south windows first. Wait, what's wrong? That's the wrong tree! I'm staring at a giant tan oak where our sentinel redwood had stood. Oh, right, we're in the new house.

I pop out of bed, join Peter at the window, and see a layer of soft new snow on the roof, trees, and bare ground where our garden will be. The snow has muffled all sound except our breathing. We tiptoe downstairs to find stirring bodies in sleeping bags, just rolling over, peering out and discovering the white blanket on the deck — so reminiscent of back-east winters, as it never snows here. Then the sky is full of huge flakes that blow sideways, like flocks of white doves silently sweeping the dawn.

Heidi's guests depart after lunch, and the snow continues on and off all day. Peter and I, with Heidi and Stuart, plan a small ceremony to move the spirit from our old house to the new one on this Solstice day. Under a bit of blue sky, we collect our flutes, a drum, a shovel, and a garbage can lid, and wind our way up the hill. At the old house, the embers still glow. We carefully shovel smoking red coals onto the silver lid, say goodbye to our beloved dwelling; chant and drum down the crispy, snow-packed path to rekindle the fire.

I can't help but think of Dad today, silently thank him for making this beautiful new home possible. The feeling that our ceremony has ancient roots stills our voices, except for a few words of gratitude and connection. Bits of scrap wood from the construction and small rounds from the cleared site make a blaze to warm us as we settle into the stillness. Happy winter solstice.

Writing My Story

I know what it's like, telling my story over and over in my mind. The silent weeping has bound my heart, memories nearly tear me apart; yet somehow, oddly, they hold me together. I repeat the story to be sure I'm not making it up. Am I really the "damaged goods" I felt like most of my teen and adult life? Traumas and secrets have defined me. Without them I'm not sure who I am. In order to survive, with my shields of protection, I've chosen to stay alive and heal. And now, I want to examine my past. What if I'm truly sick, mentally ill, crazy?

December 1997, a month after my father's death, I begin to write about the darkness in my past. What starts out as a writing-class exercise ends up like a confession, a release of feelings about the hospital horrors I couldn't deal with. My resistance is huge, and I fight against the memories pushing their way out. It feels like the "demonic" in me forces me to write. One night I light a candle and begin to scribble on narrow-lined notebook paper. Several hours later, the words appear barely legible, with an angry slant — details of the experiences I managed to keep secret, at bay, for nearly four decades — the saga of my descent into hell, near-demise, and survival. Why does this dark hole in my past bubble up now? Only a few close friends ever heard the story, but only in chopped-up sketchy details.

Over the next few weeks, with the coaching of my talented writing teacher, Lynne, I bring forward, in a monologue, some of the lost pieces of myself. Then in March 1998, the class culminates with a performance of our monologues at the Arena Theater: *Local Heroes.* I stand up onstage, and in front of a packed house of over 200 people tell how I was betrayed, incarcerated, shocked. And somehow I escaped.

* * *

"It was the fall of my senior year at the all-girls prep school in Massachusetts. Life was promising. I happened to walk in on two of my best friends smoking, blatantly against the rules. I was bound by the honor system to report them, but I couldn't. I went to my chaplain. When he broke my confidence, my friends and I were put on probation, and everyone was mad at me. The descent began there, and continued for seven long, dark months, the year I turned eighteen.

I withdraw into my cocoon, hide out... My parents check me into a hospital... a male orderly appears in my room... locks the door, pins me to the bed... I scream... then wake up in restraints... locked ward... switchblade... sleeping drops. Off to my first electroshock treatment, one of ten in a series. Three weeks later, New Year's Day, New York, and another hospital... I'm being left, don't see my parents for three months.

I'm in deep shit...ten more shock treatments ... total assault... wrapped in iced sheets, strapped down... later, unconscious. Run away, and fail. Punished. Ten more. I have to get out of here. Play by their rules... act like I'm cured. In June, they let me out.

To speak this story breaks the shame and silence. I reclaim parts of myself left behind on the battlefield; claim my power and inspire others to do the same. The disaster of my youth has become the gift of my life, and is now a gift I can share."

* * *

To be witnessed by my community and speak my truth out loud would, I thought, bring closure to this chapter of my life. Instead, new doors begin to open. The story takes on a life of its own. I decide I need to know more, find out and verify the details. What if I made them up?

Several months pass. It's over, right? I'm done. Relief comes, then flees like the shriveled yellow leaves on the deck, borne away by unexpected gusts of wind. Winter. Short days and the creeping darkness cast a shadow on my soul and leave me with more questions than answers. If I dig into this unholy tale, what else might surface?

For years I swore I wouldn't write about the hospital, the shock treatments. There might be other things that could seep out like badly repaired leaks; traumas that ought to remain buried, shielding me from pain. To name them is dangerous. Dragging things up, exposing them only gives them life. And I'd have to feel the pain all over again. No, leave it alone. No need to write further about my life. End of story.

The experiences I revealed in *Local Heroes* shocked my friends, seem unreal to me also. Maybe I over-dramatized, exaggerated. What if it was five shock treatments, not the thirty that stick in my memory-impaired mind? I need to know the truth, so one day I dial information and call them.

"New York Hospital, Westchester Division."

"Medical Records, please." Thirty-six years have passed. I'm shaking, not hopeful that my records can be found or even still exist.

"Yes, Miss Fisher, your file is here. We'll need your Social Security number... and a check for copying. That will be two dollars per page, thirty-five pages, so, seventy dollars in total."

I am furious! I have to pay to get my records? From the hospital that nearly bankrupted my family?

"I can't do it," I whined, "unemployed... single mom... broke...." I feel so much like a victim.

"Okay, we can waive the fee for you."

Wow, really? I can hardly believe my luck; they're actually going to send them. Now what? When the envelope arrives, I wade through the terrifying documents, decipher the notes. I learn the truth of it—their version at least. The details are scribbled in the handwriting of Miss Stern, Miss Riley, Dr. Burnes, and others, on cheap copy paper. What I see both frightens and enrages me. Devastated, I sit on this for another four years, unable to write anything.

Lynne, who helped coax the first story out of me, moves away, and my next teacher, Edie Meidav, appears. When I hear her read a passage from her new novel, *A Far Field,* I am stunned and know right then I want to learn from her. Edie's gifts inspire me to write pieces with vivid visual images, bright "broad strokes," she says, "full of pizzazz and depth." I begin to write vignettes from my childhood, just a few safe ones that feel like home. One day, I show her my monologue.

"Write it — it's good!" When she leaves two years later, I miss her encouragement and support, our connection. I again feel lost and put my stories away.

The following year, 2003, I spot a poster for a community college creative writing class, and Ida Egli shows up in my life. Her name, I discover, is like my grandmother's, Ida Mae, hers Ida Rae. Mennonite backgrounds. Both our daughters named Heidi. Her bright spirit and passion for writing quickly tell me I've found a mentor. I sign up for the class and submit my old monologue for her feedback. I begin the class with no intentions of writing further about trauma, but after a few weeks, new pieces slip in. That first exciting year, Ida gives me a clear and constant message: "You are finding your voice... your story is valuable... you must write it. Young women will relate to your experiences, will take courage from hearing your words, and know they're not alone. They too can survive and heal."

Is this my purpose, to share my story, to bring light into the dark places where people hide their secrets from themselves and others? I ponder, I write, and eventually, and not without significant struggle, I can say one day, "I am a writer."

WHEN I WAS A SMALL CHILD

Under Ida's tutelage, my courage grows. I take more risks, delve deeper. A few years ago, at my Advanced Cranio-Sacral intensive, I relived the childhood trauma of walking in on Mom just after she had cut her wrists. Before then, I doubted whether the memory was real; I never could bring myself to ask Dad. In my cranial session, details showed up, vivid as if happening in present time. *I see her... the blood... I am here, and not here... I have left my body, to be where it's safer.* So frightening! My colleagues were so caring and supportive, held me in such a way that I could release the terror I felt. This memory, sometimes called "cellular memory" by body workers, had remained intensely alive in my body, yet hidden away, buried from that time when I needed to suppress it.

I further learn the craft of writing, specifically how to bring up, write down, and describe what happened to me. The truth, as best I can remember. I'm aware that I fill in minor details, using my "imagination," yet my intent is more like that of a journalist: to record what I see accurately, embellishing details only when memory fails, but never changing the meaning or essence of the story.

I close my eyes and remember the exact color of the blood on the towels, and feel myself jumping backward out of my body to get away. And then I write it all down.

SMALL CHILD

No, no — I don't want to be here! And then at the same time, Mom, please don't leave me, I love you.

I am fixated in the moment — here and not here — time slowed to an eternity of moments filled with bloody towels as I stand frozen, not even in my body, feet stuck to the blue linoleum just outside the bathroom door. I am terrified, sucked into a black hole of the most intense fear I have ever felt, and my heart goes out to be with her. I think she is dead and I feel that I am dying too. Frozen. My legs can barely hold me up. Dad, on his knees, pushes me backward with his fear to block my view of her. He doesn't shift from his crouched position, stays with her but also urges me away to protect me from what I see.

"I've called the doctor," he says. "He'll be here soon." He's afraid for her, of what she has done. He hoarsely calls her name.

"Charlotte, Charlotte, my darling, come on, sit up now, take another breath...."

He leans into her body, slumped in the corner next to the tub; blood-soaked towels swaddle her forearms like casts. The work of pulling her forward is so hard, her body dead weight, and he doesn't feel strong.

My head whips around, hearing the piercing ring of the front doorbell. I snap out of this bad dream moment. Dr. Wadsworth appears, toting his black leather bag. He sets it down and right away kneels next to Mom. Dad gives up his position and I back away from them all, huddle by the west window, shade pulled down to hide the scene from our neighbors. The doctor's bag sits open next to him, as bandages, scissors, and tape appear and replace the bloody towels now lying in a pile under the sink.

"She's breathing better now... lost quite a bit of blood... cuts aren't too deep... she'll be okay...." Bits and pieces of their conversation float out of the bathroom.

"Let's get her onto the bed." Dr. Wadsworth takes charge, and the two of them manage to lift Mom from the cold hard corner, carefully carry her to the bed, place her sagging body on the clean white sheet and pull up the soft yellow blanket. Gauze covers both wrists, and I can see now that she is breathing. Her eyes stay closed tight; I think she can't see me. She doesn't know I'm here.

Dr. Wadsworth packs his supplies into the hinged bag. He taps tiny little capsules into one small bottle from a larger one in the top compartment where the neatly labeled bottles all line up in rows. He leaves two bottles for Mom. Before he leaves, he gives her a shot in her hip.

"I'll be back later this afternoon to see how she's doing. She'll probably sleep for a while, and feel confused when she wakes up. It's normal. I'm so sorry, Cliff. Didn't know things were this bad."

"Neither did I, John. Neither did I."

I hear his footsteps leaving, doorbell rattling as he pulls the front door shut. It's so quiet. Dad pulls up a chair and we watch Mom sleep. Dad seems lost in his grief, puts his arm around me as he chokes back tears. We stay close for hours. He goes into the bathroom to clean up, and I hear the bathwater, ice cold by now, gurgle down the drain, taking its tainted memories with it. He scrubs the tub, gets rid of the staining ring. He gathers towels and takes them to the basement. I hear the washer tub begin to fill, imagine the blood-tinged bubbles washing the towels clean. When he returns, we sit with her again to be sure she's inhaling enough air, that the rhythm is right.

"You stay here, Judy." He offers me the rocking chair, the antique one they got in Boston on their honeymoon. As I watch over her, he brings my Betsy-Wetsy doll to me from her wooden cradle. I hug her tight and patiently rock.

"I'll make breakfast. How about a soft-boiled egg?"

He sounds a bit stronger now and I nod yes, picture the comfort of sitting with him at the kitchen table, listening to her soft, steady breathing in the bedroom. I hear his every move: The aluminum pan lifted out of the cupboard, water filling it halfway. He lights the stove with a wooden match, striking it on the iron grate. The old refrigerator door clanks open, its long silver handle flops loosely as he fetches the eggs. Dishes come down from the upper cupboard where they're stacked.

Soon we sit at the table, kitty-corner to each other, eating our eggs from white milk-glass chicken eggcups with happy little beaks. We chop and stir the golden yolks and soft white pieces, mix them with butter and salt. My yellow juice glass looks almost the same color as the yolks, as the sun when it pops over the mountain. In my chair with my back to the bedroom, I can look out in three directions, see the trees that, even in their bare-naked state, hold promise: New green leaves will bud out soon and fill in all the empty spaces with life and movement. The sun will dance in their limbs. I feel scared, but will not cry or let him down. On Dad's serious face, I notice a tiny smile cross his thin lips. Then I tentatively smile back at him, hoping this means everything will be all right.

THE ENVELOPE, 1999

The day the envelope arrives, I panic. My hospital records. Oh, my God, I can't believe it! Now what? My fingers tremble. The suede-like dove-gray envelope, nine by twelve and thick, feels weighty in my hands. Yesterday at the post office I stood in line for ten minutes with my yellow card: "Item too large for PO box." I think back to my crazy idea of trying to trace my records, imagining that I could somehow verify my memory of the hospital. Another part of me still wants to forget the whole thing.

The records are most likely gone by now. Nearly four decades later, they'll tell me, "No, we don't keep them after twenty years" or "You're not allowed to see them without a doctor's release." So I was shocked when Abigail in Medical Records informed me that they existed. Now heavy in my clammy hands, the pages await my next move. My heart flip-flops as I stare at the return address: "New York Hospital, Westchester Division." April 1, my birthday, a whole year since I presented my monologue at the theater. The day stretches out, waiting to take me in its stormy rough embrace, more gripping than comforting. I feel I cannot escape.

I pick up Mom's dagger-like letter opener, black onyx and silver, and slit open the top. Stuffed inside I find a packet of thin, shiny, cheap copy paper bound with a brass clip. I sit down at the dining table and begin to leaf through the pages. At first I read quickly, devour the story: "A seventeen-year-old girl, tall, thin, pale, and serious, was admitted to the hospital for evaluation and treatment by her parents. Her general mood appears depressed."

I stare out the window at the storm brewing. "Depressed." Yes, that was clear. I remember the feeling of giving up, my life in a downward spiral of disappointment and betrayal, wondering how it would all end. I had thought I was going home after the Albany Hospital fiasco, by way of a New York weekend with my folks. Things were pretty messed up, and I knew I'd be blamed for my erratic behavior. Somehow it was all my fault. I had failed at attempts to duck out of this life, to go to a "better place." Who could help me? I was in deep trouble.

I'm riveted. Every page holds keys, answers to vague questions I've wondered about all these years. Images arise and fade away, like a fast-forward film of a lost teenage girl. Many incidents weakened her frail connection to life, could have destroyed her. Me! That I ever got out seems a miracle.

When Dr. Burnes had asked me about my mom, her sickness, I had said:

> "Mother screams or cries, shakes all over if I drop a dish or if the telephone or doorbell rings. She's always been this way, and it's worse lately. Father and I try not to make noise. She takes pills, pills, pills for pep, for sleep, for migraine headaches." Patient always felt it was better not to tell her mother about her problems, as mother would get upset.

That was me? As I read on I shiver, despite my feet being swaddled in Woolrich socks, a thick wool cardigan around my shoulders. My fingers feel like I soaked them in ice water. There are four real surprises in the records. First, a handwritten letter sent to Dr. Burnes by me, relaying some deep fears about my identity; after reading it once through, I wad it up and toss it into the fire. Second, a typed copy of the suicide letter I wrote to my parents when I was fifteen. In both cases, it's like seeing the letters for the first time.

Third, about the shock treatments: it was not thirty, as I had remembered. Only twenty-seven.

Then, the "theme" that appears over and over in the transcript, in several forms: The doctors wanted to keep me there. I had only sensed this, but with no verification. Now I see it in black and white: Two doctors, at a staff conference in late March said: "Needs long-term hospitalization, needs relationship with father and mother figures. Keep the parents away."… And, "Shows no moves toward independence. Suggest long hospitalization."

This harsh fact, which I knew nothing about, really shakes me. Now I see how close I came to not making it. In his final assessment, at the end of June, the month I got out, my doctor said: "There is now talk of the patient being transferred to a state hospital, as parents state they cannot afford further treatment here."

I need a break. Too much! I knew the part about running out of money, my college fund having been spent on the seven months… but a state hospital? I'm freaking out! Stoking the fire serves as a comforting distraction. As the fat madrone pieces hit the hot coals, they spit and sizzle. Their surfaces stay wet from the blustery squall that had blown off the tarp and exposed them to icy rain this morning. The stove's damper remains open, sucks air into the vent, feeds new flames and throws off some heat. I begin to take in the warmth, thaw, and accept its comfort. Next, I make a cup of Earl Gray tea, add milk and honey. Now I can read more of this bizarre story I hardly recognize as my own.

I reflect on the last page of the transcript for many weeks, even years, as it changes the way I remember leaving the hospital. I thought I was well enough, that they let me go based on my good behavior and mental stability. But here in capital letters, written right into the records, I see their truth:

"LEAVES AGAINST ADVICE, IN THE CUSTODY OF PARENTS.
FATHER SIGNED RELEASE.
RELEASE NOTE: Condition: Unimproved."

And so, Dad saved me after all.

BOOKBINDER'S DAUGHTER

A bookbinder wants, above all, for the pages to stay together, more secure even than the original. Pressing the leaves firmly between my palms, I imagine my effort will actually keep things intact. In this small movement, I find comfort and control. I slowly release my hands, which span the width of the cover. Tears spring to my eyes as I remember Dad cradling this book, half-open on his lap, asleep in the tall wing chair. In the past few weeks, going through his things, especially his beloved books, I've learned so much about him. I close my eyes and envision myself standing halfway up the library stepladder, reaching for a dusty volume.

The bookroom of our home in Cobleskill was my favorite hideout. As a small child this very same room, with its drab linoleum, clunking radiator, and late-afternoon sun, was my parents' bedroom. After they remodeled the house and moved their bedroom upstairs, Dad took over this room. He filled it with a mishmash of bookshelves, refinished tables, and a tall oak flat file with two banks of drawers large enough for antique maps, vintage newspapers, rare documents, and Civil War ephemera.

On every surface in that room, including the floor, sat piles of books eight to ten volumes tall. Except for the feeble warmth of one low radiator, the room was unheated, and in winter the bitter cold chilled me to the bone. Then I would drag out the old bathroom heater and plug in its black-and-white woven cord. It always sparked a little. Slowly, the horizontal coils turned from flat gray to flaming liquid orange, and time stretched out in that cozy place till darkness fell and I had to turn on some lights.

Losing myself in the world of Dad's books, I was free. So many possibilities existed. I could go anywhere, become whomever I wanted and feel myself true. Sequestered there, I seemed to find myself.

Spending time in that part of the house, with the books, soothed me. At the same time it was oddly uncomfortable, reminded me of a time long ago when I felt terrified yet couldn't quite remember why. I often avoided the back bathroom, where dusty boxes of unsorted books rested in the abandoned porcelain tub. The tall white metal medicine cabinet sat empty now; its shelves had held castor oil, heating pads, Band-Aids, and Mom's numerous pill bottles, their round rusty imprints proof that they existed. Once, I recall, I stepped carelessly into that icy-cold room; my heart raced as I stared blankly at the tub and quickly backed out. Years later Dad shut that door forever, constructing a bookcase to cover it up, filled it with volumes crammed solid to the ceiling, blocking off access to an old memory. And that felt safe.

The leather and cloth bindings fascinate me now as they did then. I find a box containing only Bibles, some dating back to the 1700s, leather covers so soft and flaky they feel like they might crumble under the slightest pressure. The books smell musky, slightly pungent, pleasant. Opening one fragile cover, I discover a treasure. Written there in a graceful hand, perhaps with a quill pen, are the words "Merry Christmas to Myra, With Love, from Papa and Mama, December 25, 1901." How sweet! This must be my Great-Aunt Myra. With the flow of these letters, I enter another time, a warm room lit only by a giant Yule log ablaze in a fireplace, and a fragrant spruce alight with tiny candles. Then... poof. Gone, like a vision of The Little Match Girl.

The bindings of Myra's Bible need to be reworked, their weakness analyzed so the repair will hold. The back cover is nearly detached from the book, binding threads simply worn thin. Tiny fibers must be woven and rewoven until the promise of stability becomes a reality. Cloth strips soaked in rabbit-skin glue fuse the spine into one cohesive whole.

Survival depends upon careful handling, and the binder knows the risks involved. A well-loved book shows its age: Softened corners, a hand-rubbed patina, and tiny crinkles like smile lines on a beautiful face. Sometimes a new cover must replace the old, to fix the damage, as when a sudden movement causes threads to come unglued, the body to fall apart. Perhaps the book was left on a shelf for years, disheveled, forgotten. Then discovered again later in life — buried treasure to be loved and cared for, reborn.

As I go through the books, ideas percolate in my head: A way to put things together, write my stories and tell the truth of it all. My grief immediately pushes them away. I succumb to the task at hand. Sorting forty boxes of books, remembering, I must decide which ones to keep and what to let go. Dad loved his books, cherished them all. How can I discard a single one?

Occasionally, long ago, he would check on me after I had disappeared into the bookroom for hours. "Hi, there... Find anything interesting?" he'd inquire.

"Oh, just everything," I'd giggle in our little ritual. Then together we'd examine each precious piece I'd chosen and talk about its essence, history, how and why he'd come to possess the book, and its value.

Now, without him, a wave of sadness washes over me. I hear the unspoken words whispered between us in those quiet spaces. I miss him terribly. Finally I allow myself to surrender to the sobs. Grief fills me, almost warms me as I sit rocking on the floor, hugging my knees, surrounded by boxes of books.

My body slackens, muscles release from days of tension. A glimpse of something in my future creeps in. I gather a few favorite books in my arms: Myra's Christmas Bible, Hans Christian Anderson, Beatrix Potter's *Peter Rabbit,* Dickens. These will go with me today. I picture them in their cloth covers and leather jackets, lined up between golden-eagle bookends on my plain pine desk. That desk awaits me, near a tall window admitting first morning light, my imagined studio, a special place where I can write.

I have come to it at last, a way to make the dream real and heal my aching heart. Put it all together. I will become the artist/ writer I have longed to be. Create a place for all the lost stories, emerging from the shadows, waiting to be bound.

I am, after all, a bookbinder's daughter.

Studio Dreams

Where did it start? How long have I dreamed of being an artist and having a studio of my own? Filled with visions from the past — snippets, like reels of film chopped up, strewn across the floor after long editing sessions — I try to reassemble my very first pictures. Little Judy. I loved my box of crayons and drew many versions of a tiny house, its windows glowing yellow. A horse always grazed nearby on a lush green hilltop dotted with pure white daisies. He was mine. I could run and jump on his back anytime, get away, escape to someplace safe and beautiful and free. And in my house, I could draw and paint and color all day.

Dreams can fade and go dormant for decades. I buried that one. At seventeen, the occasional daydream, like a fairy-tale promise, would pass through my mind — a little cabin, an art studio. I had so many hours to think with a near-blank slate, all those months sitting in the lounge of the New York hospital. My memory of those visions is blurry — a cabin in the woods, a room of my own, but not lonely, not like my childhood room or the one where I felt abandoned in the hospital.

Much later — after high school, art classes, then college and weaving, "Wilderness Weavers" — I created my first studio space. I set up a corner of the living room in Branscomb with a large floor loom, baskets of balled yarn, and skeins hung from the rafters. When Heidi turned four, we moved to the little red house on the coast, where I claimed the back room for weaving. For years I wove commissioned pieces: Large pillows, wall hangings and tapestries, even had a show in Oakland at "Just Desserts" with my weaver friend Julie Anixter. Dreams were beginning to take shape.

My fantasy cabin would stand proud, in a clearing at the edge of forest and meadow, somewhere in the mountains, like the Green Mountains of Vermont or maybe the Sierras. Outside, hanging in maples, birches, and a single cherry tree, I imagine skeins of brilliant handspun yarns. The rich hues range from deep gold, produced by half a year's worth of onionskins, to burgundy-rose dyed from beets and the leaves of an ornamental plum tree. Inside sits a floor loom, and by the window, a writing desk. Both have incredible views across the river to the far ridge.

A writer could stare into the distant hills, waiting for something vibrant and alive to reveal itself — a golden eagle or brewing thunderstorm. Inspiration. A weaver might sit on the loom's bench and lean against the front beam, feel the soft, thick wool of a tapestry against her forearms. She'd slip the shuttle through the opening of the threads, produced by precise movements of her feet, as if playing a piano. Each throw of the shuttle adds texture, color, and depth to the tapestry until it is tight and full and needs to be wound ahead to make space for more designs. The sounds of the loom's metal gears, the soft slipping of the fabric, and the changing of the light that streams in the windows provide clues that there is movement in her day, that she is alive, and that it matters.

Images from these dreams dance in my mind, create a collage, a template of what will happen. For five years, Peter has pursued his dream, studying osteopathy in Toronto, earning his "black belt" in the art of manual medicine.

"After all these years," he says, " now it's time for your dream. I owe it to you, darling; let's build you a studio."

I can hardly believe his offer, yet clearly he is serious, so I say, "Yes, of course. I accept!" I feel anxious to find the right location. Peter and I wander around the property, logically choosing a sunny spot close to his shop. The site is limited, but still works, as we're planning a 10 × 12, which meets code for a storage shed; kind of small, adequate, and has great light. While Peter's away at school, I pace the land, asking spirit and my intuition to help me find a place more right for me.

On a whim, I climb up the bank behind the house, above the parking niche, to a patch thick with bright yellow Scotch broom. I remember this exact spot, where years ago Peter and I first explored our new property, stood on this same redwood stump, realized that through the thick forest was hidden a gorgeous view of the river valley with row after row of ridges. I get chills. Over the next two days, I sweat and struggle, pull up the stubborn broom and coyote bush, lop every sapling. My efforts result in a chest-high pile of slash next to my new site. I measure and stake out the perimeter with bright green tape. The studio will fit perfectly between the trees with a minimum of clearing. My plan has now grown to 12 × 18 (and ultimately 14 × 21!). I've always wanted more space. Now's the time to ask for what I want without feeling guilty.

Again Peter says, "Sure, let's go." Then, of course there's the money issue, so as I sketch out the elevations, I set my budget and plan to sell some family antiques to raise the funds. First, I sell my treasured Welch flow-blue dishes, ship them all the way back to Cobleskill where they started out. This covers the first materials order, the "framing package." I still need money to pay our builder friend, Roger, who's agreed to help. The three of us will work on it every weekend, all summer. I take a deep breath and we begin. Considering I've built two houses, this will be a piece of cake.

SECRETS

From my window, the familiar fog-dragon slithers south down the valley; the shroud peels off in layers, its back illuminated all night by distant starlight. The horizon undulates. At dawn, images come sharply into focus: Tall black redwood silhouettes, backlit with a dozen shades of gray. Then, deep lavender cloud-beings show tinges of pink at their edges, signs of new life in this changing, promising landscape. The colors of morning always bring me back to myself: The saturation and intensity of moving prisms, the sunrise I observe from my perch. What is there, then, besides the Light? Ah, her beloved sister, the Darkness. Granted, I am a lover of the Light — attracted, pursuing, hopeful. Yet I acknowledge value in the shadow side. When I have probed the depths of my soul, spiraling even into the "pit" of my early years, I always return knowing the freedom of embracing both.

To connect with my inner child brings such anguish. In a recent Voice Dialogue session, I heard the soft wailing of a girl-child under the bed in my room. Finding the nerve to look, I discovered a gangly three- or four-year-old with knobby knees and lank blonde hair, lying on her side trying to hug herself. So sad! Squinting, peering into the darkness, I seemed to recognize her.

"Come on," I urge, feeling sorry for her. "It's all right to come out." Large blue eyes stare back at me, wet lashes betray her fragile fear. She stays silent, stretches in tiny movements, as if awakening from a long sleep. Her long skinny arms tentatively reach out to me, and as our hands touch, I pull her, ever so gently, toward me.

She feels light, as a bird is light, and bony, slightly cool. As the daylight touches her pale skin and wrinkled clothes, I weep, realizing how long she's been there, waiting. Decades. Keeping quiet so I wouldn't be bothered. Being still, doing her part. We cry together. Now I hold her on my lap in my arms, in Grandma's rocker. I dry the tears, stroke her fine blonde hair, caress the faintly rosy cheeks, and surround her with my warmth. She wants to tell me everything.

She has waited so long to speak that at first her sentences come out in chopped-up bits and pieces, like hiccups, beginnings but no middle, making no sense. I listen carefully for each piece she has saved for me, like a collection of precious beads: Gems, smooth and faceted, crystals, stones both rough and burnished. In the end, they will string together, making sense of seemingly random stories. How she has cared for and hidden these tales! With each one I love her more. My guilt for ignoring her is at last balanced by my joy at having her with me now.

She reminds me there were a few times when I did hear her. She popped out for brief moments, to shake me up, get my attention. I just couldn't allow her a place in my life out in the open. Now she poses no threat to me, like before, when she could make everything topple over like a row of dominos. Now it's just the opposite. I need her as much as she needs me. Her sky-blue eyes glisten as she teaches me how to cry. Now and again she giggles, like a typical four-year-old, bouncy yet content to sit on my lap. I sniff the crown of her head, inhale a mild sweetness in the matted, pale-yellow cap of hair. A smile starts to play across her lips, mixed with the serious intensity of old, old secrets being told to set things right. She knows so much, this small girl, wise beyond her years. Sometimes she just hints at the past, and then rambles on, needing to let me in on all the details. She wants to tell her secrets, but only to me.

I trust her here, snuggled in my arms. Part of me. She will not leave me now; we won't leave each other. She seeks only to be honored, treasured, and loved. No small matter! She no longer hides out, but she worries. Her leftover anxiety hovers like a hummingbird. Then she gets my attention, and I bring her right in, enfold her, and ask forgiveness. She touches my heart deeply, and I will never abandon her again. This I promise as I hold her tight, rocking, rocking, hearing her whispers, bathed in sunlight.

Epilogue

Fifty years ago, in the darkest time of my life, "my black period" — fourteen to twenty-one — I wore black almost exclusively. When I think of it, this seems appropriate, as I nearly died several times, and saw myself as victim. I barely survived. At twenty-one, I stood up and walked away from being that victim toward an undefined Light that provided the spark I needed, not only to stay alive but to embrace every part of my past. I would eventually learn forgiveness; to recognize, trust, and choose the right path as it appeared.

Trusting and believing in myself has proven the most difficult part. I made some grave mistakes, especially in choosing men. I became afraid of my attractions, the heat and passion that pulled me toward promises of connection and love. Need and desire overrode good judgment, despite obvious warning signs. I repeatedly got myself in trouble. When would I learn? Could I ever find that special man, the love of my life?

A decade and more has passed. Days fly by like the wind, ground disappearing below as the plane ascends. Years, history, memories fade, become tiny green patches, clouds whipping by as I fly into the future, the clear-blue unknown canvas that I will create.

My vision of myself growing older has transformed with each turn of events and what I call destiny. I was innocent, damaged, hopeful, near death, rescued, and healed. By fifty, I began a new phase, moved into healthier ways of seeing myself as healer, builder, lover, and wife — creator of my own dreams, powerful and at peace with myself. When life as a single woman ended, its lessons deeply embedded in my soul, I could open my arms and my heart to Peter. We would learn together on the path of relationship. I feel so much gratitude for this gift.

Our life together thrives, deep, rich, and surprising. In 1995, we designed and created a new Healing Arts Center, the office where we work together. That same year, next to our house on the ridge, we bought a four-acre parcel. The plan: to someday build a larger house with a woodworking shop for Peter. Over the next three years, we cleared, and opened up the views of the river valley and ridges of forest beyond. Then we staked out our dream house.

When Dad passed away in 1997, there was enough money from his estate to build our new home. We adored our old house, so we simply adapted its plan to the new location. I was building again, but this time with my partner. By winter solstice the house was done. Seven months start to finish.

At fifty-five my body felt strong, vibrant, even young, like anything was possible. Walk five miles? No problem. On vacation in Puerto Vallarta, we hiked five miles up and down steep, cobbled streets, hardly a peep from my arthroscopically repaired right knee. I believed I had fully healed from my injuries, no longer the "damaged goods" of my earlier life. I loved my strength, my ordinariness; I could pull Scotch broom for hours, clear a hillside, build a fence, a home, stack wood, climb scaffolds. No limitations, only possibility.

At sixty, the balance shifted. Suddenly I was vulnerable. My heart fluttered erratically, pounded out-of-the-blue rapid rhythms, scaring me, putting me at risk. Six months of tests and questions. Is it Lyme disease from a tick bored into my chest? Poisoning from toxic paint fumes? Menopause returning, or a heart attack? After several EKGs and a failed stress test, my doctor declared, "Angiogram, right now."

My sixtieth birthday party turned into a healing circle with a dozen or so of my close women friends. In Native American style, they opened a sacred circle, calling in the Four Directions and my healing guides. Each friend, "sister," offered a blessing-prayer for a good outcome and full healing from my mystery plight. My daughter sent a bowl she turned from an ancient cherry tree, a fingertip of pure gold embedded in the side. The angiogram a few days later, perfect, my arteries proclaimed "pristine!" by my doctor. In desperation, I consulted with Peggy, my friend the homeopath, and with a single constitutional remedy, all my symptoms disappeared. So what was that all about? Mystery and deep healing.

This outpouring of love overwhelmed me. My women friends are such a gift — companions and guides on this journey. I was sensing a strong connection to "Spirit," felt watched over and guided. A new path was opening to me, a continuation, really, of everything already implanted in my heart, growing and evolving for nearly forty years. I had made a choice at twenty-one: the commitment to live, to stay here on the planet and play some meaningful part in healing others and myself.

As the wheel turns, this decade of my life brought challenges, explorations and lessons about healing and my ability to persevere when faced with surgeries and long-term pain. Will I survive? At what cost to my work, freedom, marriage, sanity? Questions tumbled through my pain-medicated days and months at home, following knee-replacement surgery and, just a year later, back-fusion surgery. For nearly three years I endured: months of rehabilitation, debilitating pain, delayed bone fusion. I wanted desperately to write, be able to complete this book, but my addled brain, fuzzy from the meds, interfered with my ability to concentrate.

My life seemed defined by loss and limitation. I grieved for my lost career, my beloved massage, believed I might never be able to take it up again. Several months after each surgery, I returned to the office, able at least to manage the business I had nurtured since 1988. Gradually I recovered, bones finally knitting and fusing after two long years. My strength returned. Each massage session now feels joyful as I move in the old familiar ways, calming and releasing the stresses of others in tandem with my own. I feel such gratitude, a coming back to myself.

Sunrise. Here I sit in bed with my husband; we drink our morning coffee, snuggle, munch sourdough toast and cheddar, our waking-up ritual. Reflecting on our twenty years together, we feel more deeply in love than ever. We talk of our children, six grandchildren, and future trips to visit them, road trips in our Euro Van. Dreams of adventure. Just turning seventy, we struggle with the balance: work, retirement, some of each. Time, money, play, health. We want it all.

This book, complete. The tale I set out to tell, finished. Bits and pieces, stories from my life's journey, fitted, patched, and stitched together like a colorful Amish quilt, sewn and bound at last. I continue on this incredible journey, open to what lies around the bend.

I thank you kindly, dear reader, for your company. Here we shall go our separate ways, for this is my stop. I leave you to travel your own sacred path, infused with and illuminated by your inner beauty, your Light, and your choices. Walk with your head held high, heart open. The gifts on the trail will be many, and through the laughter and tears, you too will find your way.

Go forth in peace,
Be still within yourself, and know
That the trail is beautiful.

May the winds be gentle upon your face,
And your direction be straight and true
As the flight of the eagle.

Walk in beauty and harmony
With God and all people.
— Navajo blessing

Acknowledgments

I begin by expressing deep gratitude to the women who taught me the craft of writing, and the many friends/sisters who sustained me, with their loving support, through a decade of creating *Bookbinder's Daughter.*

Many thanks to my very first writing teachers, Lynne Abels and Edie Meidav, who spurred my interest to write my stories. Special thanks to Ida Egli—my teacher and friend, who inspired the book—for believing in me.

Gratitude to our writing group of the past six years, Linda Lambert, Ida Egli, and the late Elle Waters, for their valuable advice and generosity of spirit.

Deepest thanks to my daughter, Heidi, who took a collection of pieces in longhand and typed the first twenty-five chapters. She is always there for me.

Special acknowledgment and thanks to my earliest readers for their friendship, honesty, and encouragement from the beginning: Nita Green, Joel Crockett, David Skibbons, and Anila. Much thanks to the additional readers of my manuscript: Valerie Barber, Linda Mininger, and Ginny Mott, and to Katie Atherton for the final proofing. Thanks to Joe Shaw, editor, who taught me the value of "less is more."

Kudos to the staff of the Mendocino Coast Writers Conference, who gave me courage and showed me how to go out there and present my story.

Much gratitude to my extraordinary publisher, Cynthia Frank, for her patience, enthusiasm, and expertise in walking me through the birth of my book.

And to my husband, Peter, who has supported me every step of the way in fulfilling this dream, I am forever grateful.